MERCY
WITHOUT BORDERS

The Catholic Worker
and Immigration

Mark and Louise Zwick

D1051399

Paulist Press
New York/Mahwah, NJ

Cover art by Mario Armando Torres
Cover design by Sharyn Banks
Book design by Lynn Else

Library of Congress Cataloging-in-Publication Data

Zwick, Mark.
    Mercy without borders : the Catholic Worker and immigration / Mark and Louise Zwick.
    p. cm.
    Includes bibliographical references.
    ISBN 978-0-8091-4689-5 (alk. paper)
    1. Church work with immigrants—Catholic Church. 2. Church work with immigrants—Texas—Houston. 3. Immigrants—Services for. 4. Emigration and immigration—Religious aspects—Catholic Church. 5. Zwick, Mark. 6. Zwick, Louise. 7. Catholic Worker Movement. I. Zwick, Louise. II. Title.
    BX2347.8.I46Z85 2010
    259.086´91209227641411—dc22
    [B]

        2010009727

Published by Paulist Press
997 Macarthur Boulevard
Mahwah, New Jersey 07430

www.paulistpress.com

Printed and bound in the
United States of America

CONTENTS

To all the Catholic Workers
who have served immigrants at Casa Juan Diego

INTRODUCTION

The Catholic Worker movement was founded during the 1930s when economic crisis made life difficult, if not unbearable, for many people. Dorothy Day, Peter Maurin, and the many who followed them protested injustice and responded to people in need with the fourteen Works of Mercy as opposed to the works of war. Like the saints before them, Peter and Dorothy refused to stand by and accept evil.

Over the years, the movement has continued to respond to changing situations in the United States and the world. In 1980, inspired by Peter Maurin and Dorothy Day, we opened the Houston Catholic Worker, Casa Juan Diego, to receive refugees and immigrants. Giving hospitality to thousands of men, women, and children from many countries, especially Central America and Mexico, has been an adventure, with countless interesting stories, many hours of work, and rarely a dull moment.

In attempting to follow the Gospel in a particular historical situation, using the approach of Dorothy Day and Peter Maurin, we have listened to the stories of people who have undertaken incredible journeys to get to the United States. The stories are often sad or tragic but also contain small joys and moments of grace. People tell us of walking for days and nights; encountering snakes, fire ants, and wild beasts; enduring hunger and thirst; and being subjected to beatings, robberies, or rapes during their journey—often only to find more suffering after they arrive in the United States. Each one also tells us of good people they met as they traveled, who gave them food or water or a place to stay. The stories told to us by our guests over the years since Casa Juan Diego began include stories of joy and sorrow, violence and benevolence, crosses and small miracles.

Our work combines the Catholic Worker ideas of hospitality and nonviolence. Not only do we protest war and face violence, but we also receive in hospitality people who have suffered violence or threats of violence in wars—including the global economic violence that has displaced so many—people who have been attacked or raped on their journey to the United States, and women fleeing domestic violence.

Each day at Casa Juan Diego brings more stories, more joy, more pain, more adventures. One never knows who will come to the door. One never knows how guests of our houses who venture out will be treated in the community. And frequently people come to join in the work. Life at Casa Juan Diego is filled with these stories and we share them in this book. They are true, though they sound unbelievable. We have changed the names of people in the stories for their protection.

In the 1980s, Catholic Worker newspapers from several houses, especially New York and Los Angeles, carried articles informing readers of the lack of wisdom and the injustice of United States' sponsorship of governments in Central America where wars were being waged against the people. However, when *we* began to receive refugees and immigrants, we were unique in the Catholic Worker (CW) movement, in that we were applying its ideas and ideals to immigration issues and to the people whose lives were disrupted by war and global economics. Little by little, however, as the situation of immigrants became more and more urgent, CW houses across the United States responded. In Redwood City, California, Larry Purcell worked with day laborers. Su Casa in Chicago, first founded to receive and aid traumatized refugees of war, branched out to serve immigrants as well. In Akron, Ohio, Sr. Catherine Walsh and others, with our help and the encouragement of a longtime CW family, the Murrays, began the Akron Catholic Worker houses to receive immigrants and refugees. The Oakland CW house focused on immigrants. In Arizona, Catholic Workers take water out into the desert where immigrants are crossing. In recent years, we have been receiving calls from Catholic Workers in other states and cities as well, sharing together about how to help immigrants in often-desperate situations.

Catholic Workers in many cities stand shoulder to shoulder with the U.S. bishops and the Holy Father in protesting mistreatment of immigrants and in seeking a more just immigration policy in the United States. Two major CW gatherings in 2008 highlighted the growing concern among Catholic Workers regarding the plight of immigrants. For the first time, the theme of the entire Midwest gathering, held in Kansas City in April, was "Beyond Walls of Fear: Faith Resistance to Unjust Immigration Policies and Practices." The Southwest CW gathering in July featured speakers, panels, and action addressing the immigration crisis. We hoped the radical young CWs wouldn't be offended by being in the same camp as the pope, whose voice rang out during his trip to the United States, encouraging those defending and giving practical help to immigrants. We presented a workshop at the 2008 national Catholic Worker gathering in Worcester, Massachusetts, on hospitality to immigrants and refugees. It was well attended, with lots of practical questions and dialogue. Catholic Worker papers across the country are addressing the situation of immigrants in their papers.

This book contains stories of thirty years of Catholic Worker interactions and life with immigrants and refugees in Houston. We want to thank those who have encouraged and helped us with this manuscript, especially the Catholic Workers in Houston and our granddaughter, Noemí Flores.

1

FROM EL SALVADOR TO THE HOUSTON CATHOLIC WORKER

As Mark drove through the streets of San Salvador to the El Camino Real Hotel to buy an English-language newspaper to catch up on the news, guns—although certainly not the last thing on his mind in that troubled place—were not foremost in his thoughts. On the way, he was stopped by two members of the *Guardia Nacional*, the ever-present special police who carried mammoth guns. They asked for his car papers. After much talking, it turned out that his papers were not in order, and they claimed that he would have to go to jail. They ordered him into his car and said to follow them. One of the soldiers got into the car with Mark, bringing his gun with him to prevent escape. The gun was so oversized that the soldier hardly fit into the car.

The *guardia*, with Mark following, proceeded a number of blocks until they arrived at a desolate area where they pulled over and roughly ordered Mark out of the car again. He stood between the two soldiers with their all-too-ready guns. Thoughts raced through his head, chief among them that there were no witnesses! He remembered Fr. Rutilio Grande, who had just been killed and whose wake we had attempted to attend, and Fr. Bernard Survil, who had just been deported. What would happen to Louise and the children? Here he was, about to be killed for being a Communist, when he had not even seen, much less plotted with, one. The guns about to kill him might even be the same ones his tax money had purchased to free El Salvador from Communism. But wherever the Communists were in early 1977, the guns his taxes had bought were not being used to kill them. These guns seemed to find only teachers, labor leaders, catechists, and priests. The bullets rarely reached their targets, the Communists.

1

Soon it was apparent to the *guardia* that Mark was not a Communist. He was obviously a capitalist, driving his own car, living with his family in a foreign country, and in possession of a pocketful of very respectable credit cards. He was, however, associated with the deported Fr. Survil and with the human rights movement in El Salvador.

The soldiers kept mentioning the car papers and going before a judge. Fearing he hadn't much time left, Mark regained his composure sufficiently to blurt out the words "... *para evitar la carcel.*" The desperation with which he asked the question, "How do I avoid going to jail?" caught the attention of these heavily armed thugs and their attitude changed. They slyly suggested that they could facilitate payment directly to the judge. Mark paid the money and was free to go home.

After this harrowing experience, Mark gained a renewed appreciation of life and family. Louise and the children received special hugs when he returned to their little place among the poor in San Salvador.

In January of 1977, we had moved to El Salvador with our two children, Jennifer and Joachim, to learn Spanish and to learn about the culture and the work of the Catholic Church among the poor in *comunidades de base* (base Christian communities). Fr. Ralph Friedrich, a friend who had spent several years in El Salvador, suggested that we might go to San Salvador where Maryknoll Associate Fr. Bernard Survil would be happy to have us in his parish. Of course, we would pay our own way.

Fr. Survil sent us a bibliography to study prior to our coming, so we could prepare for our stay and work. We also enrolled in beginning, intermediate, and advanced Spanish classes—simultaneously—at the local community college. This was rather hilarious in a way, but we captured what we could. Our language backgrounds (Louise in French, and Mark in Latin and Italian) made survival with Spanish a possibility, although with age some of those language cells in the brain dry up. We also began to buy secondhand children's books and a few new ones to take on our journey, knowing life in another country would be difficult for Jennifer and Joachim, who were in the third and first grades. They had become good readers and would at least have books to read in their own language while they began to learn Spanish. Louise would continue their violin practice. We sold our piano. A large garage sale took care of everything else, even our beds, and so we had to sleep on the floor until we left.

We had mixed emotions about going—the excitement of going to another country, but also the fear of everything that could go wrong. Our families and friends were worried that something might happen to us in El Salvador, even though they were as unaware as we were of the upheaval and violence that would occur there after we arrived.

It was strange to set out in our 1965 Chevy Biscayne, owning only the car, bedsheets and dishes, our clothing, two hundred children's books, and two little violins. We still had a bank account. We drove down from California, where we had been living, through Mexico and Guatemala all the way to El Salvador. Sanborn's, a company that sold car insurance at towns along the Mexican border, helped us find places to eat and stay. Their trip guide not only gave mile-by-mile descriptions of the journey, even down to bumps in the road, but also recommended inexpensive hotels and restaurants where we hoped that our unaccustomed intestines would remain at peace after frequenting foreign places. In our inadequate Spanish, we tried to make conversation related to necessities as we went, proud of ourselves when we were able to rent a motel room the first night in Mexico.

When we arrived at the border in El Salvador after crossing Guatemala, customs officials made us take everything out of our car. This would have been easy had we brought suitcases, but to save space we had refrained from using them. We faced the daunting task of removing all of our clothing, sheets, dishes, pots, pans, and books, which had been packed loose in the trunk and car. The Salvadoran soldiers went through this mammoth pile of things. Several children's religious books, especially the *Taizé Picture Bible*, upset them. Obviously suspicious of things Christian and Catholic, the soldiers in their spotless, starched uniforms had a lengthy discussion in rapid Spanish while we waited a little nervously. Finally, about two hours later, they allowed us to pack everything back into the car and to continue on our way, even allowing us to keep the books.

Fr. Survil welcomed us in the capital, San Salvador. He had rented half a house for us at $50 per month in a poor neighborhood. At this low price, we could have stayed for years. We had electricity and running water. Most of our neighbors had electricity, but had to carry water some distance. Others had to make do with cardboard huts and cooked outside on open fires.

The poverty was striking. Unemployment was at 50 percent. Many people walked the streets with small items to sell, trying to eke out a living. Some men gave up hope and responded to the poverty by drinking pure alcohol and collapsing in the street.

Our hearts went out to the poor with whom we lived in the city. Out in the countryside, the *campesinos*, farm workers, were under a system more cruel than any serfdom, which kept families barely on the edge of survival.

We chose to live with the poor. The streets were not paved and there were open sewers. The holes in the streets made it impossible for us to drive our car to our house, and so we rented a space for it on higher ground. The danger of parasites was so great that we were warned not to wear sandals. In spite of many precautions, however, we were soon struggling with intestinal illnesses.

We had anticipated changes in lifestyle, but as North Americans accustomed to middle-class living, we couldn't anticipate all of them. We thought there must be at least one public coin Laundromat in San Salvador where we could wash our clothes. There was a "Laundromat" all right—a community center for washing clothes by hand, heavily used by those who lacked running water in their homes. The house we rented had a built-in place for washing clothes by hand, and so we became accustomed to washing each morning with the special soap commonly used there for washing clothes. Our eight-year-old daughter, Jennifer, also helped with the washing.

Small differences made the adjustment a challenge for the children. They had been accustomed to using a bathtub, but there was no bathtub in the house. At first, Jennifer screamed when we washed her hair under a hose. What bothered us most was the dust from the street that poured into our house. In that warm climate, there was no glass in the windows of the house, and the walls didn't quite meet.

Being overprotective parents, we monitored our children's activities very closely, taking them to school early each morning and picking them up when school ended at noon. In the beginning, they were a neighborhood curiosity as foreigners, but gradually the children of both cultures grew accustomed to one another. Our children were homesick. They did not know Spanish when they arrived, but were immersed in it at school.

Jennifer attended the school run by the Sisters of the Assumption, who worked with us in the base communities. She was very shy and cried often until the sisters came up with the great idea of placing her in a lower grade and assigning an outgoing young girl to be with her. Joachim attended a small Protestant school across the street from our house. He still tells the story about how he waited desperately for his father to pick him up from school on the first day. When Mark appeared, Joachim quickly asked him how to say bathroom in Spanish and then dashed into the school to find it. Little by little, the children adjusted, made friends, and learned Spanish. Because of the language gap, they didn't learn much else at school, but learning Spanish was a great gift.

Louise rationed the children's books they read in the afternoons after school so that they would last. All were of interest to the kids, from the fairy-tale collections to the entire set of the illustrated Golden Encyclopedia that we had found in a secondhand store before we left for El Salvador. Jennifer especially liked to read about the different states in the United States, each of which had a separate entry in the encyclopedia. We didn't realize how effective all those books were until later, when we noticed that the children's reading proficiency, good to begin with, had improved greatly. They had no difficulty adjusting to their appropriate grade levels when we returned to the United States. They did not even miss a year.

Louise also worked every day with the children on violin practice so they would not lose too much ground and forget what they had learned in the States. There was also a little time for treats, for an occasional movie, or a drive out for ice cream. We remember seeing *Cinderella* and *The Bluebird* in Spanish, as well as *Gone with the Wind* and *All the President's Men* with Spanish subtitles.

The adjustment to a dusty, poor neighborhood was not easy for the children. Both children had an awful time adjusting to the water and food, and they were very sick. We adults were not immune to illness either. We became friends with the Assumption Sisters, who had a medical clinic and school in our neighborhood, and Louise worked closely with one of the sister-nurses when the children were ill. One time, Joachim, age six, shocked a sister from Spain with his serious insubordination: hearing that he was to receive a shot, he locked himself in the bedroom and would not come out. With coaxing, he did emerge and he received the shot.

Once we discovered that the water was not good for us to drink, we tried to have large glass containers of water delivered to our house. However, the trucks did not venture into poor neighborhoods, probably because no one else there could afford to have water delivered. We had to drive to buy our water, transport it in our car, and carry it into our house. When Mark's shoes were resoled in El Salvador, the soles were thicker than in the States. As a result, he tripped while carrying a large glass bottle into the house, and the big bottle broke on his arm. The cut in his left forearm was an inch deep. We were shocked. What to do? There was no 911. The neighbors cried, "¡La Cruz Roja! ¡La Cruz Roja!" ("The Red Cross!") By this time, we had moved into an apartment where we could park our car close by. Mark wrapped a towel around his wound, and we all hurried into the car, with Mark driving with his right hand only. Fortunately, as soon as we were on the street, we came upon one of the sisters walking on the sidewalk. She got into the car and directed us to the office of a doctor she knew. We waited two hours at the doctor's office, not because of long lines, but because in that part of the world water is scarce, and at the time there was none to clean the wound. Thank God, the broken glass had not hit an artery.

We thought all was well after the doctor had sewn up the wound, and then Mark lost consciousness. It might have been a reaction to the anesthesia. When the doctor couldn't find a pulse, we were all very concerned. What a great relief it was when he came to! After all the excitement, while Mark was still lightheaded, the sister asked, "Luisa, do you drive?" Louise answered, "Yes, but not here." San Salvador was crowded with pedestrians and cars, and the traffic went so fast that the very idea of driving there had been intimidating to her. She had not planned to drive in El Salvador and had not registered her license with the government. Nevertheless, it seemed the only way to get everyone home, and we all arrived safely. In the days that followed, Mark's arm became infected and he had to go each day for weeks afterward to the sisters' neighborhood clinic for antibiotics.

We were surrounded by poverty, families struggling daily to survive and maintain a human and Christian existence. We were impressed by the people. They lived in poverty and great oppression, but with the aid of the Church, and the spiritual and conscience formation of the base communities, the people found hope.

We had approached El Salvador unaware of impending violence. At the time we arrived, there were no serious open conflicts in the country, so we thought things would be fairly safe. We had not counted on the elections, which occur every six years and were due to take place not long after our arrival. Salvadorans in the neighborhood said to us with some concern when we arrived, "You have come just in time for the elections!" Little did we know how explosive elections could be in Central America. It quickly became clear. If we had known what was to follow, we would not have made our journey, but the deed was done.

The people told us that there was a movement to challenge the repressive government. Its aim was to support social interests and to elect someone who would represent the people—and not only the rich. It was hard for the people to hope for social transformation through the electoral process, but they wanted to try. Most of El Salvador was owned and controlled by fourteen wealthy families, while most people were desperately poor. The community members recounted for us the history of the 1930s, when members of the indigenous population attempted to challenge the injustice of the status quo and were massacred.

We were firsthand witnesses of the violence and repression of the government of El Salvador and of the exclusion of the poor from any chance for a better life. People were terrified by the words *escuadrones de la muerte*; these were the government-sponsored death squads that collaborated with the government in killing civilians who were considered enemies of the establishment.

We found that the Church was the only force left in El Salvador to counteract the oppression and violence of the government—a government that, sadly, was funded by the United States in the name of stopping Communism. Leaders in the United States were still preoccupied with the domino theory, which postulated the idea that nations would fall to Communism one after another if social justice movements were not stamped out.

Thus began the deportation by the government of foreign priests who were working with the poor and with social movements in El Salvador. When Fr. Mario Bernal was deported to Colombia, presumably because of his popular and controversial radio program, Jesuit Fr. Rutilio Grande celebrated an outdoor Mass protesting his deportation. Fr. Rutilio, a close friend of Archbishop Oscar Romero, had left his position at the university to live in smaller towns and the countryside, where he organized small base communities and cooperatives for *campesinos*. He publicly criticized the injustice of those who owned huge portions of the land and yet didn't pay enough so that their workers could feed their children. Powerful landowners in the area saw Fr. Rutilio as a threat; all labor leaders in El Salvador were seen as threats to the security of the large supply of cheap labor and so were targets for violence.

Fr. Survil—who had not yet been deported himself—invited Mark to take pictures of what turned out to be Fr. Rutilio's last Mass. When Mark parked the car, he noticed that the one next to ours was a shiny new car with a pistol on the seat. The presumption was that the new car and the gun belonged to a government agent. Mark thought it fortunate that he had forgotten his camera. He was already noticeable at the Mass as a North American. If he had been actively taking pictures, the thugs keeping record of the participants would have noticed him even more.

Fr. Rutilio was smiling, but visibly agitated. At that last Mass on February 13, he challenged the government, and Mark heard him say the words that led to his martyrdom: "If Jesus came to El Salvador today, he would be arrested as a subversive—and the Bible would be considered a subversive document."

We were probably not considered innocent bystanders. It was obvious that we were connected with Fr. Survil, who kept upsetting the authorities by leafleting our neighborhood with peace-and-justice materials. He would walk through the *colonia* (the neighborhood), talking to the people and passing out *Justicia y Paz*, a very moderate publication of the Archdiocese of San Salvador that was considered subversive because it advocated for the poor. He also wrote letters to newspapers in the United States about the injustices in El Salvador.

He was soon picked up and jailed. The authorities stripped him of his clothes, blindfolded him, and strung him up so that his feet did not touch the floor as he was interrogated. He spent a night naked, with his hands restrained. As soon as he was released after being given a stern warning, he cranked up his mimeograph machine to make copies of a letter describing his ordeal and put them in the mail to many newspapers in the United States He came to our house to tell us what happened and to discuss plans for our stay in El Salvador. It was not until many years later he told us that, in spite of intense psychological pressure, he had not ratted on Mark when questioned over and over during the interrogation: "Who was there? Who was that *gringo* at the protest Mass in Apopa?"

What he did tell us at the time, and mentioned again years later, was that he could hear an American voice in the background guiding the Salvadoran interrogators. Of course, the military government read the letters he had tried to mail, and plainclothes agents picked him up for the second time right after he left our house. This time he was deported directly. It was February 18, 1977. He was lucky they didn't kill foreign priests at that time.

The leaders of our base community in Barrio Lourdes in San Salvador thought it was important that members of the community go to Archbishop Luis Chavez y Gonzalez to report that Fr. Survil had been detained, psychologically tortured, and then deported. They asked Mark to accompany them, which he did. After sympathetically hearing the report, the archbishop jokingly suggested that they would just have to ordain Mark to replace Fr. Survil.

In the eyes of the government, the Bible study groups and small communities of the Catholic Church were subversive. It was true that priests and lay leaders were challenging the status quo and organizing groups among the very poor, and that those in the oligarchy and the government were concerned about what they saw as a threat to their existence. But in the Bible study group we attended in the community of the poor, we heard only the Gospel. There was no talk of violence or of Communism in those church meetings, only reflection on the Scriptures.

The national elections took place on February 20. On February 28 the people organized a protest against what they said was a fraudulent election; several hundred marched through the streets and took over the *Parque Libertad*—Freedom Park. The protesters had asked Fr. Alfonso Navarro to celebrate two outdoor Masses for them. He celebrated Mass there before troops came to dislodge the protesters with guns and machetes. For many present that day, it was their last Mass. Bodies were carried off in trucks to mass graves. The neighbors in our *colonia* came to tell us that two hundred people had been killed for protesting. Tension filled the atmosphere. The government silenced the newspapers on the subject of the possibility of fraud in the elections and the truth of what happened that day.

As we walked through our neighborhood late one afternoon, people ran from their homes to tell us that the government had declared martial law. Though our Spanish was very limited at that time, and we did not know the local words for martial law, we soon understood that everyone must be in their homes by 9:00 p.m. Soldiers would shoot any group of more than five gathered together. Thank God, the neighbors helped us understand.

The Salvadorans were dissatisfied with the situation after the elections, and a few began to speak about violence. The government was clearly aware of the threat. Our neighbors spoke frequently of the influence the United States would have in any upcoming conflict. They did not perceive our country as being on the side of the vast majority of the population, which was poor, but, rather, allied with the rich; they knew that the United States gave money to what they now believed was a fraudulently elected government. Neighbors began to caution us about the *orejas* ("ears," or government spies) who might be lurking, listening to any conversation, or trying to draw people into conversation critical of the government. Being reported by an *oreja* might mean death. We, of course, would not have thought of or spoken of overthrowing the government, but that extreme was not required. All one needed to say was that large landowners should pay a just wage. That would have been enough.

Monseñor Oscar Arnulfo Romero was appointed archbishop of San Salvador on February 3 and installed on February 22. Some priests who were working in El Salvador told us that at the time they thought the appointment might be a disaster. Romero had been leading middle-class movements in the Church, instead of working among the poor. He was considered by the oligarchy and by the other Catholic bishops in El Salvador to be a safe, conservative candidate for archbishop at a time when questions were being raised about the injustices in the social system. The concern on the part of our priest acquaintances was that he might identify with the rich and powerful and be distant from the poor. Some local priests had openly tried to lobby in favor of the auxiliary bishop of San Salvador, Monseñor Arturo Rivera y Damas; nonetheless, they accepted the new archbishop and began to work with him.

On March 12, Fr. Rutilio Grande was gunned down, along with two Salvadoran laypeople. At first we thought that perhaps the murder had been committed by the owner of the car with the gun on the seat at the Mass, but then we learned that the weapons were machine guns. We were on the way with our children to Fr. Rutilio's wake at the parish in Aguilares where he had worked, some distance from the capital where we lived, when an incident happened that dramatically brought to us the reality of the tension and fear among Salvadoran Catholics at this time. We were following the sisters and members of the *comunidades*, who were driving in front of us in an open Jeep. The Jeep overturned. We watched in horror as bodies were hurled through the air. We learned later that the road had been made slippery by the sugar cane transported earlier that had dripped on the road. We were concerned that our small children had seen the accident. It was bad enough that people were injured and that our children witnessed this, but the paramount feeling among the people was fear that the *guardia* would find out about the wreck— and that we were on our way to Fr. Grande's wake. It was dangerous to go to the wake or funeral of someone who had been killed by the death squads.

We never did arrive at the wake because of the accident, but went to the hospital to visit the injured sisters. When we arrived at the hospital, however, the sisters were not there. The driver's wife and children, who had been riding with us and were still with us, were worried sick that the authorities had picked up the people in the other Jeep and detained them. Finally, they appeared at the hospital, having taken a long detour through country roads to avoid detection and questioning by the *guardia*. Fortunately, the injuries were only minor, and our children were reassured.

When his friend Rutilio Grande was killed, Archbishop Romero went to the church and celebrated Mass during the wake where the three bodies had been laid. We learned later (never having arrived at the wake) that he spent hours there listening to stories of the suffering landless peasant farmers from the area, and hours there praying.

The archbishop became convinced by this experience, by his priest advisers, and by the people that he must protest this senseless murder. He closed all the churches of the archdiocese the Sunday following the death of Rutilio Grande and had one memorial Mass. We walked some distance from our parish with the other parishioners and gathered in the square in front of the cathedral to celebrate with the archbishop the one national liturgy commemorating the life and death of a great Jesuit, who was already canonized in the minds of the people. Even the Catholic schools where government officials sent their children were closed.

At that Mass, Archbishop Romero spoke of the importance of Fr. Rutilio's work in accompanying the poor, relating his work to the Gospel. It was clear as he spoke that the new archbishop was against violence. He put Fr. Rutilio's work in the context of Matthew 25:35–46, Jesus' teaching about Judgment Day and the poor, and cautioned those in social movements to center their lives and work in Catholic social teaching as Rutilio Grande had done. When Jesuit Father James Brockman compiled and translated Archbishop Romero's sermons in a book entitled *The Violence of Love*, he included an excerpt from the homily of that memorial Mass we attended:

> The Church's social teaching tells everyone that the Christian religion does not have a merely horizontal meaning, or a merely spiritualized meaning that overlooks the wretchedness that surrounds it. It is a looking at God and from God at one's neighbor as a brother or sister, and an awareness that "whatever you did to one of these, you did to Me."
>
> Would that social movements knew this social teaching! They would not expose themselves to failures, to shortsightedness, to a nearsightedness that sees no more than temporal things, the structures of time. As long as one does not live a conversion in one's heart, a teaching enlightened by faith to organize life according to the heart of God, all will be feeble, revolutionary, passing, violent. None of these is Christian.[1]

During the time before and after Fr. Rutilio's assassination, people advocating social change in El Salvador, especially Catholics, were picked up on the streets and disappeared. With his life changed by the murder of Fr. Rutilio, Archbishop Romero found himself on the side of the poor, those threatened by death squads, and those detained by the Salvadoran government—the wrong side if one wanted to stay alive. He used the Catholic radio station to immediately protest, as soon as each incident occurred, the arrest of people who had committed no crime. At that time there was a better chance of their coming out alive if he announced that they were detained before they disappeared. He also publicly denounced and condemned human rights violations in his weekly homilies broadcast on the Catholic radio station. The archbishop spoke beautifully and clearly about the need to live according to the New Testament—so clearly that we could understand even with our rudimentary Spanish. As we walked through our neighborhood, we could hear the radios in all the houses tuned to that one station, and his voice from many radios came through as one. In the middle of what had become government terror in the country, people were given hope as the archbishop spoke of the Gospel and Jesus' care for the poor.

The war had begun. There were small guerrilla groups, but they were not organized on a national level. At that time, it was war on the people and on anyone organizing among the poor. Catholic events were suspect and a campaign of rumors was begun against Archbishop Romero. We remember whole-page fake ads taken out in local newspapers supposedly sponsored by "Catholic Mothers of El Salvador," attacking the archbishop for his protest against oppression and the torture and disappearances of Salvadoran people, and for his concern for human rights, human dignity, and decent wages. We never met any of these "mothers"; nor did anyone else. We only met mothers who were concerned about their children having enough to eat and having the opportunity to learn to read and write.

Before long, certain members of the armed forces began a campaign in the Salvadoran media to kill a Jesuit a day, but international pressure halted that—until more than a decade later when, in 1989, six Jesuits and two women were killed at the University of Central America.

To gain as much of an upper hand as they could in the impending violence, the Salvadoran Army quickly began forced recruitment, driving trucks around the city and picking up young men off the streets. Many young men disappeared into those trucks to be inducted in the army and ordered to fight—in the name of stopping Communism—for the very system that had made their lives so difficult. Much later, the guerrillas strengthened, and they also began forced recruitment.

Everyone expected us to flee, to leave for the United States immediately, since our American patron had been forced to depart. Concerned about the danger of staying in El Salvador, we checked with the American Embassy, where they assured us that there were no serious problems and no reason to leave. They had received no guidelines regarding the departure of U.S. citizens. Tourism was still a major industry in El Salvador, and people from European countries still visited regularly. Given this reassurance, odd as it seemed, we felt we should stay if we could, in order to provide some encouragement and symbolic support for the Catholic community. We could afford it and would not be a burden to the community or the archdiocese. We still felt somewhat secure as American citizens in our educational venture, although our education had taken quite a different turn from our original expectations.

Before Fr. Survil was expelled, he had introduced us to his community and they accepted us. Along with laypeople, the sisters emerged as leaders and were an important presence in the neighborhood. We carried on with our Scripture study group. Soon, however, one of the mothers in the group told us that her policeman-son had asked her to stop the meetings because the police had orders to shoot first and ask questions later if they came upon any meeting of more than five people. They claimed they had the "right" to do this because martial law had been declared. In the light of this development, the sisters and the group decided not to meet any more.

Lent was an occasion for spiritual growth. Every Friday we wound in procession through the narrow streets of our *colonia*, making the Way of the Cross, meditating on the final hours of Christ's suffering and death. The people of the neighborhood took turns sponsoring one of the fourteen stations, decorating a simple altar in front of their homes. The political situation was so bad that even this religious act was considered subversive. As we went along, some bystanders yelled ugly words at the religious procession. The continuation of the sufferings of Jesus in his people, in the Body of Christ, in the Church that St. Paul wrote about, became a stark reality in the lives of the people in our neighborhood, some having already lost family members to the death squads that roamed at will.

The washing of the feet on Holy Thursday took on special significance. A French Jesuit priest, harassed by the *orejas* for even being in our neighborhood, performed the Holy Thursday ritual. He washed our feet and the feet of poor mothers who had already lost or would soon lose husbands in the oppression. His own church was a just a shed a few feet from the railroad tracks.

The violence escalated. Between January and May, six priests were deported and seven were exiled. Many laypeople were tortured and killed. Fr. Alfonso Navarro, the priest who had celebrated Mass for those who protested the election fraud, was assassinated on May 11. It was after this that the people we had come to know in El Salvador advised us to leave, especially because of the children. The local Maryknoll superior insisted as well. We were not under his jurisdiction, but he probably felt responsible for us, since we had worked with a priest who was a Maryknoll Associate.

The Maryknoll Sisters spoke with us about returning to work with them if conditions improved.

Our grand finale in El Salvador was a weekend retreat Mark made. Members of *comunidades* from several parishes gathered with one of the parish priests and his team for talks and discussion. The meetings were in Spanish, but because they were from the New Testament, it was possible for us to understand them. The discussions and presentations went well, but nights were somewhat hysterical because the participants were beginning to fear that the government soldiers would come and arrest them, at the very least. The group tried to cover up their fear and anxiety by talking and laughing—giggling—all night at anything, including our Spanish. They had reason to fear. After our return to the States, we learned that government soldiers broke into one of the retreats in the same building and killed the priest and four participants.

We left El Salvador before Archbishop Romero was gunned down at Mass. We left before the four American churchwomen were killed. We left long before the Jesuits and their housekeeper and her daughter were killed. We left El Salvador enriched by our experience, both chastened and inspired by the experience of the Church under siege. Our Catholicism and our faith would never be the same.

We learned lessons in El Salvador that we have never forgotten. In addition to our experience of the culture and the *comunidades*, we were greatly impressed by the life of the Church. We had been part of the religious and social turmoil of the sixties and seventies in the United States. Our spiritual needs had been met in small groups more than in the parish structure, though we did participate in the sacramental life of the Church. We discovered that the Church was the only force left in El Salvador to counteract the oppression and violence of the government. The Church defending the poor and being persecuted but still speaking up was the institutional Church: not a dissatisfied, marginal leftist clique, but the Church of martyrs—lay, religious, and clerical. We began going to daily Mass with the sisters. The liturgy and the paschal mystery—the death and resurrection of Jesus—took on a completely new significance. The modern swinging liturgies we had sought out in the States paled in comparison.

The people who lived in those one-room homes and cardboard huts were people of profound faith and culture in spite of the poverty in which they lived. We had wanted to learn about *comunidades de base*, but we learned much more. It seemed strange that people who had little formal education and were living on the margin of existence were enlightening us, with our masters' degrees and financial security. We had not expected to have such intelligent conversations, since in the United States poverty is often associated with a lack of culture. One example of this was when Fr. Survil arranged for a man from the community to talk with us each week to improve our Spanish. His first question was, "What would you like to talk about? How about the prison system in the United States?" As we sat in his little one-room house, we were surprised at the question and the discussion that followed.

In the United States, we are influenced by Calvinist ideas that the "elect" are the upwardly mobile and the "unelected" sinful are poor. In El Salvador, we learned that the people who make up 80 to 90 percent of the population, though poor, have a depth of culture that we never expected to encounter. We returned to the United States with a deep respect for the people, although with the awareness that the wealthy in their country did not appreciate the culture of the poor and peasants either.

Our months in El Salvador had a great impact on us, not only in our understanding of what was going on in the country, but in our spiritual lives. While there, we read books by Dorothy Day, which helped our reflections. We were confirmed in our commitment to be New Testament Christians despite our human weaknesses. What limited talents and abilities we had, we would use to serve others in some way.

We hadn't given up on Central America, so we found ourselves, still feeling ill and having lost a lot of weight, on our way to Antigua, Guatemala, to study Spanish. The language school we attended there, in a city full of language schools, was famous and well respected. Ironically, many of the students at that school were studying for a position with the U.S. government in Latin America. Their understanding of what was going on in Central America was quite different from ours. They thought it was strange that we identified with the poor, when the United States government was funding the Salvadoran government's war.

One of the first things we noticed in Guatemala was the difference in the newspapers. The Salvadoran papers were controlled by the government and printed nothing that could have been construed in any way as critical of the government. For the first time in months, we read—in Spanish—what was happening in El Salvador. Our source of news in that country had been the *Miami Herald*, which Mark had been driving to buy when stopped by the *guardia*. In Guatemala, they could print articles about the problems in El Salvador, but not what was happening in their own country. We had not left violence behind in El Salvador. On the day we passed through Guatemala City on our way to Antigua, a labor leader was killed.

In Antigua, we lived with a Guatemalan family for two months while attending the language school. Louise attended class in the afternoons and Mark in the mornings, so that one of us would always be free to take care of the children. Our classes were one-on-one with a native speaker, an excellent way to learn. The teacher refused to allow us to speak any English in the class. If we wanted to discuss a movie, wonderful—but we had to do so in Spanish. One of the first lessons we learned in Antigua was that one does not call the people native to Guatemala *indios*. The word is an insult, coming from centuries of prejudice and oppression, in which the word *indio* had been used as a pejorative term.

Living with a Guatemalan family helped because we took all of our meals with them and any communication was in Spanish. It also helped us to learn about the culture of the country, such as customs and daily diet. We grew to enjoy black beans prepared in various ways, as well as fried plantains. Our children played with the children of the family with whom we lived, which helped them with their Spanish. They loved the bilingual Montessori school they attended in Antigua because they could speak English as well as Spanish and participate in a variety of programs.

In the sixteenth century, Antigua was the first capital city of all of Central America, but it was abandoned as such after several devastating earthquakes. It is filled with old universities, churches, and monasteries now in ruins. Antigua seemed tranquil while we were there as students, but this was only on the surface. After we left, the head of the Franciscan order there was found dead in a ditch on the road to the capital. He had made the mistake of being an advocate for a young man, attempting to participate in a government-approved amnesty program.

While in Guatemala, we received word from the Maryknoll Sisters that their order was no longer going to accept laypeople, especially families, to work in El Salvador, because the situation deteriorated daily. We then decided to apply for admission to volunteer groups in the United States. At the language school, we found some interesting addresses in the booklet of an organization called International Liaison, which listed volunteer opportunities in the United States and in other countries.

(International Liaison is now called the Catholic Network of Volunteers. They publish *The Response*, where Casa Juan Diego is now listed as a place for volunteers to come and work.) We wrote to some programs in Texas and indicated to them that we could begin to work when we finished our language studies. We weren't very worried about our financial state. We still had most of what we had planned to be our children's education money to use in case of an emergency. We felt we would be comfortable being part of a Catholic Peace Corps type of organization.

Every member of the Zwick family was eager to return to the States. After experiencing the application of laws in El Salvador and Guatemala, we felt better about our country and its laws. We just wished that the United States would not send guns to Central America because they were being used to kill the wrong people, especially civilians. It would be better to send aid in the form of people and programs.

We began the long drive back to the United States. Driving home was easier, since our Spanish was better and border crossings were not as tense. It was not all roses, however. Our car was twelve years old, and we had a feeling we were going to have trouble. Before beginning our trip to Central America, we had heard horror stories about motorists who had been stranded with car trouble on the western coast of Mexico; in fact, we had changed our original route through Mexico for that reason. We asked the Lord to just get us to the United States, where it would be easier for us to have the car repaired.

Our Sanborn's guide advised us again on restaurants and motels. One night, way out in the country in Mexico, we found the only motel for miles—a $5.00 rate, with partial water services, a bed for each child, and a narrow single bed for the two of us. Even though we weren't newly-weds, we didn't complain! However, it wasn't exactly comfortable.

Our trouble began outside of Vera Cruz when we backed our car into a streetcar track and discovered later that our rear tire was rubbing against the fender and burning up. It was Sunday, but we were able to find a tire repair shop operating out of a home to assist us. They fixed the problem, accepted no money, and we headed for Tampico to spend the night. North of Tampico, well into a desolate area with no gas stations for a hundred miles, we were unpleasantly surprised to discover that our car had lost all of its oil. We asked the Lord again to just get us to the States, just across the border, before we broke down.

Fortunately, as we drove down the highway, we noticed a large flatbed truck with an enormous piece of machinery on it that had stopped along the highway. Hoping this was the answer to our prayers, we stopped to see if they had any extra oil. They didn't. But as we were leaving, with our optimism rather wilted, one of the truck drivers suggested that we take oil from the big machine on the truck, and he siphoned some off for us. We offered to pay, but again, the Mexicans refused payment of any kind. We got back on the road and drove north through the countryside toward Matamoros and the U.S. border.

The Rio Grande River (called the Rio Bravo on the other side) was a beautiful sight to us, especially since our car was still running. Going through United States customs was no problem (we only had our old things), and we arrived in the United States, entering Brownsville. We were happy to be back.

Just a few hundred feet into the United States, in Texas where we had never set foot before, the car sputtered dramatically and died. It would not move another inch. The Lord answered our prayer—no more, no less. We had all the preconceived ideas about Texas that Northerners have, but we didn't see any cowboy boots when looking for a garage. The car was fixable, thank goodness. It turned out it was a clogged gas filter that stopped the car, apparently common for those who have driven through countries where gasoline is refined a little differently.

We returned to the United States on the Fourth of July; our lives changed. Grateful to be alive, we had to get reoriented to living in the United States and we had to make a plan for the future. Our first night back was pleasant. The kids could hardly believe they could drink the water from the faucet in the motel. TV was another luxury long foregone, and they very much enjoyed watching fireworks and other Independence Day celebrations.

We began to visit the places we had contacted. In Austin, we spoke with Archie Gress, founder of Volunteers for Educational and Social Services (VESS) under the auspices of the Catholic bishops of Texas. He welcomed us warmly and assured us that there would be a place for us in McAllen, Texas, on the border of Mexico.

Before beginning work, however, there was one thing we had to do—visit our families in Ohio and Pennsylvania, who had spent over half a year worrying about us in war-torn Central America. After visiting our families—who were glad to see us alive, even though we looked like skeletons because of the dysentery—we drove back to McAllen. As VESS volunteers for two years, we were in charge of a program for 1,000 children in a religious education program at Our Lady of Perpetual Help parish.

These two years were a relatively calm period in our lives. The parish had liturgies in both English and Spanish. We added to our repertoire of Spanish songs that we had learned in El Salvador and that we would later sing at Masses in Houston. As VESS volunteers, we had summers free and a stipend of $500 each for educational purposes, so we took advantage of this and drove to California, where we had lived for ten years before going to Central America. During the summers, we took classes in theology and spirituality. Friends let us use their house in Livingston. There the kids took lessons and became good swimmers. As we drove to California and then to visit family up north again, we developed travel traditions with the kids, driving all day and then finding a motel with a swimming pool. We topped it all off by cooking dinner on a hot plate in the motel room.

In 1979, VESS invited us to transfer to St. Theresa's in Houston to work in parish social services and various other ministries. At the same time as we arrived in Houston, refugees began pouring into Houston from El Salvador, and then Guatemala and Nicaragua. The parish social ministry program at St. Theresa's could address some of the things the refugees needed, but not their basic needs like a place to stay until they could begin anew. When we began to receive requests for help, we were dismayed because we could help only those within the geographical boundaries of the parish. We had to send people back to parishes that did not yet have outreach programs for Latin American Catholics, and some parishes that had no social programs at all.

Things were worsening with the war in El Salvador. Archbishop Oscar Romero received death threats. The Catholic radio station, where he had defended so many, was bombed into silence early in the war.

Archbishop Romero had desperately tried to protect his people, going so far as to write to President Jimmy Carter to ask him to stop sending millions of dollars a day in military aid to El Salvador, letting him know that it was being used to repress the people and that the government's reign of terror was attempting to destroy social movements meant to defend fundamental human rights. Romero preached love, nonviolence, and agrarian reform, but he was maligned and criticized by those who wanted to keep the status quo. It was a time when dead bodies could be found everywhere, thrown in garbage dumps. Relatives were often afraid to claim them, lest they be next.

Archbishop Romero personally saw the carnage and faced down the military to claim bodies. Years later, the journal *Sojourners* printed a Salvadoran woman's remembrance of the archbishop's visit to the morgue after Father Octavio Ortiz was killed. Fr. Octavio was the first priest that Archbishop Romero had ordained. He was killed along with four young laymen when gunmen broke into their retreat: the same type of retreat Mark had attended before we left El Salvador.

The Isidro Menendez Morgue was famous. That's where the bodies went after they were found on the streets, in the ditches, or in the garbage dumps of San Salvador. There were times when there were six, seven, eight bodies every day. The garbage truck would pick them up and take them there until someone came to identify them. Sometimes no one came. They were afraid of reprisals.

That's where they took Father Octavio and the four boys after the National Guard killed them in El Despertar. The news spread quickly through the neighborhood. I went with my father, Beto, who had been a friend of Father Octavio since I was a girl. We went to the morgue looking for our dead.

The entrance was totally militarized. Monseñor Romero arrived the same time we did, and he went in right away, racked with sorrow. "Where are they? Where are they?"

No one stopped him or anything. The guardsmen just looked at him from the door, curious to see the archbishop going into such a place of ghosts. We went in behind him.

The floor was one big puddle of blood. The five [bodies] were there, thrown on the floor. Streams of blood were still coming out of them. Around them were some of the people from the community that had arrived before us.

"Where is Octavio?" "Here, Monseñor. This is him." They pointed to him. You couldn't tell it was him. His body was completely flattened, his face destroyed to the point that it looked like he didn't even have one. I had seen Father

21

Octavio in my house eating with my father so many times…and I couldn't even recognize him.

Monseñor Romero knelt on the ground and held his shattered head. "It can't be. This isn't him. It's not him.…" Tears streamed from Monseñor's face as he held him with deep tenderness. "They ran him over with the tank and smashed his head, Monseñor." "I can't believe that they could be so savage," he said.

The guardsmen looked in through the door. Monseñor's cassock was covered with blood and he was crying, cradling Father Octavio in his arms. "Octavio, my son, you have completed your mission. You were faithful.…" Marichi came in, completely distraught. "You don't have a camera, do you?" Monseñor asked her. "Not here, it's at home." "Go get it. Take pictures of Father Octavio for me, with his face like this, the way they left him."—Carmen Elena Hernández[2]

In his sermons, Archbishop Romero tried to give hope and courage to the people in the middle of all the violence and terror. He told them that Matthew 25:35–46—seeing Christ in the poor, in the prisoner— still applied in this terrible situation, even if it required tremendous courage to go to those who were in prison, and tremendous courage to bury the dead. Fr. Brockman's collection of Romero's homilies includes one given in March 1980, a few days before he died:

God as Christ dwells near at hand to us.
Christ has given us a guideline:
    "I was hungry and you gave me to eat."
Where someone is hungry, there is Christ near at hand.
    "I was thirsty and you gave me to drink."
When someone comes to your house to ask for water,
    it is Christ, if you look with faith.
In the sick person longing for a visit Christ tells you,
    "I was sick and you came to visit me."
    Or in prison.
How many today are ashamed to testify for the innocent!
What terror has been sown among our people
    that friends betray friends whom they see in trouble.

If we could see that Christ is the needy one,
    the torture victim,
    the prisoner,
    the murder victim,
and in each human figure
    so shamefully thrown by the roadsides
[if we] could see Christ himself cast aside,
we would pick him up like a medal of gold,
    to be kissed lovingly.
We would never be ashamed of him.
How far people are today—
    especially those who torture and kill
    and value their investments more than human beings—
from realizing that all the earth's millions
    are good for nothing,
    are worthless, compared to a human being.
The person is Christ,
    and in the person viewed and treated with faith
we look on Christ the Lord.[3]

It was Archbishop Romero's very last sermon, the one that precipitated his death. His insistence on soldiers' laying down their arms was too much for powerful people in the government and the military, and among the wealthy landowners. In that homily, he addressed the men of the army, of the *Guardia Nacional*, and of the police, and asked them to refuse to shoot. This quote has become so well known that it is widely used in any commentary on Archbishop Romero:

> Brothers, you are part of our own people. You kill your own *campesino* brothers and sisters. And before an order to kill that a man may give, the law of God must prevail that says: Thou shalt not kill. No soldier is obliged to obey an order against the law of God. No one has to fulfill an immoral law. It is time to recover your consciences and to obey your consciences rather than the orders of sin. The church, defender of the rights of God, of the law of God, of human dignity, the dignity of the person, cannot remain silent before such abominations. We want the government to take seriously that reforms

are worth nothing when they come about stained with so much blood. In the name of God, and in the name of this suffering people whose laments rise to heaven each day more tumultuous, I beg you, I ask you, I order you in the name of God: stop the repression![4]

Archbishop Romero was martyred the next day, shot in the heart as he celebrated Mass. At his funeral, the thousands of people who could not fit into the cathedral with the dignitaries gathered in the square in front of it. A bomb was set off and shots rang out from atop adjoining buildings. The people stampeded for the safety of the church. The Mass was never finished and Romero was buried quickly.

Soon afterward, hundreds and then thousands of refugees began arriving in the United States from El Salvador, escaping what was becoming a full-blown civil war.

People challenged us at our work at the parish to do something for the refugees. Even members of the Houston City Council called on us to go down to the bus station and take care of the refugees coming in. We knew something had to be done. We complained. We wrung our hands. We prayed.

We began saying to each other: "If we had any guts, we would open a Catholic Worker house to serve the Salvadoran refugees." As it turned out, we also needed to serve refugees from the terrible war in Guatemala, not to mention from Nicaragua, although the political situation was different there. In all of these countries, forced recruitment was pushing young men to come to the United States to avoid war. We were conscious that we, too, had fled the war in El Salvador with our children in 1977, with the same concern that so many migrants have about their own children.

We knew the Catholic Worker movement. We knew one could simply start a House of Hospitality to help refugees begin anew: no permission was needed to respond as laypeople to the crisis. Civil disobedience and conscientious objection to unjust laws are at the heart of the movement. While immigration and refugees had not been its number-one emphasis, we knew that the principles applied. Resistance to injustice and the practical application of the Works of Mercy were exactly what the situation needed.

But we were not ready to start a Catholic Worker house or refuge center. We used our children as an excuse. By October 1980, though, we knew our lives had to change. We still had no courage, only excuses, until Louise, with her library science degree, learned that there was a position available for a Spanish-speaking children's librarian at Houston Public Library. She had been trained in children's literature and storytelling and wanted an opportunity to put it into practice. She applied, passed through the stages of the process, and arrived at the crucial final interview. Before leaving, Louise asked Mark to pray that it go well. At the appointed hour, Mark stopped everything and began praying for a good outcome. Becoming a little restless, he decided to pray the Rosary while walking up and down in the large social service office at St. Theresa's. While he was doing that, an inspiration came to him. If Louise had a job as a children's librarian, maybe it was the time to start a Catholic Worker house.

When Louise returned home that evening, her smile and good mood made it clear that she had received the job. Her studies in Spanish in Central America helped to secure it. Encouraged, Mark shared his idea with Louise. It sounded good to her, too. We talked at length about the possibilities, as the idea of starting a House of Hospitality for Central American refugees began to take shape. Louise's employment meant that we would have enough money for our children, who were now in the sixth and fourth grades. They could continue their music lessons and go to Catholic school if we chose that route.

We are prudent people. We usually pray about our impulses before taking action—or we pray for healing after making an impulsive decision (better late than never). This was October 1980. We decided to think and pray about the Catholic Worker house until December 31 before mentioning it to anyone or taking action.

Another option emerged when Mark was offered a job in his field as a social worker. We had left an opening in our prayers for the possibility of Mark's seeking work again in the mental health field, if this was the direction in which the Spirit was leading us. If we both worked, we could live on one salary, save the other, and one day have enough money to really help the poor. This is the great American Catholic cop-out—but we considered it.

We made a decision of the heart. The *Catechism of the Catholic Church* tells us that, concerning prayer, Scripture speaks sometimes of the soul or the spirit, but most often of the heart (more than a thousand times). According to Scripture, it is the *heart* that prays. The *Catechism* says: "The heart is our hidden center, beyond the grasp of our reason and of others; only the spirit of God can fathom the human heart and know it fully. The heart is the place of decision, deeper than our psychic drives. It is the place of truth, where we choose life or death."[5] We were searching deep in our hearts.

Dorothy Day died on the last day of the Church year, November 29, 1980. We are pretty sure she went to heaven and arranged for us to be ready to begin the Catholic Worker house at the end of December. Her prayers were obviously with us as we were becoming more committed and being forced to pass from love in dreams, to love in action. It was a time of *metanoia*, a change of heart.

By the end of December, there was not a doubt left—only anxiety. In our hearts, we had chosen the Catholic Worker. That the work of hospitality to illegal refugees and immigrants would itself be considered illegal was most definitely not foremost in our thoughts. We would be doing this work not to break the law, but to keep the law of the Gospel and the law of love.

2

JUST READ THE
LIVES OF THE SAINTS
Casa Juan Diego Begins

We had taken the risk and decided to start a Catholic Worker house in Houston. But how to begin? It isn't a franchise, like McDonald's or Domino's Pizza. We knew that we could simply rent a cheap place, put out our sign, and start a Catholic Worker house. There are many such operations. The challenge would be to live the Gospel.

To help us, we turned to Dorothy Day and Peter Maurin. When the founders of the movement met in the 1930s, Peter, a brilliant but shabbily dressed Frenchman, proposed the idea of the Catholic Worker program to Dorothy. The young woman listened intently as he told her about personalism and voluntary poverty, and about the prophets of Israel, the Fathers of the Church, and the saints. Peter outlined his program of action: roundtable discussions, Houses of Hospitality for the practice of the Works of Mercy, and agronomic universities. To top it off, Peter wanted a newspaper that would bring Catholic social teaching "to the man on the street." He had heard that Dorothy was a Catholic convert and had newspaper experience. She had been writing articles for *Commonweal* and *America*. He hoped that she would help him carry out his ideas in a practical way.

Dorothy had been searching for a way to put her concern for social justice for the poor together with her Catholic faith, but she wondered about the practicality of Peter's program. How could it be carried out? Dorothy understood the importance of starting a program, but asked, "Where would we get the money?" Peter's response determined the future basis of the Catholic Worker movement: "In the history of the saints, capital was raised by prayer. God sends you what you need when you need it. You will be able to pay the printer. Just read the lives of the saints." He told her how St. Francis de Sales scattered leaflets like any radical, and St. John of God sold newspapers on the streets. When Rose Hawthorne started a hospice in New York for the poor suffering from cancer, her method of raising money was to simply tell people what she was going to do. That appealed to Dorothy. She thought that perhaps she could start in a small way. This seed grew into *The Catholic Worker* newspaper, Houses of Hospitality, CW farms, work for peace, protests against injustice, and a way of life that has inspired generations. The methods of the saints proved to be practical for Dorothy and Peter. We hoped they would be for us, too.

Catholic Workers take the personalist approach, which is not to be confused with individualism. Our methods are different from agency or bureaucratic models. CW methods do not include applying for government funds for operation. CW houses depend on donations and the Workers are free to use them to apply the creativity and freedom of the Gospel in response to need, without writing and rewriting grant proposals. The saints taught us that we do not need such funds to serve the poor. In fact, nonfederally funded programs may be better, since government programs are so costly to administer and since they restrict services. Most of the immigrants we serve do not qualify for federal funds, so we would not have been able to apply for federal funds for Casa Juan Diego anyway. The idea was the daily practice of the Works of Mercy.

As Peter Maurin often said:

In the first centuries of Christianity pagans said about Christians: "See how they love each other." The love for God and neighbor was the characteristic of the first Christians. This love was expressed through the daily practice of the Works of Mercy. To feed the hungry, to clothe the naked, to shelter the homeless, to instruct the ignorant at a personal sacrifice was considered by the first Christians as the right thing to do.... You have to keep to a personalist approach, which is so much more profound than politics.

In one of his prose poems that, collected together, came to be called "Easy Essays," Peter described with deceptive simplicity the personalist vision of the CW:

A personalist
is a go-giver,
not a go-getter.
He tries to give
what he has
and does not
try to get
what the other fellow has.
He tries to be good
by doing good
to the other fellow.
He is altro-centered,
not self-centered.
He has a social doctrine
of the common good.

In our effort to build a Catholic Worker house, we tried Peter Maurin's methods. As he predicted—and to our surprise—after we made the decision to begin and we started to tell people about it, they helped. What we discovered, just in starting and using these methods of the saints, is that this is something the ordinary believer can do. It doesn't take a superhero, just people willing to make a commitment and begin. We learned that, when beginning, it also helps to pray, fast, and be aware of the challenge and risk of living the Gospel. We found that the best way to start a Catholic Worker house is on your knees. In our case, having a fire or two also helped to spread the word.

Before beginning, we had a meeting with several couples we had come to know, who were concerned about serving the poor. When we proposed the idea, our friends voted unanimously and enthusiastically in favor of a Catholic Worker house. These couples became a part of a long-term support group for Casa Juan Diego. Many from that original group have remained with us all these years.

The next day we arranged meetings with the diocesan leadership. We went to our bishop to announce our efforts and to ask his blessing. Bishop Morkovsky's availability reminded us of our experience in El Salvador where there was always easy access to the bishop. When we met with him and with the chancellor, Msgr. Dan Scheel, we didn't go to ask for money. We had learned years ago that to succeed in a diocese you never ask the bishop for money and never attempt to make him responsible for your ideas. Bishop Morkovsky was receptive, although he stated that he would prefer that we start a Legion of Mary or a sodality instead of a Catholic Worker. (The image of Dorothy Day was not as clear as it is now, and he may have had the mistaken impression that she had Communist leanings. Cardinal O'Connor had not yet introduced her cause for sainthood.) Mark bristled at the idea, not because he did not respect the Legion and the sodality—he had spent years with both organizations—but because he felt the Catholic Worker model was better suited to our dream of helping people from Central America.

Thankfully, the diocesan leadership was encouraging and gave us their blessing, although they were understandably concerned about the prudence of this project, because dioceses are run differently than Catholic Worker houses. We didn't ask for diocesan affiliation. Catholic Workers usually do not affiliate with the diocese, but remain independent of any other group or organization. This allows them to make their own decisions. Thus, if things go well, the Catholic Church can say, "Look what the Catholics are doing." It also provides a safety net for the diocese. If things go badly, they can say, "We are not responsible for these people. They are not affiliated with us."

We had announced that we were going to begin, and there was no turning back. Looking for rental possibilities, we began our pilgrimage up and down Washington Avenue, but there wasn't much available, just used car lots and antique shops. Finally, at 4309 Washington Avenue, we discovered an old building once used as a meat market. The building was large, but had no heat, gas, or shower, and only one toilet and sink. We rented that old ugly building; to us it represented a beginning, and a beautiful one at that.

One of our earliest contributions came with a donation of office furniture picked up by Stephen Lucas, a young railroad inspector who happened to live next door to us and had a van. When Stephen found out what we were doing, he became excited, went into his house, and brought out an envelope containing $500 for the new center. We were on our way.

A number of clergymen in Houston—though all very different—proved generous to our cause. When we visited Auxiliary Bishop John McCarthy, he congratulated and encouraged us. The bishop said humorously that three priests "owed him one," and that we should visit them to ask their help in getting started. All three had met Dorothy Day and loved her.

A Westside pastor, Msgr. Crosthwait (also known as Fr. Joe), gave us a check to help us get started. He remained a friend for many years, inviting us to speak at the Masses at St. John Vianney Church to share our project with his parishioners. Some time later Msgr. Crosthwait discovered that we operated without salaries. He became ecstatic when we spoke about giving our work as a gift.

Msgr. Al Doga also allowed us to speak at the Masses at his parish, Prince of Peace, and presented us to his people as being committed to the poor like Dorothy Day. He was generous until and after his death, remembering Casa Juan Diego in his will. His love for the poor made up for his lack of patience.

When we contacted the third priest, Fr. John Perusina, he invited us to his rectory and sat down with us for several hours as we laid out our plans for a Catholic Worker House of Hospitality. He wanted the facts and did not want to end up paying a lot of bills, as had happened with a priest he had worked with in the past. Once he decided to help us, however, Fr. Perusina was one of Casa Juan Diego's staunchest supporters. Over the years, he invited us to speak several times at his parish, St. Michael's, and if he observed that we seemed to be a little tired, he would immediately send a contribution in the mail. When a few people complained to Fr. Perusina that Catholic Workers were Communists since they worked without pay, he humorously replied, "But they're *our* Communists." Fr. Perusina also remembered us in his will.

Father Tom Sheehy, a Sacred Heart Father and pastor of Our Lady of Guadalupe church, God rest his soul, came by to tell us that he wanted to start an office of justice and peace at the Catholic Worker. After seeing the place, however, in all its poverty and simplicity, he just laughed and laughed.

The building was immediately christened Casa Juan Diego. There was an "un-grand opening." We began to give food to families who took immigrants into their own homes, and soon began a regular distribution of food and clothing to the poor of the community. Anyone who was in need could come. We became the drop-off place for things that people wanted to give directly to the poor, or for things that people didn't need. Some of it we didn't need either, but "beggars can't be choosers." People came to help, to organize donations, and to distribute food.

Young men and a few women from El Salvador and Guatemala, having fled the conflicts in their own countries, began to appear, asking to stay in the house. The first guests had been sleeping in used car lots on Washington Avenue in Houston and were grateful for a bed. They helped in the house any way they could. We began to give hospitality to as many as a dozen each night. The guests told stories of dangerous, difficult journeys, crossing several countries on foot or by freight train. Many of our first guests were young people sent out of Central America by their parents to avoid forced recruitment by either side of the conflicts in Central America.

From the very beginning, many demands were made on our limited resources. The diocesan paper, the *Texas Catholic Herald*, carried a positive article about the opening of Casa Juan Diego, and Louis Moore, then religious editor of the *Houston Chronicle*, ran a full-page article featuring the house and the work. He seemed to grasp the meaning of the Catholic Worker movement, though he wasn't Catholic. This publicity brought attention to our humble work. Several parishes, as well as a small group of individuals, began helping us with financial support on a monthly basis and have done so ever since. We could not have survived without these two groups. We still cannot!

If all we had had to do was pay our rent and refer people to agencies, our work would have been easier. There were, however, no agencies to which we could refer the undocumented, no agencies even for some citizens. We had to take responsibility ourselves to try to help refugees begin anew, with the help of the good Lord and of so many who have come to join us as full-time Catholic Workers or part-time volunteers over the years. Some of the first CWs were Salvadoran refugees.

We began without any rules for our guests, hoping and believing that love and practicality would solve all problems. Because of things that happened, however, we added some guidelines.

One of our first guests was a man from South America who came with a duffel bag. He appeared at the library branch where Louise worked and she called Mark to see if there was room for him. Although not new to the country, this man needed a place to stay. Mark came to the library to pick him up and take him to Casa Juan Diego. All was peaceful the night he arrived, but the next day problems began. In those early days, people were already donating clothing and a bag of donations had been placed on a table in the middle of the common room. Several guests were playfully tossing the clothing around when unfortunately, a piece of women's underwear landed on the new guest's head. The man became enraged, threw the underwear to the ground, and to everyone's surprise, pulled a machete from his duffel bag and attacked the man who had thrown the underwear, cutting his ear. Four Salvadoran guests were able to subdue him.

We decided for the future to ask guests to give us any weapons they had when they entered, with the agreement that they would be returned to them when they left. People arriving rarely had guns or knives, but when they did, having carried them on a long and dangerous journey, they generally turned them in. Mostly they were frightened, lonely people in a strange land. They loved the safe cocoon that is Casa Juan Diego and usually left without reclaiming weapons they turned in.

One of the surprising things to us is that violence has been such a rare occurrence within our Houses of Hospitality. Our great frustration in the area of violence has been with those who inflict violence on poor immigrants and refugees, rather than from our guests.

One guest arrived with a loaded pistol after we implemented the rule about weapons. He turned it in as required. A week later, he banged on the office door when he was roaring drunk and demanded his gun back. We refused, but he insisted, quoting our promise from a week ago that we would return it. What a quandary! It was his gun and we had no right to it, especially since we are pacifists. We hemmed and hawed. He insisted. We prayed for guidance. He demanded his gun. We suggested he could pick it up from the police. "It's not the police's gun," he said. Prayers answered: "How much do you want for the gun?" The answer, "$50." "We'll buy it." Case closed. Lives saved! Except what do you do with a Saturday Night Special?

After a few people came in sloppy drunk, we established a rule that the guests could not drink and live at Casa Juan Diego. A few men began to sleep all day and party all night, so we required them to go to look for work during the day. When a few men became too aggressive or used inappropriate language with the women guests, we made a strict rule about respecting women. The vast majority of guests, however, were highly motivated and respectful, and soon moved on to their relatives or established themselves in Houston.

Beginning a CW house on almost no funds and no staff was a very daunting task, but from the beginning, people appeared out of nowhere to help. Dr. Carol Ashton came to start a simple medical clinic in that first building. The building was so shabby that nurses refused to work with her, but she treated patients each week anyway.

Things fell into place. A rice company called and said they had one thousand pounds of rice they could not sell. Would we be interested? Silly question. A priest who knew carpentry and plumbing came down from Iowa during his vacation and installed showers and more toilets. Later, a young man who said he was "sort of" a plumber repaired four showers. A seminarian said he could do carpentry and repaired the bathroom. Another young man said he was a "shade tree carpenter" and repaired another bathroom. A draftsman from the suburbs who had been laid off came in to paint some bathrooms. A dentist accepted refugees in pain immediately at his office. No charge. A man brought in one hundred pounds of rice and beans along with onions and potatoes for the sixth time! A contractor put up drywall in a new room.

It wasn't long before Bishop Morkovsky came to celebrate Mass in that first ugly building, carrying his own satchel filled with vestments and altar vessels. He was one of the best Spanish speakers in the diocese at that time. When Mass was over, it wasn't easy to find him, because the great man was mingling with the guests. The bishop's celebration of the liturgy was the beginning of our long-standing tradition of having Mass with our guests on Wednesday evenings. Fr. Mario Arroyo, who at the time was the vocation director and coordinator of the missionary cooperative program for the diocese, came almost every week for years. Msgr. Scheel came each Tuesday and Thursday morning to celebrate Mass with us and with the people who came for clothing. We called it *la Misa de la ropa*. Spanish-speaking priests from the Galveston-Houston Diocese still continue the Wednesday evening tradition, taking turns in celebrating the breaking of the bread with the immigrant guests of Casa Juan Diego. Louise, along with other guitarists when available, always plays for the Mass. It is a celebration of thanksgiving for the safe arrival of those gathered and includes prayers for those who did not make it through or who are facing great difficulties on their way.

After crossing the first hurdle of actually starting a House of Hospitality, within a few months we began our newspaper, the *Houston Catholic Worker/El Trabajador Católico de Houston*. The first issue was dated May 5, 1981. The stories of the refugees and the adventures of living and working in the houses have been recorded in it since the earliest issues, along with articles about Dorothy Day, Peter Maurin, and the Catholic Worker movement. Other articles have reflected on the violence in Central America, the wars from which the refugees were coming. In the earliest years, Mark wrote many of the stories and articles for the paper. Louise was working at the library; she typed stories and articles in the evenings, and on weekends she assisted with editing. At other times, the guests, who had various levels of education, wrote down or dictated their own stories.

Later we began to study and reflect on international economics, globalization, outsourcing; we also looked at "free trade" and how it was uprooting the immigrants who arrived at our doors. We put this, too, in our newspaper. Like Dorothy Day's *Catholic Worker*, our paper also tries to expose the root causes of the sufferings of the poor. Like our founders, we try to present the great traditions of the Church in bringing God's love to the world in a practical way, as an alternative to the consumerism that can grip the soul of our people. We understood, with Dorothy Day, that a newspaper could fulfill several of the fourteen traditional Works of Mercy, such as educating the ignorant and admonishing the sinner. From the very first issue, the paper was bilingual because most of our guests were Spanish speakers. People interested in the work have always included those who have contributed articles and helped with translation of articles for the paper.

Stephen Lucas and his wife Lillian, our neighbors when we began, became an important part of Casa Juan Diego. They have always maintained the mailing list for the paper, updating it with all the additions and corrections, as it grew over the years from 1,000 to 67,000. Gradually, our paper blanketed Houston and its suburbs, but with time, half of the copies began to go to other states and even a number of other countries. Bulk copies go to local parishes and to Catholic schools and universities across the country, where interested faculty members have requested them.

The newspaper has been our main way of communicating with others the needs of those who come to us. Most readers are touched by the stories of the refugees and immigrants who often suffered terribly, not just on their journey, but also on the streets of Houston.

So many people have helped Casa Juan Diego, sharing their money and the goods of the earth, from rice and beans, to diapers and baby wipes, to school supplies. People bring very nice clothing, toilet paper, soaps, rosaries, wheelchairs, furniture, and almost anything else. The donors come quoting the Fathers of the Church: "The extra coat you have in your closet belongs to the poor; we must help the poorest not out of our excess, but until it hurts." We use their gifts in the CW houses or give them to the poor of the community. Tons of clothing, food, and furniture are distributed at Casa Juan Diego.

When a famous restaurateur wanted to help, he asked us what we most needed. We thought a little and mentioned we often lacked fresh milk and eggs. He has been sending forty gallons of milk and a case of eggs for our guests each week for years.

We try to be as unbureaucratic as possible, giving as donations are given, providing basics for the guests who live with us and then to the poor of the community. We try to distribute the gifts fairly, not giving only to the best storytellers. We have always been conscious that, in some situations, the best storytellers get help and those who can't tell a good story starve and go naked. Everyone who comes to our weekly food distribution receives the same: rice, beans, vegetables, fruit, canned goods, and bread. At Thanksgiving, we give a chicken or turkey.

All kinds of requests come in. People need more than food. "Do you have a bed, or a sofa that could be used for a bed? Could you help with immigration fees so that we do not have to live in fear any more? Could you help with a wheelchair or adult diapers for my brother who was seriously injured? Could you help us survive a little longer? Could you help me travel to my relatives?"

Our help is on a very practical level. We don't throw cash around, but try to encourage refugees and immigrants in crisis to stay at our Houses of Hospitality. We encourage people to come to the food distribution each week so that they can use any funds they have to pay their rent. Buying food at the grocery store makes it difficult for those who make the minimum wage or less to pay their rent and utility bills.

We have been known literally to give the shirt off our back. One day an old friend came to give us his change of address and a $500 check. Mark put the check in his shirt pocket, as well as the change of address. On his way out of Casa Juan Diego, he encountered a young man from the United States who said he was hungry. In a hurry to pick up another person, Mark quickly made some sandwiches and wrapped them. Next, the visitor said he needed some clothes. He did smell bad and his clothes were dirty. Mark simply took off his shirt and gave it to him. After Mark went to the clothing room to find another shirt, it struck him—the check was in the pocket of the shirt he had just given the young man! He lost no time looking up and down the streets of the neighborhood for the man in his shirt. But he couldn't find him! Finally, it occurred to him that the man might have gone to a local fast food restaurant to have a Coke with his sandwiches. The manager there said that a young man fitting the description had just left. Mark dashed between cars at the corner of Washington and Shepherd, caught up with him, and offered him the shirt he had just selected from the clothing room, "Could I ask you to exchange that shirt for this beautiful shirt so that I could have mine back?" As he received his shirt, Mark was relieved to find the check still in the pocket. When someone donates by check, Mark's shirt pocket remains our best temporary filing system before going to the bank.

Some of our supporters especially like the idea that no one is paid a salary. One of the great strengths of the Catholic Worker is voluntary poverty (keeping in mind that voluntary poverty, no matter how precarious, is not as bad as involuntary poverty). Those who contribute financially are pleased that their donations go directly to the service of the poor. Each person who contributes money, whether it is one dollar or a much larger donation, receives a thank-you note.

One day, after we had been in operation for more than a decade, a couple who were good friends of the house rushed into Casa Juan Diego, very agitated and asked to speak to us privately. They mentioned that they had just been reading the story of Ananias and Sapphira in the Acts of the Apostles, in which those who did not share their goods, especially those who lied about having goods to begin with, were struck dead. The couple had just received a legacy. Not wanting to end up like Ananias and Sapphira, they wrote a check to Casa Juan Diego for $10,000.

When friends of Casa Juan Diego tried to get large foundations interested in donating to us, the representatives of foundations laughed and asked where our endowment was? They said, "We see that you have money for this year, but where will the money come from in the years to come?" They expected us to have millions in the bank for a rainy day—and live off the interest. Though prudent and realistic about what kind of help we could give people with the money donated, we tried to follow Dorothy Day's example of using the funds as needed during the year and then sending out a letter of appeal each Christmas, in the hope and trust that the Lord and good people would provide for the future.

We accepted Peter Maurin's and the centuries-old teaching of the prophets of Israel and the Fathers of the Church that usury is immoral, although we have not been able to be absolutely pure in that. We do have bank accounts. Even though we are uncomfortable with the whole system of usury—borrowing money at interest, receiving interest on money, and following the general practices of banks—it is not possible to keep all the donations under the mattress.

In the early years, sometimes our money ran out before we sent our letter of appeal in December. Several times, we were out of funds in October or November and had houses full of people living with us. We were not sure what to do. The money was gone, and Christmas had not arrived. We didn't want to flirt with usury through credit cards, but we did still have a credit card from when we were working. We charged the limit on the card (thousands of dollars) to provide funds and then paid off the charges when the response to the Christmas letter of appeal arrived—before interest would be charged. Later, after some of the priests who had originally helped us remembered Casa Juan Diego in their wills, we were able to survive better until the end of the year. An article in the *Houston Catholic Worker* titled "The Dead Priests' Society" tells about those who helped in this way.

People often ask us if the diocese funds Casa Juan Diego. The answer is no, not directly, but the diocese (now an archdiocese) has been very helpful. In 1984, Joseph A. Fiorenza became bishop of Galveston-Houston. While we didn't have the miracle of the roses from a wintery mountaintop to present to him, we did have thousands of immigrants, our own Juan Diegos, who had passed through our doors. The new bishop's response was very positive. For the guests of Casa Juan Diego, Bishop Fiorenza did the best possible thing by allowing us to participate in the Diocesan Missionary Cooperative Plan. This has given us the opportunity to speak in several parishes each year at the Masses about our work and to sign up people for the newspaper. It is through these talks that many people have become interested in Casa Juan Diego. They have not only been generous in their contributions, but also volunteered to help. Some who would have considered our work too radical were more comfortable with us as participants in the Diocesan Missionary Cooperative Plan: it was a sign of the bishop's approval. Our new Cardinal Archbishop Daniel DiNardo has allowed us to continue the missionary talks in parishes.

St. Thomas Aquinas says that if you accept one grace, others will follow, like links in a chain. Many refugees and immigrants have come, and many graces have come. Since its foundation in 1980, more than seventy thousand refugees and migrants have passed through Casa Juan Diego, staying at least a night. Often some 150 guests have stayed the night in our Houses of Hospitality at a single time. It has not been unusual for 50 to 100 new homeless people to arrive each week. At the time we write, 500,000 meals are provided each year.

With time, migrants and refugees from many nations joined the Central American refugees seeking a place to stay. In addition to those from the wars in various countries, many were refugees from the global economic crises that hurt the poor so much. Families of the deported and families of prisoners came to stay with us. Battered women from Central America or Mexico arrived asking if we could help them, too. Pregnant women began to arrive, telling us how their coyote (someone who smuggles people into the country) had raped them. Could we give them a place to stay?

We will never forget the day that Gloria, one of our guests, started down the stairs to tell us it was time to go to the hospital. But before she could get to the bottom, the baby was born right there on the steps. Some frightened women guests received the baby. Having never assisted at a birth before, they thought the ugly, purple baby was dying, which they told Gloria's three daughters. In their anxiety, the women thought the mother might be dying as well. This they also told the girls. While waiting for the ambulance to arrive, we sat with the weeping girls, trying to comfort them. When the paramedics came, they reassured everyone that mother and baby were fine and took them to the hospital to be checked. Ever since that day, we have reminded women about to give birth to tell us as soon as they have their first labor pains, so we can transport them to the hospital in time. Even with this precaution, a baby was born several years later in a car on the way to the hospital.

Faith and the approach of personalism—taking personal responsibility —demands that you don't just let things go, that you can't ignore problems. Ignoring problems, small or great, is what gets people (guests) hurt. Maybe we're softies. Maybe we should let people fend for themselves—all, of course, in the name of Christian anarchism. But we're probably not good anarchists in this regard. When we receive a nine-months-pregnant woman who has never seen a physician, we insist that she see one. When a baby has diarrhea, vomiting, and fever, we can't say, "Go and be thou healed." (We may start with a bottle of Pedialyte.) When a woman is sick at 2 a.m. with violent stomach cramps and vomiting, we can't say, "*Hasta mañana*." When a young man has painful urination and pus in his urine, we don't pass it off as a little prostate problem. When a person is drunk, we don't let it go. When people who run *cantinas* try to recruit our women guests to become prostitutes, we don't let it go. Our problem is the necessity we feel to stay with a problem until it is resolved.

We try to keep the perspective that, as the Gospel of St. Matthew tells us in chapter 25, Jesus himself comes to us in the guise of the poor, who today are often refugees and immigrants, and it is by how we respond to him in that guise that we shall be judged. In that Bible passage Jesus tell us what it will be like when he comes again, how he will separate us into the sheep and the goats—sheep on the right and goats on the left:

> "Then the king will say to those on his right, 'Come, you who are blessed by my Father. Inherit the kingdom prepared for you from the foundation of the world. For I was hungry and you gave me food, I was thirsty and you gave me drink, a stranger and you welcomed me, naked and you clothed me, ill and you cared for me, in prison and you visited me.' Then the righteous will answer him and say, 'Lord, when did we see you hungry and feed you, or thirsty and give you drink? When did we see you a stranger and welcome you, or naked and clothe you? When did we see you ill or in prison, and visit you?' And the king will say to them in reply, 'Amen, I say to you, whatever you did for one of these least brothers of mine, you did for me.'" (Matt 25:34–40, NAB)

We hesitate to mention the second half of Jesus' teaching on judgment, the fate of those on the left who have not helped the Lord in the poor: "Depart, you cursed, into everlasting fire" for not performing the Works of Mercy.

We are grateful to Dorothy and Peter for making Matthew 25 the center of the Catholic Worker movement and applying it to more aspects of life and experience than are generally considered in its light. For example, Dorothy taught us that as the Lord is present in others, we cannot drop bombs on them.

It is easier to do this work without compensation if we remember what Peter Maurin called the shock maxims of the Gospel: Going the extra mile, giving your extra shirt to the one who asks, loving your enemy, forgiving in the face of criticism and persecution, turning the other cheek, seeking first the Kingdom of God. The life of the Catholic Worker, of Casa Juan Diego, is a reversal of values seen in society. In the Kingdom, the greatest are not the most powerful, not the richest, not the strongest, not the smartest. The Lord told us that he is present in the poor and the weak.

When we pray and meditate, we keep this perspective. We see the poor and homeless as ambassadors of the Lord. When we meditate, we keep our sense of humor. For example, when people ask us if our efforts at Casa Juan Diego are our full-time work, we answer, "Of course not. We just spend a hundred hours a week with Casa Juan Diego and fritter away the rest of the time."

Life in Catholic Worker houses, centers of hospitality, is not easy. Since there is no pay, one must be compensated in some other way. If Workers are not compensated in some way—for example, through knowing that we are doing the work of Jesus and the Gospels or are helping our fellow human beings—then anger and frustration might set in. The guests or others who come for help might become the enemy, interfering with our lives. Sometimes we and the other Catholic Workers get tired or grouchy. One trouble in our work is that some people expect us to be saints all the time, whereas in reality we are not saints. We are not angels. We are imperfect people who become impatient and who need to eat and occasionally rest. Somehow, to give one's all is not enough for some critics. A constant effusion of blood, sweat, and tears is expected whether it's midnight or 6:00 a.m. The plain fact is, one has a limited amount of blood.

Catholic Workers who come to help in the work full-time are at the heart of Casa Juan Diego. Inspired by the movement, some come for a summer or for a year or two after college to give a time of service, to learn about Hispanic culture, and to improve their Spanish. Some stay a few months, others have stayed for years. Many have been a real inspiration to us. A few have gone on to start other Catholic Worker houses. Others have made lifelong friendships or have even married fellow CWs.

When people first come to join in the work, in the hustle and bustle and in the middle of so many needs and so much suffering, it can be very challenging for them. It is hard at first to accept our limitations. We can help each person with hospitality and in other small ways, but the consequences of the injustices done to undocumented immigrants, such as their lack of any rights, can be overwhelming. When new volunteers accept personalism and the simplicity of a Gospel approach, and are able to be flexible without a lot of structure, we have a Catholic Worker. While some have found the best expression of their faith working at Casa Juan Diego, others have found it too difficult.

Combining the personalist approach of taking personal responsibility with voluntary poverty means that we do not have paid people to maintain the property. One day we might be addressing 1,500 people at Mass, being interviewed on television, or helping solve a person's difficult problems. The next day we may be cleaning up someone's excrement.

Our guests have always helped us in many ways. As in the tradition of the Catholic Worker, they help with cleaning and cooking and with the mailing of the newspaper. After the house had been in operation for some years and we already had more than one building, this contribution of guests was expanded to include a team of *ayudantes*, assistants, developed at our men's house. These men come from among the immigrants and refugees who live in the houses and stay longer than other guests. The team of fourteen lives in the men's house and dedicates a full day each week to the house. Because they came here to help their families and still need to send money to those who depend on them, they are free to work the other days. There are two in the house each day. Seven men take turns cooking and enlisting the help of other guests with cleaning, while seven others take responsibility for the door, the phone, and receiving new guests. The adult male guests sleep on bunk beds, between four and six in a room. There is an *ayudante* in each room; this enables them to more easily identify problems or let us know if someone is ill.

Should a visitor come by the men's house on Monday or Thursday evening, they would see the fourteen men bent over white books entitled *Dorothy Day y el movimiento del Trabajador Católico (Dorothy Day and the Catholic Worker Movement)*, published by the Houston Catholic Worker. Mark and the other men who are full-time Catholic Workers are always there too. The conversation, in Spanish, becomes very intense as the men talk about nonviolence, Dorothy Day's conversion, serving the poor, personalism, voluntary poverty, and giving your work as a gift. Matthew 25, the Catholic Worker mission statement, is often read on meeting nights; knowing it by heart helps "the fourteen" understand the CW movement.

Volunteers who do not live in the houses are always coming and going, literally dozens of them, to assist in various ways—not to mention the many who contribute financially to keep the work going. Volunteers from parishes come individually or in groups to help. As we write, a parishioner from St. Cecilia's is redoing the bathrooms in the women's house. When there was a bad freeze in Houston (a rare occurrence) and the frozen pipes broke, a friend of the house who was retired arrived at the door with his tools and asked if we needed help with the plumbing. We did! Parish youth groups organize donations, help with the newspaper, and provide arts and crafts programs for the children. Those involved in programs for the RCIA (Rite of Christian Initiation) often come to learn about the Catholic Worker and about immigration issues and sometimes paint several rooms or prune the trees and shrubs on the property. Several Presbyterian church groups also help. A hundred and fifty families from one Catholic parish have been involved for several years in making lunches for the men of our house who go to work and also for men in the neighborhood who are looking for work. Others take up collections of items needed at the houses or the clinic or call to see what we need at the moment.

While we have always been encouraged by people who support and help in the work, our work has not always been praised. In fact, it has made some people furious. A large crowd comes for the food and clothing distribution. Things are not always neat outside when they leave with their food or clothing and this, of course, disturbs the neighbors. We have always tried to respond to the neighbors' criticisms as best we could. We started sending out a cleaning crew each day to make sure there was not a lot of debris on nearby streets. One businessman in the neighborhood attacked us with great furor in the early 1980s, picketing in front of Casa Juan Diego. He referred to Mark mockingly as "Saint Zwick." Very angrily he would say, "You are trying to be some kind of saint—yeah, Saint Zwick—how does that sound? You just want to be canonized. Hope you're happy in being a saint at our expense, trying to make a name for yourself!" Or, "You are trying to make points with the pope—you just want to gain jewels in your crown with the pope!" This man complained that Casa Juan Diego was a plot of the pope to bring more Catholics into the United States. Little did he know that often the majority of the guests of Casa Juan Diego are not Catholic.

Dorothy did not proselytize the guests in Catholic Worker Houses of Hospitality. We have always accepted people without any religious test and washed their feet without proselytizing. We don't require people to speak with us or laugh at our jokes or even pray with us in order to receive food in our food lines. We do continue to have weekly liturgies where guests and staff from all of our houses gather, and we invite guests to go to Sunday Mass at a nearby parish. As a community, we pray Morning Prayer from the Liturgy of the Hours, but guests are not required to attend. If some guests want to be baptized or make their first communion, we are glad to help them get in touch with a parish to do so, upon request. If immigrants ask us, as they often do by telephone, where they can find a Catholic parish in Houston where there is a Spanish Mass, we are glad to provide the information.

We preach at Casa Juan Diego, but generally not with words. Our wordless sermons are hard-hitting, and at times they overwhelm people. Some who listen are never the same. But again, no words (or very few). We do not intimidate with words or gestures. Our preaching is pantomime. We preach only by our actions and by the way we live.

Our work is a blessing to us because it forces us to pray. There are so many tragedies in people's lives and in the failure of our abilities to resolve all problems and meet all expectations that we are brought to our knees. Sometimes all we have to offer is our emptiness and helplessness. Do-gooders, we are. We really want to do good. Peter Maurin emphasized that we need to make a world where it is easier to be good.

Some, including a former Salvadoran government official, have described us as a bunch of bleeding-heart liberals. We don't allow ourselves to bleed. If we did, we would bleed to death quickly. If we absorbed the suffering, fears, doubts, and loneliness of the refugees, the immigrants, the battered, or the pregnant and homeless mothers of even those who came yesterday—we could not stand it. It would be overwhelming. If we allowed our hearts to bleed for our guests, we would hemorrhage to death. We do not often ask about feeling, suffering, desolation, or pain. We would drown as the floodgates opened. We address the situation and meet the immediate need in some small way, if we can. We guarantee our commitment to help—not our tears. We have much more energy than tears. Working and weeping are like oil and water.

Once when we made a presentation at a Methodist church in Houston and talked about our work and CW ideas, the reaction surprised us. After a less-than-perfect presentation about work, personalism, and voluntary poverty—and about the refugees, about mothers coming without their children in order to earn money to support them, about the young teenage refugees—they seemed very moved by the whole thing. One member of the group finally said, "This is so radical, so primitive." We were taken aback, but felt complimented. We did not feel radical or primitive. We felt very ordinary, with a lot of work to do.

We know that Matthew 25, our mission statement, is for everyone, not just for those who start Houses of Hospitality or who stay there. And that is essentially what we tell our guests, when they ask how they can repay what Casa Juan Diego has done for them. We do not accept money—they are in no position to pay or to make donations, nor will they be in the near future. They come to us with only the shirts on their backs, and while they have more shirts, pants, shoes and socks, and jackets when they leave, thanks to the generosity of many, they still have little. If they are moving into an apartment, we give them donated dishes and silverware, food, and a mattress if we have one at the time. After a few days of work, they will be able to begin a new life, but with few resources. They can come back for food each week until they get on their feet. Donors who have been able to build up more of an earthly treasure willingly help Casa Juan Diego, but many of them do not often meet really poor people in person. However, the immigrants who leave our houses will meet the poor in the neighborhoods in which they'll live. There they will have the opportunity to help their brothers and sisters. We remind our guests that one day, after they leave Casa Juan Diego and have a job, a poor person in great need will cross their path. We hope that like a flash of lightning from the heavens, it will strike them: "Now is the time to repay Casa Juan Diego! It's my turn!"

Instead of sending out rugged individualists from Casa Juan Diego, we are sending out seventy thousand people who, we pray, will use the methods of the saints.

3

WHY JUAN DIEGO?
A Saint for Nobodies

To answer the phone at Casa Juan Diego you need three things: Spanish, English, and a sense of humor. Occasionally someone calls and asks, "Is Juan Diego there?" or "Could I speak to Juan Diego?" After we tell callers that, unfortunately, Juan Diego is not here, some push for Mrs. Juan Diego. With a smile, we tell them apologetically that Juan Diego died more than 450 years ago. They noticed the name of the house, but they may not have known that it was named for the man to whom Our Lady of Guadalupe, the mother of Jesus, appeared several centuries ago near Mexico City. We named the first house Casa Juan Diego (House of Juan Diego) and as more houses were opened over the years, the name Casa Juan Diego became an umbrella name for all of them.

People have often been curious about why we chose Juan Diego as our patron when we started the Houston Catholic Worker. He wasn't even "blessed" when we began. The bigger question—which is really the answer—is why did God choose Juan Diego to receive the apparitions of Our Lady of Guadalupe in 1531. If it happened today, we might ask why God would choose a Native American who was not a successful CEO, nor a college graduate, nor a theologian, to be the one to carry the message of Our Lady of Guadalupe to the local bishop. Not only was this poor Native American unfamiliar with the historical-critical method in biblical studies, with neoliberal economics, or with United States democracy, he didn't even know how to read and write in his own language. She chose the lowly over the exalted.

Mark had visited the Basilica of Our Lady of Guadalupe in Mexico City before he and Louise met. He told Louise, a new Catholic convert, the story, explaining that Mary had appeared to Juan Diego at a time when missionaries had been very unsuccessful in convincing indigenous people about Christianity during the conquest of "New Spain." He told her how scientists had visited the basilica and examined the cloth and her image left on cloth so many years ago, and how they were unable to explain how they had remained intact for centuries.

In Catholic tradition, there are a number of stories about the Mother of Jesus appearing to certain individuals and giving them a specific message, such as calling people to repent or to build a shrine. These appearances are not on par with Sacred Scripture. They are considered private devotions, which can be accepted or rejected by the faithful, although most Catholics tend to see the revelations approved by the Church as part of Catholicism. The Church investigates each one; only in a few cases have the apparitions been declared authentic.

Historians and anthropologists have varied reactions to these revelations. They tend to see them as rooted in hysteria and believe that they flourish because of Church connivance. Some Catholics see them as pious fantasies of the unlettered. Whatever our beliefs, the message is clear. In every apparition approved by the Catholic Church, the Mother of Jesus appears to humble, lowly, poor laypeople, including children. To some believers, this points to the authenticity of Guadalupe. Another matter of authenticity is that, if the Church had invented these stories, surely the Blessed Mother would have appeared as a white woman to send her message to a bishop of Western culture.

Devotion to Mary under the names given to her in these appearances —such as Our Lady of Guadalupe, Our Lady of Fatima, or Our Lady of Lourdes—is a part of what is often called popular piety, which includes praying the Rosary, processions, and an emphasis on the Communion of Saints.

Our faith-filled experience in Central America helped us to appreciate popular piety and understand its importance to ordinary Catholics. Some have thought that those interested in building small base communities and making the very poor aware of human rights did not emphasize faith. Maybe this was so in some countries where a percentage of the groups eventually became secular. Our experience was different in El Salvador. The Maryknoll priests and their associates there made a conscious effort to include popular piety in their work with the poor. They did not attempt to stamp out the noble, simple faith of the people, but built on it. Archbishop Oscar Romero defended popular piety and devotions.

Our Lady of Guadalupe inspires and gives encouragement to countless people whom others have tried to keep on the margins of society.

On the occasion of the retirement of Archbishop Patricio Flores of San Antonio, the first Mexican American bishop in the United States, a documentary was made for public television in Texas. His story is impressive. He had grown up as a migrant worker, and like other children of migrant workers in Texas, he did not return to school until November each year. While the civil rights movement made everyone aware of the enforced discrimination against African Americans in the South, most Americans continued to be unaware that in states like Texas, Mexican Americans were treated almost as badly. In the documentary, one of the brothers of Archbishop Flores told of having been refused service in restaurants unless he ate in the kitchen. Even in parish churches, they had to sit in, as he somewhat humorously put it in spite of all the pain, the very "first" pews as they entered—which meant, the *back* of the church. *La Virgen Morena* (the "Brown Virgin," that is, Our Lady of Guadalupe) sustained them through these times: "She looked like us, she was one of us."

Why did Our Lady of Guadalupe appear at that place and that moment in history? The story reveals that God intervened with Mary's gentle love when oppression and injustice were so bad the indigenous people as a group had asked to die. They had come to think that death might be preferable to what they were suffering.

Our Lady of Guadalupe's identification with the messenger, Juan Diego, was an important aspect of the message. She brought the Gospel to his people in a way that they could understand. It has been said that her intervention is the best model for what is called enculturation. Mary, who had generally been depicted as a white Westerner, appeared to Juan Diego as an indigenous Nahuatl woman with brown skin. She would always be known as *La Morenita*. She told Juan Diego of her love for his people. She asked him go to the bishop of Mexico and request that a church be built in her honor. The chosen one belonged to the race of people not accepted by some of the conquistadors as human beings. Our Lady of Guadalupe's appearance was the answer to the prayers of the few native people who had become Catholic and to the prayers of the Franciscan missionary priests who had accompanied the conquerors. The story of Juan Diego reminds us that liberation theologians did not invent the preferential option for the poor. Mary has always practiced this.

When we came to Texas, we saw Father Virgilio Elizondo's movie about Our Lady of Guadalupe. Using the themes of cultural-ethnic identity, faith, and social concern, the film tells the ancient story of the apparition of the Virgin Mary to Juan Diego. Elizondo's film is a combination of popular piety, the traditional story of Our Lady of Guadalupe, and reflections on what her appearance meant—not only to the poor at that time, but also to people of all times. A larger theme in the film is how, throughout history, God has used the poor and the powerless to bring his message to the world.

Elizondo's film influenced our choice for the name for the Houston Catholic Worker house. When we started in 1980, we had nothing except the heritage of Peter Maurin and Dorothy Day. Juan Diego was a perfect match to be our patron. Juan Diego was poor, powerless, and a nobody in the worldly sense, an important symbol for those who are nobodies in the eyes of the powerful but who are greatly appreciated by God. The people we would serve, the refugees and immigrants from Latin America, were considered nobodies. Those who came and continue to come to us are wanted here only for their cheap labor, but are not considered human beings by many, as was true of Juan Diego. Like him, they do not speak the language and have no rights. We hoped that God's care for the poor and for those from other cultures shown by Mary's appearances to Juan Diego would somehow shine forth at our new house. We, too, were nobodies as we began taking in refugees from the wars in Central America. We identified very much with Juan Diego. We remain nobodies in the eyes of the world.

When Europeans traveled here after Columbus "discovered" the Americas, many of the invaders thought the indigenous people did not have souls and therefore did not have the right to own anything, but should be subject to the conquerors. That attitude is present today in what Pope John Paul II called a "new colonialism." Those who have manipulated international finance, as well as wealthy landowners in the south, appear to have the same attitude as the conquistadors: the poor do not have the right to own anything, but should be subject to those who own the most.

Sometimes the story of the Blessed Mother's appearance as Our Lady of Guadalupe has been told as if there were no receptive Spaniards at all, that every one of them was as cruel as Cortés. With the conquistadors, however, came missionaries burning with the ardent desire to share their faith with the people. It was very hard going at first because of the terrible treatment the natives were receiving at the hands of the conquerors. The Franciscans defended the indigenous people and worked hard to share their faith with them. They wrote to the king of Spain and to the pope to argue that the indigenous people of New Spain were human beings with souls. They described the cruelty, corruption, and hardness of heart of many of their own countrymen. One of the Franciscans who defended the native people was Juan de Zumárraga, bishop of Mexico. A book by Eduardo Chavez Sanchez, the postulator of Juan Diego's cause for sainthood, shows how the apparitions were amazing encouragement for Franciscans. The book was sent to us by the priest from the parish that operates our Casa Juan Diego House of Hospitality in Matamoros, Mexico. The book has more recently been published in English as *Our Lady of Guadalupe and St. Juan Diego: The Historical Evidence.* Quotations from the book later on are our own translation from the Spanish-language original.[1]

As the people were enslaved and their women taken by soldiers, they came weeping to the bishop, who denounced the behavior in his weekly sermons in the church where the conquistadors attended Mass. Bishop Zumárraga complained that Cortés and other leaders then fled from his sermons, no longer going to church. Because of his strong critique of the injustices, cruelty, thievery, and corruption, especially of those in charge of the government of Mexico City, Bishop Zumárraga was threatened, and lies were made up to discredit him and to try to have him replaced.

There is a strong parallel between what happened in Mexico all those years ago and what happened in El Salvador in the seventies and eighties. When Archbishop Oscar Romero defended the poor and criticized in his sermons the oppressors who were torturing and killing people, he was threatened. Lies were made up to discredit him and some people, even his brother bishops, tried to have him replaced.

In 1529, one year and four months before the apparitions of Our Lady of Guadalupe to Juan Diego, Bishop Zumárraga wrote in desperation to the king. He said that the situation was insupportable, that only a miracle of God could save the situation and the earth: "*Si Dios no provee con remedio de su mano está la tierra en punto de perderse totalmente.*" ("If God does not provide a remedy from His hand, this land is about to be totally lost.") The missionaries prayed for God to intervene. They prayed for a miracle. Chavez wrote:

> The situation which resulted from the Conquest and the discord which existed among the Spaniards gave no possibility

of a way out; it could have resulted in a cataclysm of one world against the other—the Spaniards who felt questioned by their consciences and the indigenous who showed in their sorrow a profound fatalism. Only an intervention of another magnitude could create a new people, a new race.

Shortly thereafter, God did provide the remedy to what might have been the total destruction of a civilization and culture. In 1531, a *Señora del Cielo* ("Lady from Heaven," as Juan Diego called her) appeared to a humble Native American at Tepeyac, a hill northwest of what is now Mexico City. Mary identified herself as the "ever virgin Holy Mary, Mother of the True God for whom we live, of the Creator of all things, Lord of heaven and the earth."

The remedy that the bishop had prayed for was accomplished through Mary, Mother of Jesus, Virgin of Guadalupe, who sent Juan Diego to bring God's message to the bishop, and through him, to all of the Americas. She left her own image on Juan Diego's *tilma* (cloak) as a sign. The image shows her pregnant with the child Jesus as a sign of new life. That is the image preserved today in the Basilica of Our Lady of Guadalupe.

Juan Diego was one of the few indigenous people in New Spain who had become Christian. He, with his wife, had been baptized and frequently received the sacraments. His faith was an example of the sincere and profound conversion hoped for by the missionaries. Devotion to Mary was very much a part of the evangelization that Juan Diego had received. With her help, Juan Diego and his people could become comfortable with this religion from across the ocean.

When Our Lady appeared several times to Juan Diego, the *Señora del Cielo* affirmed the dignity of an oppressed people in an unmistakable way. Mary, who had so often been depicted as blond and blue-eyed, appeared with brown skin and spoke Nahuatl, the language the conquistadors had forbidden. Stunned, Juan Diego asked Our Lady to send a nobleman instead of him, someone the bishop would listen to. But she wanted him. Instead of asking a more important person, she simply asked him again and encouraged him.

The story has been told to many generations of Mexican people: When Juan Diego went to the bishop, the bishop asked him for a sign in order to verify the authenticity of the apparitions. So Mary instructed

Juan to return to the hill upon which they had first met. He followed her instructions and went. To his surprise, he found roses blooming in the dead of winter. He gathered them in his mantle and went to see the bishop. When Juan Diego unfolded his mantle, the bishop and his assistants saw not only roses but also, imprinted on the mantle, the image of Our Lady of Guadalupe that we know today. The bishop believed and the church was built, as Our Lady had asked.

Our Lady of Guadalupe did not come in her own name only. When she spoke to Juan Diego, she said she was Mary, Mother of the True God, that she came in God's name and that she would exalt and manifest God in the sacred house that Juan Diego would ask the bishop to build. She promised that she would hear the cries of those who cry out to her, who look for her, who trust in her to remedy all the different sufferings, miseries, and pains.

It was only ten years before the apparition at Guadalupe that the capital city of the Aztec empire fell to the Spanish forces. And it was only ten years after the apparition that nine million of the inhabitants of the land had converted to Christianity—and not by force. It was a historically unprecedented conversion. After the appearances of Our Lady of Guadalupe to Juan Diego, the indigenous people flocked—literally by the millions—to Catholicism. This changed the face of the Church and radically renewed it. There was a newfound, unheard-of dignity for the indigenous and the poor.

Without a doubt, writes Chavez, quoting early sources, this massive conversion of the indigenous people was a surprise for the missionaries:

> It was their seeking of not just the sacrament of Baptism, but also Confession [as they began to practice their new faith]. It occurred that—said Mendieta (Fray Gerónimo de Mendieta, *Historia Eclesiastica Indiana*)—by the roads, mountains and deserted spots a thousand or two thousand Indians followed the religious, just to go to confession, leaving behind their homes and properties; and many of them pregnant women, and so many that some had their babies on the way, and almost all carrying their children on their backs. Other elderly people who could hardly stand even with a supporting stick, and blind people, walked 15 or twenty leagues to search for a confessor. The healthy came thirty leagues, and others went

from monastery to monastery, more than eighty leagues. Because on every side there was so much to do, they found no entry. Many of them brought their women and children and their little food, as if they were moving to another area. And they sometimes waited one or two months....

The numbers seeking baptism were so great that the missionaries stopped the baptisms to write to Rome to ask how to proceed in such an unprecedented situation, concerned about their ability to prepare so many in the knowledge of the faith. They were encouraged to continue.

In her lifetime, Dorothy Day made a trip to the Basilica of Our Lady of Guadalupe and wrote about her experience there. Dorothy also mentioned several times in her writings the beauty of little parish churches dedicated to Our Lady of Guadalupe.

At Casa Juan Diego, we have always celebrated a special Mass on her feast day in December with the special songs known to the people of Mexico for generations. At our Masses we point out that at the time Our Lady of Guadalupe appeared, there were no borders between the United States and Mexico or between Mexico and Central America. All of the southwest United States, Mexico, and Central America were included in New Spain. Our Lady appeared for all. The Church has declared her the patroness of the Americas, which is perfect for Casa Juan Diego because those who come to us represent so many countries in Latin America. As we tell the story, we emphasize how Our Lady of Guadalupe affirmed the dignity of the people, especially the poor, which is the great gift God made through her to the powerless of this world.

When Fr. Mario Arroyo helped us to develop a chapel, the stained glass window was of Juan Diego. More than one guest who has arrived at Casa Juan Diego has rushed into the chapel to give thanks to Our Lady of Guadalupe for their safe arrival at Casa Juan Diego.

Our ten-year-anniversary celebration on her feast was an interesting one. The mariachis had already begun to play and the *matachines* (indigenous dancers) were ready to dance. The bishop and priests were lined up, ready to enter the dining area for the thanksgiving celebration for ten years of Casa Juan Diego. Three hundred people were waiting (and sweating) to begin—when someone came in, shouting, "The guy who stabbed Gonzalo is outside! Call the police!"

Somehow, the Mass went on. The "new" building at 4818 Rose Street (completed in 1986) was overflowing. It was standing room only, because not only friends of the house but also readers of the *Houston Catholic Worker* came. We had also invited all those who come for food and clothing each week. Former guests heard about it as well, and they came in large numbers. Some of the children came dressed as Juan Diego. While Mark was making sure that everything was ready for the Mass and trying to deal with the crisis outside, the adults were listening to the Scripture readings and Bishop Fiorenza's homily. During the first part of the Mass, Louise took all the children (about forty) in the long back hallway and told them the story of the apparition of Our Lady of Guadalupe to Juan Diego. When it was time to return to the Mass, the children brought up fruits and vegetables at the offertory as a symbol of the fruits of the earth, as is the custom in the celebrations of the feast of Our Lady of Guadalupe. In our celebration, every child, in procession, brought a fruit or vegetable to the altar. After Mass, the celebration continued. The mariachis stayed to play more music and the *matachines* danced again. Tamales made by the women who come to the food distribution were served. As the bishop was leaving, a man on crutches with one leg amputated to the hip wanted to speak with him. He accosted him, asking for financial help. We were embarrassed, wishing he had asked us instead of the bishop for money.

Years later, in 2002, Casa Juan Diego was filled with joy over the canonization of Saint Juan Diego. Mexico's welcome for Pope John Paul II when he canonized Juan Diego reverberated in Houston, where several television stations celebrated the Holy Father's visit to Mexico and put it together on their programs with presentations on Casa Juan Diego. Channel 2 (NBC) had a beautiful half-hour special in which Casa Juan Diego and clips of Pope John Paul II and the canonization in Mexico were alternately featured. At one moment, the TV anchors would be speaking with people visiting Mexico for the canonization, and the next moment they would show conversations with immigrant guests of Casa Juan Diego. Then back to the Holy Father and the *matachines* at the Mass in Mexico City and the enormous cascade of roses that fell over the pope and those celebrating with him. Anchor Bill Baeza of Channel 2 went so far as to say that miracles are required for a canonization, and that one of Juan Diego's miracles was Casa Juan Diego in Houston.

Local FOX-TV also featured the story of Juan Diego's canonization and Casa Juan Diego together, and Channel 45 in Spanish had a news segment as well. The television programs showed our early morning food distribution to the poor of the community, our English classes, our medical clinic in action, and our guests recounting their stories. These programs enabled us to tell the people of Houston how much Juan Diego has meant to us, and why his name was chosen for our work when we began.

Our celebration at the time of the canonization was marred by an unfortunate event. Catholic Workers at the women's and children's House of Hospitality heard strange noises very late at night outside the chapel. Some drunken men were throwing rocks at the stained glass window of Juan Diego. The window was ruined. We later replaced the window with another of Our Lady of Guadalupe. Archbishop Daniel DiNardo (now a cardinal) later came to celebrate a special Mass, complete with mariachis, to bless the window.

Though we were not able to attend the canonization in Mexico City, we have visited the Basilica of Our Lady of Guadalupe a number of times since Casa Juan Diego began. The shrine is always overflowing with pilgrims from all over Mexico and the rest of Latin America. Once we went to Sunday Mass at there at noon. What a mistake! We were almost crushed by the crowd when we went to communion. Many also brought forward religious objects to be blessed.

Sometimes one can spot a few English speakers at the shrine. Once a tourist asked us what the place was all about and what its significance was. We glanced around the basilica and saw it filled with the poor who had come to receive all the love, compassion, help, and protection that the mother of Jesus had promised them so long ago. We explained to the tourist that it is Juan Diego's original *tilma*, the cloth with the image of Our Lady of Guadalupe, that is given the place of honor in the Basilica. That kind of cloth usually lasts only thirty years, but it is intact today and the colors are as clear as they were in 1531. In the brief exchange we tried to introduce him to the significance for the poor of the appearance to Juan Diego, but we are not sure he understood.

The basilica we visited was very beautiful, but the more modern one is different from the older building Mark had visited years ago. The old structure—but not the original—was sinking and was no longer safe.

Once when we visited, we climbed what seemed like a thousand steps up the hill of Tepeyac to the site of the original apparition and the original small church built in response to Our Lady's request. We were overwhelmed by a sense of the presence of God and Our Lady of Guadalupe among the poor, brown-skinned people on pilgrimage with us. We also visited the place next to the basilica where Juan Diego had moved to live for the rest of his life after the original shrine was built. There in that place we were struck by the impact of Our Lady of Guadalupe on an entire life, an entire people.

The poorest of the poor continue to flock from all corners of Mexico to La Villa, as they call the basilica. Through Mary, they know that they are people of dignity—loved and important in the eyes of God, however humble their lives. Some walk on their knees into the basilica, fulfilling promises they have made to Our Lady of Guadalupe.

Sometimes we wonder if the prayers of those first missionaries could have caused the Spaniards to leave so many indigenous people in Latin America alive so that Our Lady could appear to one of them. Compare this to the English in the United States, who decimated the indigenous population and left few Native Americans alive.

We live in a time when the emphasis is again on a master race—when anyone who might be disabled, imperfect, depressed, old, sick, or poor is not considered worthwhile and who might be killed even before birth with the blessing of society. Today, immigrants, who contribute so much and receive nothing in return from the taxes they pay, are denigrated—but thank God, not by the Church and not by Our Lady of Guadalupe. When we visited the basilica after years of receiving immigrants in Houston and advocating for them, we were conscious that those who filled the shrine were the people who should not exist except perhaps in very small numbers, according to the followers of Margaret Sanger and those who run Planned Parenthood. These are the people that the Minutemen—self-appointed guardians of the border between Texas and Mexico—try to keep out. They wish these remarkable people would go away. Our Lady of Guadalupe's message is the opposite of racist eugenics and politics.

Even today, indigenous guests of Casa Juan Diego from Guatemala or Mexico become very frustrated and angry when someone, in a voice meant to insult, calls them the pejorative name *indio*, which over the centuries still conveys the condescending tone that the cruelest conquistadors used to characterize a native person. Guests whose first language is not English are hesitant at first to admit this to us, because they are apprehensive that they may be criticized or looked down upon. We, of course, rejoice with them and congratulate them on speaking two languages.

When we commemorated the twenty-fifth anniversary of Casa Juan Diego, Auxiliary Bishop Vasquez celebrated the Mass of Our Lady of Guadalupe. This time everyone gathered to celebrate the Mass at our men's house. In his homily, Bishop Vasquez welcomed the immigrants. His reflection on the importance of Our Lady of Guadalupe in revealing the dignity of the people included the story of his grandfather, a devout Catholic who, a couple of generations ago, had to sit in the back of the church at Mass in west Texas because he was a Mexican immigrant.

This time the *matachines* were to be the children of families who come to our Casa Maria in southwest Houston for food each week. They wanted to give back to Casa Juan Diego. Seven o'clock came, however, and though the *mariachis* were there, the *matachines* were not. We had to begin without them. As Bishop Vasquez was finishing the Prayer of the Faithful after the homily, there was a noise at the door. When we went to investigate, there were the *matachines*, dressed in their bright Native American costumes and headdresses. It is the custom for them to dance reverently at the Offertory and after communion, so they had come in time. When we walked up to Bishop Vasquez, he looked at us and we said, "*Los matachines han llegado*" ("The dancers have arrived"). The bishop responded, "¡*Que pasen!*" ("Let them come in!"). The young people came in very reverently, bowing as they danced, reminding us of how the Aztecs had adapted their customs to their new Christian beliefs and worship.

In our technological and globalized society, where having is much more important than being—and speed, innovation, and material success are prized at any price—immigrants are considered by some to be nobodies, throwaways. But for those who come to know them even briefly, they are human beings, made in the image and likeness of God, with hearts and caring personalities, with the same worries that middle-class people have for their husbands, for their children.

Each day, in addition to the new migrants, we receive at Casa Juan Diego destitute families whose breadwinners have been deported, and those who have been injured working in dangerous jobs in Houston for a small wage. We need the prayers of Our Lady of Guadalupe to counteract the hatred and oppression of immigrants and the global economic oppression of the poor today. We also need the prayers of Our Lady of

Guadalupe for ourselves and for those who collaborate in the work. Even in working with the poor we can be tempted to let our desires for success, visibility, and influence dominate our thoughts, words, and actions to the extent that we might lose our vocation. We want instead to walk in the steps of Saint Juan Diego and his people, who were brought closer to Jesus through his Mother: as Dorothy Day called it, the downward path to salvation, to the humble, and to the poor.

4

CAN THE WORKS OF
MERCY BE ILLEGAL?

In 1980, when we announced that we would begin a House of Hospitality to receive refugees from the Central American wars, not everyone understood. Some were less than enthusiastic and could not imagine that we would start such an operation. What if the refugees from violence, coming over the border and into Houston, were illegal in the United States? We might get into trouble since it was against the law to harbor or transport "illegal aliens." Leonel Castillo, the former director of the U.S. Immigration and Naturalization Service (INS), who was active in Catholic circles in Houston, questioned the wisdom of starting such a House of Hospitality for undocumented refugees.

Although to some the idea seemed radical, if not subversive, our familiarity with the Catholic Worker movement and Dorothy Day's way of doing things made it the logical thing for us to do. If we were to be true to our beliefs, faced with the reality of the Central American wars and the refugees, we had no choice but to act. We knew that being a good or even ordinary Catholic is challenging, to say the least. Living out our faith could hardly be illegal, but even if it were, we would still have to try.

The Bible tells us that at times we may have to take a prophetic stance. The Catholic Worker tradition includes resisting injustice—following the law of Christ even if it means being arrested and going to jail. The founders of the CW movement believed that we must do what is right by making difficult moral decisions and by protesting wrongs even though at times the protests are against the civil law. While we sometimes join with others in protesting and picketing, our own resistance to injustice more often takes the form of the Works of Mercy. We took the risk of taking in homeless refugees even if our government did not recognize them legally as refugees, and we have continued to do so every day.

We began this work because people were homeless, and we knew that if they were deported back to their countries, many of them would be killed. Our experience in El Salvador taught us that this was a real possibility. We soon discovered that the new refugees had little chance of attaining legal status. Because the United States was funding the wars in El Salvador and Guatemala, and advising their militaries, it was not giving political asylum to refugees from either country.

Giving hospitality to refugees who are fleeing oppression and starvation has always been a work of the Church. Some risked or lost their lives helping refugees during World War II and in similar situations. From the beginning, we have understood our work in this context.

People sometimes wonder about our work with people who do not have papers. Once in the 1980s a reporter from one of Houston's major TV stations called. His first request was, "We want to know about your smuggling operation." We were aghast at the accusation; we'd been accused of being Communists, but never of smuggling. As we told the reporter, we do not bring people across the border: "At Casa Juan Diego we do not help people who shouldn't be here. Casa Juan Diego was started as an attempt to be biblical in the face of vastly increased immigration to the City of Houston."

We reflected on the reporter's question as we went about our daily work. Did he think we should throw all our guests into the street? We wrote about it in the *Houston Catholic Worker*, in December 1993:

> It was Saturday morning and there was much to do. A volunteer youth group from a local parish was visiting. Martha, a battered woman who had taken refuge at Casa Juan Diego, abruptly interrupted our work to insist that she go to visit her newborn at Lyndon B. Johnson County hospital. Concern was written all over her face. The hospital had sent her home without the baby because the newborn had respiratory problems.
>
> We decided we should take her to see her baby—a mother separated from her newborn suffers the pain of birth all over again in her empty arms.
>
> As we were driving to the hospital, it dawned on us—like a bolt out of the blue, or like Paul being struck off his horse.

Is Martha legal? Are we transporting an "illegal alien"? We don't believe any person can be illegal, although they may be undocumented.

Are we breaking the law? What should we do? Should we put Martha out of the car immediately—right there on 59 North on this overpass and not break the law another second? Should we rush over to a nearby church and go to confession—and how do you confess such a sin, since it is no sin in any examination of conscience books that we know of:

Bless me Father, for I have sinned. I have harbored and transported illegal aliens? What would the priest say? He would probably say, "My child, our Holy Bible says that we should welcome the stranger—go and sin no more." Or: "If you have trouble, bring her to our sanctuary. It may be illegal to help her, but it is not a sin."

Later, we would have answered the reporter differently, explaining that we had not only war refugees staying at Casa Juan Diego, but also three men with such serious head injuries that they had to shuffle instead of walk. Other men were confined to wheelchairs. Two men living with us had each lost a leg and were awaiting prostheses so they could walk and work. We had men who were mentally ill. We had men and women on dialysis because their kidneys had failed. We had three pregnant women who refused abortions; one had complications that frightened us. We had people with AIDS. We had people with liver problems that made them look like they were pregnant. In addition, we had almost a hundred healthy immigrant men, women, and children in our houses.

The reality is that at any moment, from the very beginning, we could have been arrested for our work with refugees and immigrants under the guise of "harboring and transporting illegal immigrants."

To this day the most common question regarding the work of Casa Juan Diego is this: "How can you help people who don't have papers?" When we speak to groups, some comment, "We love that you are helping the poor, but you are breaking the law. We have mixed feelings about your work." One Protestant church group had been helping us financially, but when they discovered that we had developed a house in Matamoros, Mexico, for those who were stranded on the other side of the border, they accused us of running an underground railroad and cut off all aid. We were surprised, because the truth is that we do not run an *underground* railroad, but an *overground* railroad. We do not sneak in people in the middle of the night or at any other time—although some guests do arrive late. We do not bring people in at all.

People ask us how we stay open. While we openly receive refugees and immigrants who have managed to arrive in Houston on their own, we are cautious and realistic. We tell new Catholic Workers what they should not do while working here and representing Casa Juan Diego, even though in their enthusiastic idealism they might consider taking the risks. We ask our Catholic Workers not to marry people in order to obtain papers for them. We ask them not to go to the border and bring people across or try to sneak them through checkpoints in the trunks of our cars. They may not pay coyotes, dangerous people who are paid to smuggle people in. We caution staff that on a couple of occasions coyotes have managed to stay at our house for a few days, presenting themselves as new immigrants. Our *ayudantes,* or guests, soon identified them and they were asked to leave. Though we work with a population that lives underground, in the shadows, we do not participate in shady deals. We do not work with coyotes. The majority of them are violent thieves who specialize in impregnating women who are at their mercy. Just as we never go to the homes of battered women without a police escort when they need to retrieve important papers, we do not go where coyotes are holding people or meet coyotes anyplace.

If there is a way to assist guests by signing forms to prove their address or their lack of income so they can get medical care or other help, we do so. If we can help those who once lived in the house prove that they have lived in the United States for a certain number of years for when they apply for legalization, we do so, but we do not lie as we fill out the forms.

When people come to our door who have just arrived from a terrible journey, we try to remember that beneath their old clothes and tired faces is Jesus; in their humble flesh they are a manifestation of the splendor of God, and they share in his suffering. How could we turn them away? Rosa, for example, came from El Salvador. She began to tell her story to Louise, but broke down and started sobbing when she began speaking about her children. Three of her sons were killed in El Salvador. She was homeless and didn't know a single soul in Houston. That, in our opinion, was the issue.

Why do people come? What do they say? Their blisters and tears speak for themselves. As we talk with new guests, it becomes clear that they must be very desperate since they have been willing to suffer so much to get here.

Immigrants have often come to us with swollen, shredded feet from walking for days. Their flesh is visible through their tattered shoes, which have been soaked going through rivers, and have dried and split. Sometimes their feet look more like watermelons. Whether people find their way through on their own or have been released or abandoned by coyotes, they have often walked for days without a break. They may lose their toenails and often have legs full of thorns from walking through the brush. Men, women, and children arrive dehydrated, exhausted.

José's feet looked like they were about to fall off when he arrived. They were swollen, gray, and rotten looking. He asked whether he could see a doctor. Apparently, José had walked to Houston all the way from Brownsville in ill-fitting shoes, or else he had spent a long time in the water. He probably walked across Mexico, too. His feet reminded us of the stories Mark's older brother, Pat, used to tell about the trench foot of World War II soldiers.

One day in December, two refugee families entered Casa Juan Diego. They walked very slowly and didn't say anything. As they walked over to the sofas in the entrance and sat down, their feet did the talking. They were red, raw, bruised, and blistered. We didn't ask many questions of the group, but it emerged that the two families had walked three hundred miles on their way to Casa Juan Diego. One of the women was pregnant. A three-year-old who could not keep up had to be carried all the way. They couldn't remember the last time they had eaten. Slowly, they shuffled into the dining area and began to eat slowly. Their eyes brightened as they ate and became comfortable in the large dining room, savoring the simple and long foregone pleasure of sitting down. Since they had arrived with only the clothes on their backs, we soon invited the family with the sore feet to visit the clothing room to find a change.

For those who have not been here to greet new arrivals, it is hard to imagine the joy and peace in the eyes of immigrants who arrive dirty, limping, and exhausted, having walked for days to arrive at Casa Juan Diego. They experience a great sense of relief when they realize they have a place to stay and will be cared for, at least for a few days. They may immediately fall asleep on the three sofas in the entrance, dirty clothes and all, while Catholic Workers prepare beds. Visitors to our houses are sometimes scandalized to see men sleeping during the day on the couches instead of working. Forgive them: they may not have seen a bed in several months. They never rest long, though, before seeking work.

The immigrants and refugees often do not know Casa Juan Diego exists when they leave their homes (except sometimes Hondurans or guests whose relatives had come earlier), but learn about it on the journey or in their search for a place to stay. Churches, schools, police, hospitals, and many individuals in Houston know Casa Juan Diego and often direct people to us.

The next arrival that day was Roy. Someone had beaten him to a bloody pulp, and his face was swollen and discolored and looked like a black-and-blue rubber ball. We hoped he wasn't a man who had gotten drunk and into a fight.

Dorothy Day always helped us to respond to those who come to our doors. "The mystery of the poor is this," she wrote, "that they are Jesus, and what you do for them you do to him."[1] Peter and Dorothy taught us that Jesus comes to the door of a House of Hospitality in many disguises. They followed the tradition of St. Benedict of Nursia, who told his monks to receive the guest, especially the poor person, as Christ himself. The words of our faith encourage us and give our work of hospitality meaning: "Let mutual love continue. Do not neglect hospitality, for through it some have unknowingly entertained angels" (Heb 13:1–2, NAB). We know that the classic sign of our acceptance of God's mystery is welcoming and making room for the stranger. We have the example of Jesus, who was a refugee, and the entire Holy Family, who were refugees, to inspire us. Ironically, the Good Samaritan himself was an unwelcome alien from the north—an illegal. We have the example of Peter Maurin, one of our founders, who was French and undocumented, and who brought so much with him to the United States in faith, culture, and ideas.

Most homeless shelters turn away those without identification. No ID is required at Casa Juan Diego. We have searched the Scriptures and have not been able to find any time when Jesus required identification from the people he helped. There is no mention in Matthew 25 of demanding legal papers for helping others, only a clear description of what followers of the Nazarene are to do.

One in four U.S. citizens is a baptized Catholic, and many others are Protestant followers of Jesus. All are people of the Word, but apparently only of certain words. The Hebrew Scriptures (the Old Testament) ask us to receive the alien, those from foreign lands, into our homes. Exodus states clearly that we must not oppress the immigrant (chapters 22 and 23). Deuteronomy 10:18 asks us to participate in the Lord's work of caring for immigrants and strangers: "For the LORD your God...loves the stranger and gives him food and clothing," and in chapter 24, "You must not pervert justice in dealing with the stranger," and again, in chapter 27: "A curse on him who tampers with the rights of the stranger" (Deut 10:18, 24:17, 27:19; NRSV). The New Testament affirms the Old, to say the least.

Regarding questions of legality and illegality, we remember Martin Luther King, Jr., who famously said: "We should never forget that everything Adolf Hitler did in Germany was 'legal' and everything the Hungarian freedom fighters did in Hungary was 'illegal.'"[2] In this light it seems strange that some are very upset by the presence of immigrants and refugees and accuse those who give them any help of breaking the law, but do not mind too much when our government or CIA does illegal things in other countries in order to "win."

For example, the School of the Americas run by the United States government has taught methods of torture and repression to soldiers and law enforcement of other countries for decades. Those who tortured church people in El Salvador were trained at the School of the Americas. If that is not against civil and criminal law, it is certainly against the law of love and morality. It is no wonder then, given its bad reputation, that the School of the Americas changed its name. (It is now the Western Hemisphere Institute for Security Cooperation.)

Dorothy Day used to say it is strange that people rebel at the idea of obedience to the Church, while giving unquestioning obedience to whatever the State, the government, tells them to do. She suggested that it was better to listen first to the Church. "Holy Mother the State" may say that the undocumented cannot be helped, and if you do help, you may be arrested. The Bible and Holy Mother the Church say you must help immigrants or run the risk of losing eternal salvation.

Our one arrest, though surprising, was not dramatic or romantic.

After a second fire at Casa Juan Diego, we built a new building of concrete and steel in the 1980s. The city insisted that our kitchen be registered and inspected by the Houston Health Department. Mark wrote in the *Houston Catholic Worker* of his arrest after an encounter with the Health Department:

> I feel like a common criminal. I have just been arrested. But why? We can't always choose our form of protest and arrest, but why couldn't we have been arrested for a better, more noble cause? We had not been arrested for helping poor people or for peace or for getting people jobs who can't always prove their legality. We had not been arrested for protesting against those countries sending arms to Central America, but for a kitchen violation.
>
> What will I tell my grandchildren? That one of my great acts of living the Gospel, of walking in the steps of Dorothy Day, of non-conformity and non-violent resistance registered in the annals of the history of the City of Houston, was being arrested because several (5) live cockroaches attacked a city health inspector (about to lose her job because of cuts in the city budget).
>
> Why couldn't we have been arrested for protesting the new immigration law? Why couldn't it have been for encouraging our son to think carefully about the draft law before register-ing? Why couldn't it have been for helping refugees?
>
> No! No! None of the above! The violation charges under the ordinance code and law of the City of Houston section 20–21, item 21 reads: Effective measures not utilized to min-imize the preserve of roaches in food preparation area, offense date 03-09-88, time 2:40 p.m.
>
> What would I tell my mother? She has always insisted that only dirty housekeepers have roaches. (She is from the North.) But she was very forgiving.
>
> What will my relatives say? They are already disappointed that I am engaged in manual labor with all that education. They don't mind my being like a garbage collector, but do you have to do it without getting paid? That's un-American!
>
> What will the Bishop say? The inspector got confused and wrote that the owner of this property was the Houston Catholic Church instead of the Houston Catholic Worker. It is now history and on the record.

What would Dorothy Day say? "Problems with the health department? That shows Casa Juan Diego is pure Catholic Worker."

The staff has been generally supportive. One member thinks I have staged the whole thing just to get publicity for the sanctuary movement, but the others said they would visit me in jail and bring some of the day- (or 2 or 3) old-bread we receive. Others think that I am grandstanding, but they don't realize that though I was the one arrested, some of their names are on the charge list.

The visit of the health department was providential. While we had been winning the battle against roaches (although they have us outnumbered 100,000 to one), we had never really won the war against them except in 1982 and 1985 when our houses were destroyed by fire.

The arrest has had its benefits. The staff has come together in its efforts to overcome the enemy (roaches). Roaches have been a boon to community spirit, because staff has united in their efforts to do battle with a common enemy and thus forget about less important things that divide people.

Well, that was the city and not the Immigration and Naturalization Service (INS). Folks have sometimes asked the Immigration Service why they do not arrest us. In fact, during the 1980s, when Mark participated in a public panel discussion, the district director of the INS (recently renamed a part of the Department of Homeland Security called Immigration and Customs Enforcement, or ICE) also was on the panel. One man in the audience, pointing at Mark, asked the district director: "Why don't *you* arrest *him* for harboring illegal aliens?" The INS man mumbled something about not bothering churches, and then surprisingly said: "They really are not harboring anyone. What they do is wide open. There is no secret about what they do."

The government has always been ambivalent about the way they relate to Casa Juan Diego. In the early 1980s when several people involved in the sanctuary movement were arrested and jailed, it seemed that our opportunity for serious arrest and jail time was at hand, but it never happened. For many months during this time Mark took responsibility for driving immigrants and refugees to airports and bus stations en route to relatives or friends so that new CW volunteers (who hadn't always signed up for such consequences) wouldn't face arrest for "transporting illegal aliens."

The irony during so many years of our work was that the Immigration Service would sometimes release immigrants from detention and send them to Casa Juan Diego. Before the media built up scapegoating and hatred of immigrants, it was common for us to receive referrals from the Immigration Service. We still occasionally receive referrals from ICE.

In the early 1980s, we got a call asking us to receive fifty Mexican men who had been released because they had agreed to act as witnesses in a trial of smugglers. Of course, we said yes, but we also explained that we were not a locked facility and could not return people to detention. The officials said they understood that and had communicated directly with the men regarding the future. They had actually released them and given them each $50.00 to make their way to their homes in Mexico.

Sometimes we would receive a call from Laredo or other parts of Texas to receive a pregnant woman. The officers were loath at that time to deport or jail pregnant women, especially if they had difficult pregnancies. We received injured people from Immigration, sometimes with legs cut off by a train. In every case, the government asked us to pay the bus fare. We paid.

Once, however, day laborers—who were not guests of Casa Juan Diego, but others who come into the neighborhood for jobs—became too numerous in our neighborhood, and the Immigration Service raided the streets, including in front of Casa Juan Diego's men's house. In 1993, on All Souls' Day—the Day of the Dead—Immigration came onto the property of Casa Juan Diego at 6:00 a.m., posing as labor contractors (offering $5.00 an hour), even trying to drag men off who refused to leave their home at Casa Juan Diego. We didn't find out what had happened right away because the raid took place so early. At 8:00 a.m., our guests told us what had happened.

It was hard to believe that the City of Houston had set up Casa Juan Diego as a target for Immigration's raid. After all, we had already existed for thirteen years and had been receiving people directly from Immigration. We called some friends of Casa Juan Diego who were active in immigration issues and had a meeting at our men's house to consider our response. As we talked with the group, we discovered that one of our guests, who had a paper saying he was temporarily legal, had been released because of that document and had come back to stay at the house. He told us that he, along with the other men picked up in the sweep, had been taken to what he thought was a school, where their documents were checked on computers. Some at the meeting were indignant that a place of learning had been utilized to expel people from our country. The guest told us it was just a few blocks from Casa Juan Diego and that he could take us there. We all quickly piled into several cars and followed his directions. The place turned out to be a city park, at this time almost empty except for a couple of families walking through. The immigrants had been detained in the tennis courts while their documents were checked—a clearly inappropriate use of a public park. We saw that the fence around the courts where they were detained could be featured in a demonstration. We demonstrated inside the fence at the tennis courts the next day with supporters from the community against the use of city parks as detention centers or jails. This brought out the Houston press. Their interviews with several demonstrators looking out of the fence appeared on television and in the newspapers.

The day of the raid was filled with ironies. The drug dealers, prostitutes (male and female), and pedophiles who cruised the area looking for an AIDS-free population were still on the street, but those who wanted to work were being deported by Immigration. The troublemakers were even on Spanish TV giving their commentary, still free because they are legal. A woman called whose husband had been detained in the raid. "Isn't it strange?" she sobbed. "They took my husband who was struggling to make a few dollars for food and rent, but still on the street corner in front of Eckerd's on Washington is the man who put a pistol to my chest to steal the little chain around my neck."

We didn't know until later that day that the principal from the local elementary school had been instrumental in calling Immigration. We found out when a supervisor from the school district called to apologize. Did that principal know that some of the men who were picked up for looking for work were also parents of children in her school? Hundreds of children from Casa Juan Diego have attended the school of this principal. What would happen to them if their fathers were deported? Do children pay for the sins of their parents?

Every time we sat down to discuss the attack we were interrupted by various city, county, school, and United Way agencies asking for help with their various unsolvable problems. On that day, we received all of the following calls:

> The Harris County Psychiatric Hospital called, asking us for travel funds to help an undocumented patient.
>
> The Houston Police Department Family Violence program called, asking us to take in a battered Honduran mother and her child.
>
> Harris County Social Services called, asking us to provide housing for a family of six who were living in their car while waiting for the inspection of their Section 8 public housing.
>
> St. John Vianney parish called, asking us to take a mother and child who had been living in a small apartment with nine people.
>
> AVANCE, a group that provides parenting classes and other programs for Spanish-speaking parents, called, asking us to house a woman who had nowhere to go.
>
> A Cuban American woman called, asking us to give hospitality to a friend who has six little children and an abusive husband.
>
> Memorial Hermann Hospital social workers called, asking us for housing for an undocumented paraplegic man who was in that hospital.
>
> An HISD elementary school called, asking us for help for a battered woman.
>
> The Texas Department of Health called, asking us to assist with $60.00 for temporary legal papers so that parents who are from Mexico could stay with their seriously ill, hospitalized child.
>
> St. Stephen's Catholic Church called, asking us for help with travel for a family.
>
> Another church called, asking us for information about medical care for a Spanish speaker.
>
> The Harris County Probation office called, asking us to accept an unaccompanied minor.

In addition, we received numerous calls from neighborhood mothers whose husbands had been picked up; other family members also called in desperation. They had been calling Immigration and various detention centers, trying to locate disappeared family members. Some women begged us to help them find live-in jobs, since they could not survive without their husbands or brothers.

Whom would the city and Immigration target next? The battered, homeless women who are brought to us by the police and school principals? The homeless men on crutches and in wheelchairs who are sent by Houston hospitals? The homeless babies? The six hundred immigrant women who come for food each week? The three hundred immigrant women who come for clothing every other week? The sick and those with serious dental problems who come to our free clinics? The people who come to Thanksgiving dinner? The people who attend English classes?

What could we do?

We decided we would continue to serve the many thousands of people sent to us by the agencies and the churches of Houston. We would continue to work with the families of the disappeared of Houston, just as others have worked with the families of the disappeared in Central America. We would continue to bind up wounds and console the suffering and take in the strangers who come to our doors. We would continue to accept the pregnant women, and women with children, that Immigration sent us after apprehending them. We would continue to distribute food and clothing to families on the margin to help them stay in their own homes. We would continue to meet with people of goodwill who want to work toward a positive solution.

And we would pray. We would pray for those who made the decisions to persecute the most humble and vulnerable.

First, we asked the help of Bishop Fiorenza, who wrote to the district director of the Immigration Service and to the City of Houston to protest the raid on Casa Juan Diego, a religious work of mercy. Then, at the request of community people who had picketed with us at the tennis courts, Mark spoke at a meeting of the Houston City Council, putting a human face on the people targeted in the raid, especially those of Casa Juan Diego. All of this must have had some effect, because nothing like it ever happened again.

In 1998, when Hurricane Mitch hit Central America and destroyed so much, the Immigration and Naturalization Service turned to Casa Juan Diego for help. After protests from the Central American consulates, President Clinton had decided that it was not possible to deport people back to Central America with a good conscience after the tremendous destruction of the hurricane. The damage was so bad that there would be no place for the deportees to go upon their return.

71

Would we accept immigrants who were imprisoned in the detention center in Houston? Their only crime was being born on the wrong side of the Rio Grande. The detainees had said they had nowhere to go and had no telephone numbers of anyone they might know in the United States. Because Immigration could not put all of them on the street with no one to receive them, we gave our *fiat*—our yes.

One might say that after eighteen years, Immigration in Houston called Casa Juan Diego with a Christmas present. Known as Operation Overwhelm in 1999, for us it echoed the song the "Twelve Days of Christmas":

On the first day of Christmas (Operation Overwhelm), the Immigration and Naturalization Service sent 44 guests from Honduras to Casa Juan Diego. On the second day of Christmas, the INS sent 47 guests from Guatemala. On the third day of Christmas, Immigration sent 67 Central Americans from various countries. On the fourth day of Christmas, Immigration sent 91 from various countries. On the fifth day of Christmas, Days Inn allowed us to pick up 100 mattresses. On the sixth day of Christmas, not much happened. On the seventh day of Christmas, we stopped counting.

One group arrived in the middle of an RCIA group from a local parish. RCIA is the parish program that instructs people who want to be Catholic. The RCIA group had come to Casa Juan Diego to learn why we as Catholics did this work. You can imagine their surprise when they discovered that part of being Catholic means taking homeless immigrants into your home. We prayed that none of them would abandon their path to the Catholic Church because of our reckless hospitality.

The twelve days of Christmas continued, with several guests arriving each day from Immigration, along with others who came on their own—20 one day and 50 on another.

We wrote about this in our paper on January 6, the real twelfth day of Christmas, when Latin Americans celebrate Christmas, as do we at the insistence of our guests. Three wise men did not come from the East, but 39 immigrants came from the South—39 "Christs in the poor" from Laredo Immigration. More would come if we could figure out how to get them to Houston. Letters began arriving at Casa Juan Diego from other immigrants among the several hundred in detention in Laredo, begging us to send bus tickets so they could be released.

San Antonio Immigration also called to tell us that they had 200 immigrants to send. They could try to put them on buses, they said, but thought the newly released men might not even board the buses if they didn't understand that they weren't being sent to another jail. Casa Juan Diego could pay the bus fare, but we needed someone in San Antonio to help put people on the buses. We called Catholic Charities in San Antonio to help facilitate their transfer to Houston, but this seemed to be out of their usual line of work. Bishop Fiorenza called the Archdiocese of San Antonio to explain the situation, and San Antonio Catholic Charities began helping to put people on buses to come to Houston. Auxiliary Bishop Tamayo lent us his name to find assistance in Laredo, where he had been a pastor prior to coming to Houston. Catholic Charities in Laredo was delighted to cooperate and put immigrants on the bus for Houston. Some also came from the Rio Grande Valley, from San Benito. We paid the fares. We were picking up people at the bus station at all hours of the day—and night.

The District Office of Immigration in Houston was a model of efficiency, courtesy, and cooperation in the process of releasing people to us day by day, and keeping us informed minute by minute of all the details. They even transported people to Casa Juan Diego. One courteous INS employee would have liked a tour, but we reminded him that it would make our other guests too nervous. Some deportation officers said they wouldn't enter the property because it was a sanctuary. It was hard to believe these same INS employees were imprisoning people.

When they arrived, many of the immigrants from hurricane-wracked Central America suddenly remembered phone numbers of friends and relatives in other cities. Perhaps their contacts were undocumented and they had not wanted to hurt them by giving out their addresses. There were long lines of people at our phones.

The team of *ayudantes* at the men's house responded immediately to the arrival of so many new guests, and added more and more rice, beans, and turkey (frozen from Thanksgiving and Christmas donations) to the cooking pots. News programs on Spanish-language television stations in Houston interviewed us about the overwhelming situation. A local motel responded by bringing us one hundred mattresses. We felt like we were in the middle of a whirlwind.

Our immediate response to the overcrowding in our men's house was to send people on buses wherever they wanted to go. If they had a contact who would receive them, we sent them. We had already purchased literally tens of thousands of dollars worth of tickets over the years at Greyhound with our checks to help immigrants. These folks now had documentation that they had permission to travel legally in the United States.

But suddenly Greyhound began refusing our checks. They said Telecheck wouldn't allow it. When we called Telecheck, they responded, "Your account is good. There is no reason why your checks would not be accepted." But Greyhound still said no. Our new Catholic Workers—recent college graduates from up North come to serve the poor in Houston—were not daunted by Greyhound. They whipped out their credit cards and purchased several thousand dollars worth of tickets to send immigrants to their families. Casa Juan Diego would reimburse them later. Families also began sending money to help with travel expenses for relatives.

We were glad to hear that the U.S. government was allowing Hondurans and Nicaraguans to apply for temporary permission to work so that they could send money to their hurricane-ravaged countries. Unfortunately, only those who arrived before December 31, 1998, could apply. The journey from Central America takes so long that most people—who had lost their family members, homes, and all worldly possessions—would arrive too late and have no possibility of any legal status.

After a few weeks, things calmed down and we continued at a more normal pace, still regularly receiving quite a number of immigrants and refugees each week, many of whom had lived through the hurricane. They had almost no possibility of legalization now, but they had left a desperate situation.

The guests who arrived after Hurricane Mitch had powerfully moving stories to tell. Mitch had devastated more than one country in Central America. One woman from Belize told of the hours she spent in the top of a tree waiting for the floodwaters to recede. She excitedly told of the help that arrived for her country from *La Reina* (the queen). It took us a few minutes to realize that she meant the Queen of England, helping a former colony.

Refugees from Hurricane Mitch, like all the other immigrants who arrive at Casa Juan Diego, immediately tried to find work. They had no desire to sit on their hands. Our guests are always anxious to begin work to earn money for their families.

The Immigration Reform law of 1986 allowed many undocumented people who had been here for a long time to become legal if they could provide proof of employment. It also included a prohibition against hiring undocumented workers and large fines for doing so. When we discovered that there was a provision in the law leaving room for day labor and cooperatives, our workers became a cooperative. Everyone who lives at Casa Juan Diego participates in the co-op. While few other groups took advantage of this provision in the law, Casa Juan Diego has provided such a cooperative in Houston for years. We sent notices to parish bulletins announcing that workers who do yard work, moving, construction, furniture finishing, and so on, could be found at our St. Joseph the Worker center. Eventually even larger businesses began to work with us.

Individuals who hired workers for a day often paid cash. With the cooperative, employers who wanted to hire more people for longer periods would give us a record of the hours worked. They would make out a check to the Padre Jack Davis Co-op, and we, in turn, would pay the workers. As the numbers of workers in the cooperative increased, the tradition of where to keep the money in the hours before paying the workers would change. For a while we kept it in the office of the men's House of Hospitality, and it was there that robbers demanded the money at gunpoint. The thieves spoke English. As they leveled the gun at Matt, our Catholic Worker from Arizona, they kept saying, "Don't get smart!" We were glad that he turned over the money, rather than be killed. The thieves got away with several thousand dollars. We did not keep the money at that location again.

In 2005, the Minutemen—self-appointed armed civilian guardians of the Mexican border, with suspected links to the Ku Klux Klan—decided to confront Casa Juan Diego, which they said was an illegal operation. They announced that they would confront the day laborers who wait for work in the area. They also took pictures of everyone coming and going at Casa Juan Diego. Housewives bringing donations of clothing wondered why those scary folks were taking their pictures.

In 2007, Minutemen protestors began to regularly target Casa Juan Diego, carrying signs with inflammatory lies, such as one announcing that immigrants murdered 10,000 people a year. They shouted racist comments as they picketed us. They didn't wear sheets or burn crosses, but their message of hate was clear. They camped out in the parking lot of the Jack in the Box across the street from our men's house.

Houston Indymedia reported on the World Wide Web that the Klan had placed Casa Juan Diego under siege with protests and cameras and hostile shouting. Their reports were picked up by Indymedia in Ireland, Germany, New Zealand, and other countries. One commentator said,

> This past Wednesday, the 14th, the KKK showed up near Casa Juan Diego to harass clients and staff. They were in the parking lot of the Jack in the Box at Shepherd and Washington, yelling racist insults to any brown-skinned person who was within shouting distance. This eventually grew to the point of yelling insults at anyone they thought had anything to do with Casa Juan Diego. They appeared to have the approval of Jack in the Box management for use of their parking lot, as some sort of staging point.[3]

Both Indymedia and the *Houston Catholic Worker* mentioned the connection with Jack in the Box. The Minutemen came every Saturday morning for a few weeks—apparently with no permits to hold a demonstration. Because of the publicity and their concern that the group was attempting to stir up violence, the criminal division of the Houston Police Department sent several police cars one Saturday morning. After that, the Minutemen did not return.

Not long after the publicity about Minutemen incidents, we received a call from the legal representative from Jack in the Box headquarters San Diego, California. Not pleased with the negative publicity, he assured us that Jack in the Box opposed any kind of racist activity and would not allow such demonstrations on their property in the future.

We know that refugee work and care for immigrants must go on, even in the middle of hate campaigns against them. One cannot stop giving food to the hungry. One cannot stop helping mothers find their children, brothers find their brothers, or husbands find their wives. One cannot stop providing coats and sweaters in Houston's winter weather or fans in the hot summer. How could we not give a desperate person a place to stay? The day we start requiring hungry people to prove their legality is the day the Gospel is denied. Christians can no more stop carrying out the Works of Mercy any more than they can stop breathing.

As Dorothy Day said:

If we hadn't got Christ's own words for it, it would seem raving lunacy to believe that if we offer a bed and food and hospitality for Christmas—or any other time, for that matter—to some man, woman or child, we are replaying the part of Lazarus or Martha or Mary and that our guest is Christ. There is nothing to show it, perhaps....

But he did make heaven hinge on the way we act toward him in his disguise of commonplace, frail and ordinary human beings.

Did you give me food when I was hungry? Did you give me to drink when I was thirsty? Did you give me clothes when my own were all rags? Did you come to see me when I was sick or in prison or in trouble? And to those who say, aghast, that they never had a chance to do such a thing, that they lived two thousand years too late, he will say again what they had the chance of knowing all their lives, that if these things were done for the very least of his brethren they were done to him.[4]

Our goal has never been breaking the law, although one could say that we break it many times a day. Our problem, our challenge, is keeping the law, the law of charity and justice, the law that demands one does not repeat the behavior of those who passed by the injured man in the story of the Good Samaritan.

5

CASA JUAN DIEGO RISES
FROM THE ASHES

We discovered the fire when it was time to sing the closing hymn at the Wednesday night Spanish liturgy. Forty people were there. The priest said, "Go in peace and live the faith," but no one heard because they were all pointing at the ceiling. The shouts began: "*¡Arriba! ¡arriba!*" ("Above!") and "*¡Humo!*" ("Smoke!"). Everyone scattered as smoke and flames came through the cracks in the ceiling.

Several men dashed upstairs to try to put out the fire, grabbing the fire extinguisher on their way. One young man took the garden hose to the roaring flames on the second floor. Their efforts were useless. Within seconds, the shouts changed to "*¡Bomberos! ¡Bomberos!*" ("Call the firemen!") It was unbelievable. Casa Juan Diego was burning down. It was July 7, 1982. We had opened the house just eighteen months before.

We hurried everybody out. Some of the men were frantically trying to salvage their few precious belongings from the downstairs dormitory where they had been staying, which caused us to shout: "*¡Afuera! ¡Afuera!*" ("Outside!") We immediately tried to call the fire department, but the phone wouldn't work.

In total disbelief and shock, we watched the flames leap out the upstairs windows. What do you say, what do you think, when your house is burning? Our first reaction was, "Please God, let no one be in there," although we knew no guest or Catholic Worker was upstairs during the Mass. We had a moment of panic when we could account for only twenty-five of the twenty-six people who were living in the house. Someone asked, "Where is Alfonso?" He could not be found. He was the one who had run into the building with the garden hose to try to extinguish the blaze. In the minutes before he was found, we had visions of him in the flames. We would never have forgiven ourselves if someone died in the fire.

To this day, we don't know who called the fire department, which was one block away, but they arrived very quickly, extinguished the flames within a short time, and searched the shell of the rented building. No bodies in the upstairs ruins. We were grateful. The Catholic Workers who lived on the second floor, however, could salvage nothing. All the medical equipment upstairs was also ruined.

Even as the building blazed, the Catholic Workers began to gather the overnight guests to arrange lodging. We invited all to stay together at the Catholic Worker home where we lived with our children. Our children were at summer music camp and we had extra space. Volunteers arranged the transportation and purchased drinks. Within a short time, all the guests had arrived. Spontaneously, they knelt and prayed, giving thanks that no one was injured. We had twenty-six people spend the night together on the floor. We tried to get some sleep but had little success. We tossed and turned for hours. Shortly before dawn, all was quiet, but it was time to get up; some of the men had just gotten jobs and didn't want to lose them.

In the morning, we returned to the burned-out, smoldering site, only to be stopped by poor people seeking assistance. Their pain was similar to ours. We were both homeless.

The day after the fire, Sister Kathy of Magnificat House called to offer hospitality for our guests. We accepted her offer, and seventeen guests were placed with them. Within several days, we were able to make other arrangements and move all the people from Magnificat House. We returned to the building the same day to console the landlord, whose insurance had run out ten days before the fire as he attempted to negotiate a new contract. He immediately plunged into working on the debris. He said that the building would not be safe or usable for months. Only a shell remained.

A Mass of thanksgiving was offered July 26 at the burned-out house. The staff wanted to give thanks that no one was injured in the fire.

The cause of the fire remains unknown. The arson investigator asked a few questions the night of the fire. Arson was suspected, but we had no suspects, nor could we place anyone upstairs immediately before the fire. We knew of no one who would have wanted to burn down Casa Juan Diego.

The date of the fire is indelibly impressed in our minds. It was the end of a good beginning. Much had transpired in that old ugly building in eighteen months. In that house on Washington Avenue, we had begun a major distribution of food and clothing. We had given many people a place to stay, especially young men from Central America fleeing the wars, the forced recruitment, and the death squads. We had also received a number of Cubans from the Isle of Mariel.

When a Catholic Worker house burns, it forces the staff to make a decision. They have permission to quit with a sign of relief—which is a real temptation—or they can start all over. We chose to start anew. The decision was not easy. It was a faith decision, made somewhat easier by the great interest and support from the community for the work of Casa Juan Diego.

Catholic Workers in other parts of the country encouraged us to purchase a building rather than rent, in order to be able to function independently of various pressures and have a permanency in the work with the poor. Often people prefer that CW Houses of Hospitality not exist near their homes. Would they protest? And how would we be able to purchase property, since we had used all past contributions to serve the poor? In our August 1982 paper, we asked readers of the *Houston Catholic Worker* to help us purchase a building of our own. We hoped to raise $125,000.

The devastating fire had put Casa Juan Diego out of business. It no longer existed except in the hearts of the people, out of people's garages where donations were being stored, and on the streets of Washington Avenue as we tried to continue to help with food and clothing. Workers and volunteers were becoming frustrated and impatient. Someone suggested we do what Dorothy Day would in such a situation—start a novena. If all else fails, pray harder and longer, and for nine days. We began our novena of prayer, penance, and sacrifice on August 30. People gave up television and the newspaper; some fasted, some went to daily Mass, and some said the Rosary. The novena participants gathered every night to read Scripture, pray the psalms, and sing popular Spanish hymns. At the same time, we followed an old Catholic custom about receiving help buying and selling real estate, and buried a statue of St. Joseph. With this ritual, which Dorothy Day also followed, we hoped for St. Joseph's intercession that property might be available.

Before the novena was finished, we signed a contract to purchase two houses and four small apartments for a reasonable price several blocks from the old Casa Juan Diego. The novena of petition turned into a celebration of thanksgiving. We sang the Magnificat, Mary's prayer of thanksgiving. We had much to be thankful for, from the night of the fire when no one was injured, to the purchase of the property and the generosity of many people.

The results of the fire were paradoxical. The fire had suspended our work, but the publicity drew attention and support to our work with the poor. It facilitated the purchase of property for a more permanent place of hospitality. Contributions after the fire helped us to make a down payment of $35,000 on the property. We began anew, but deeply in debt with a mortgage.

The first time we heard the name "Loyola" was after we purchased the property. Sr. Olive, a young, red-haired Sister of Charity of the Incarnate Word in Houston, visited us and asked questions about our work with immigrants. The sisters had hospitals and clinics in several states, including Texas. Sr. Olive said that her superior, Mother Loyola, was interested in helping the homeless. She didn't mention filling out complicated forms to apply for funds, just that we should write a letter to Mother Loyola, telling about our work and ourselves. We did. It was a very short, handwritten letter.

Within a week, we received a call telling us that Mother Loyola wanted to see us. Would we be available? Of course we would. Mother Loyola came with an envelope. She simply handed over the envelope as if it was a Christmas card. There were no other terms. In the envelope was a check to pay off the mortgage on the buildings. We were out of debt and on our way.

The new Casa Juan Diego included five buildings. The main building, located at 4818 Rose Street, served as the office, as well as distribution center for food, clothing, furniture, and the noon meal (soup kitchen). A smaller building was the residence for women, children, and staff. Another housed guests and served as the used-furniture garage. A second larger building at 4814 Rose was for men, and included a chapel and meeting room for clarification of thought and celebration of the liturgy. The fifth house was prepared to be a medical center with volunteer physicians.

The buildings were old and would not tolerate much wear and tear. The drywall had seen better days, which turned out to be fortunate for Marta, one of our guests. One night, at 1:00 a.m., Isidro, her husband, pushed her through the drywall of the living area for women and staff.

Isidro was built like Arnold Schwarzenegger as he appeared in *The Terminator*. The wall now had the outline of a human body on it, that of his wife.

As if pushing his wife through the wall wasn't bad enough, two pregnant women who were in front of Isidro's wife also went through the wall. His wife had hidden behind them for safety. At least the drywall gave way, thank the Lord.

Isidro had been staying at the house with his wife. He'd been overcome by jealousy and had been drinking heavily, a dreadful combination. He broke down the door where his wife and the pregnant women sought refuge. After the mothers picked up their little ones, they fled upstairs to the safety of the staff quarters.

In the seconds in which all this transpired, Jane, an English-speaking guest at Casa Juan Diego, called the police. She then escaped to the rooftop. It was the first time anyone had ever called the police, but Jane had seen enough violence. Prior to coming to Casa Juan Diego, she had lost her front teeth attempting to break up a fight between a husband and wife. (Thanks to a very generous dentist, she again has teeth.) Steve, a staff member, was soon on the scene to deal with Isidro and the police for the rest of the night. Steve, a big Notre Dame grad, was nonviolent, accepted the values of Casa Juan Diego, and could deal with the situation.

When the police came, Isidro had already left, but they found him later in the neighborhood of Casa Juan Diego. Apparently he resisted them fiercely, which resulted in his going to jail. The following morning we received a call from Isidro saying that he was in jail and wanted us to come and arrange for his release. His wife begged us to do it. The Lord said we should visit the imprisoned, not necessarily bail them out, although we do our share of that. In this case, we declined. Isidro was released that morning through a woman he had been working for. This woman insisted that we accept Isidro back at Casa Juan Diego, but we decided not to. Christians we are; masochists we are not.

Isidro got back on his feet. He is a skilled and hard worker. He returned to being gainfully employed and has avoided jail. Thank the Lord that there were no serious injuries as Isidro expressed his jealous rage against his wife. Violence is not common at Casa Juan Diego. When it does occur, it is usually related to alcohol consumption. Our experience with Isidro and his wife confirmed our rule against guests drinking.

The old buildings served us well for several years, with most of the drywall intact, but not for long enough. As if one fire had not been enough, a second one struck on June 20, 1985, at 5:00 a.m.

"Mark! Louise! Mark! Louise!" The nervous voice kept calling while rapid knocks came through the door just a few feet from our pillows. "What now?" we wondered. "Probably an abusive ex-husband or boyfriend trying to break into the women's house to beat up 'their woman' again."

We opened the door. "There's a fire in the office," the Catholic Worker said. "Please call the fire department." In a few seconds, we were on the phone with 911.

We got dressed as fast as we could. We figured it was a small fire and would soon be out. Not so! The office was in flames and the women's house behind the main house was on fire.

We could not believe what was happening. We felt like this was a movie or TV show, and we would turn it off and life would return to normal. We joked about the fire being a good way to get rid of cockroaches, a challenge in Houston.

Reality sank in when a cameraperson from Channel 13 arrived, and a neighbor reminded us that this was the second fire. When poor people came asking for help during the fire, we responded with a smile and proceeded to help them as much as we were able. Even if your houses are burning, you must serve others. Our pain doesn't lessen their pain. It didn't help us when one of the neighbors commented while the building was still smoldering, "Mark, you must be doing something wrong over there."

One of the first concerned people to arrive at the fire was Auxiliary Bishop McCarthy, who offered to send a check, which was brought later by the diocesan chancellor, Monsignor Scheel. Father Mario Arroyo, our "chaplain," brought two more checks from the diocese, one a personal check from Bishop Fiorenza.

Refugees, whom we had helped settle in the neighborhood and who came to volunteer, burst into tears when they saw the house where they had cooked and eaten in flames. "¿Qué pasó, Marcos?" ("What happened?") Other friends came by. The ministers from the local Baptist and Methodist churches in the neighborhood came to Casa Juan Diego and offered to help. They invited us to speak with their congregations.

Three television channels and two newspapers soon came to the scene. (The media loves fires.) They were polite and interested in our work and were patient, despite our disjoined efforts to respond. On camera, the first question was, "Mark, why are you doing this work?" With the house still smoking, the answer did not come easily.

The fire gutted the main building. No one was hurt. The neighboring building, which housed the volunteer staff, was damaged but not destroyed. All the blankets and many sheets and towels were burned, along with a donated washing machine and dryer. A great quantity of cooking oil, which we had stockpiled in the attic because it was so essential for our daily food preparation, was destroyed. We learned that if you hoard food, the Lord might take it away, might burn it.

We knew we could no longer house and feed guests until we had reorganized. Within hours, we called in dumpsters and trailers to haul off the mountains of debris outside the house. Refugee families who formerly lived in Casa Juan Diego and other volunteers had the rubbish cleaned up by nightfall.

Of the guests still living in the houses, many had already planned to go to their families or work in other cities. We purchased tickets for two young teens to go to their families in Bakersfield, California; a ticket for one guest to Miami; three to work in Austin; and two to Dallas, where they were to be accepted as refugees in Canada. Several days before, we had arranged for three families to go to New York, Newark, and Los Angeles. A mother and newborn remained with us, along with several teenagers who were with us more permanently. Otherwise, we were closed for some time.

The cause of the blaze was not certain, but firefighters at the scene told us that it appeared to be an electrical fire. The fire began at 5:00 a.m. Before noon, we had decided to rebuild. We decided to resolve our despair by looking to the future. We made plans to build a two-story structure of concrete block and steel on the two lots to shelter the homeless, especially families. We trusted that this structure would not burn, or if it did, it would burn very, very slowly. To this day, we are so concerned about fires that the only candles allowed in Casa Juan Diego are the sanctuary lights for the Blessed Sacrament in our chapels. No smoking is allowed in the buildings, either.

Before the embers were cold, we received a call from Mother Loyola, who invited us to a meeting of her Council of Sisters. We don't recall saying anything profound as we participated in our smoky clothing, but they voted to give us $150,000.00 for a new building. This amount might have done the job on the construction of a building made of wood, but we insisted on concrete block and steel. We were tired of fires and worried that one day we would not be so fortunate as to be without casualties. Many other generous people made the completion of the building possible, even though the plans for the new House of Hospitality continued to get bigger.

We planned for special bedrooms for CW staff, three sets of adjoining rooms with a shared bathroom and doors that lock. The second floor would be mainly bedrooms, with a laundry room and storage rooms, as well as a playroom for children. We called on refugee mothers who were former guests to advise us on the design of the bedrooms for the women at the new center. They insisted that two single beds in each room would be sufficient. We included two large rooms for larger families. On the first floor, a large dining room and all-purpose room would be the center of the building, with more bedrooms along the back hallway.

With the help of the community and the sisters, we were able to build a two-story structure on adjoining lots at Rose Street and Durham Avenue. It was a great challenge, however, to convince the Catholic contractor to start the building. He worried that being called Catholic Workers might mean that we were socialists. We think the bishop helped to convince him otherwise. One man who worked for the construction company insisted on making a very large sign, which he placed in the yard where the building had burned while waiting for the construction to begin: "Casa Juan Diego Will Rise from the Ashes!"

We stopped construction before the final details were finished because it was becoming too expensive, deciding to finish the final details like painting inside with the help of our Catholic Workers and volunteers from the community. The building is a strong structure; it withstood a hurricane soon after it was built and later Tropical Storm Allison, which parked over Houston for three days pouring down rain. We hadn't thought about the frequent threat of these storms on the Gulf Coast when planning the construction, but the building has turned out to be a refuge from them. Now when a hurricane threatens, immigrants and refugees who live in Houston ask to come to stay with us for a few days until the storm passes. We have quite a crowd during these times. We did not realize when we purchased the property that it is in one of the rare areas in Houston that does not flood during storms.

During the time the building was being built, we heard about thousands of refugees and immigrants without papers living in southwest Houston, where there were few, if any, services for them. The huge apartment buildings, which had been built while Houston was booming economically, had emptied out with the oil bust and lack of jobs. Refugees from the north of the United States had fled Houston and returned to their homes up north. Now the new refugees filled the apartments. We thought we should try to help. We talked with Bishop Fiorenza and he encouraged us to go out there as well.

When a man named J.R. visited Casa Juan Diego, he was almost in tears. We had just asked him to pray for our efforts in southwest Houston. "Yes," he said, "my wife and I noticed the note in the last paper and she wondered how in God's name you could ever handle another place. Won't it be too much?"

We immediately pointed to the other staff helping unload the fruit from J.R.'s ranch. "We couldn't do it without these folks," we protested. It is true that we were busy day and night, and a new place would mean many headaches, but we had more Catholic Workers to help. A few headaches in the name of serving the poor is not all bad.

We didn't start an extra house because we had extra money. We were broke and still owed Linbeck Construction $25,000, which we couldn't seem to reduce, but thank the Lord they were patient. Several dozen families, some individuals, and several parishes kept us going during lean summer months.

Our money went to pay for the utilities in our buildings, and to buy food, tons of rice and beans for consumption and distribution, disposable diapers for the children of our guests, medicine, soap, rent (for homeless families to get out on their own), gasoline, bus and airplane tickets to send refugees to their families, and anything that was needed to help the poor. At that time the staff received a stipend of $10 a week (later it was increased to $100 a month). We survived from week to week.

The new house, Casa Maria de Guadalupe, opened in a rented storefront in 1987 to offer distribution of food and clothing and to provide English classes. It wasn't long, however, before complaints poured in to the landlord about the crowds of poor people. From the moment the Catholic Worker staff heard of the complaints, they made every effort to keep the poor in front of their building and away from other properties, but it was too late. The landlord closed our operation. He insisted that the Catholic Worker vacate the property immediately, even though a six-month lease had been signed. The landlord charged that the poor people gathered in front of Casa Maria for food and clothing distribution would frighten off potential renters of other properties in the area.

We agreed that seeing hungry women and children standing in line for food was disturbing, if not unsightly. In fact, it is an awful feeling, seeing hungry mothers and children, poorly dressed, standing in line asking for food in the name of the Lord. Even after all the years since Casa Juan Diego opened, we still found it disturbing and were unable to look into people's faces as they waited in line. We survived by pretending they were there for other reasons or forced ourselves to think they were not really hungry. We said we hoped the landlord would feel free to join the food lines if he was ever in need. At least he refunded all our rent money.

While we were looking for another house for Casa Maria, the pastor of Holy Ghost Church, which was served by the Redemptorists, came to the rescue, offering to allow our food and clothing distribution in his parish. He not only made the offer—he welcomed us warmly. He was delighted to have Central American Catholics who lived in the shadow of his parish come to his church and mingle with the other Catholics, so they could get to know one another as members of the Body of Christ. He felt it would be enriching for his parishioners at a time when there was conflict between English-speaking and newer Spanish-speaking parishioners.

We continued searching for a house, knowing we would have to purchase one in order to avoid eviction. God would provide! We were able to find one not far from a busy intersection, and arranged to purchase the house in 1987. Catholic Workers lived in the house and traveled back and forth to share with other Catholic Workers at Casa Juan Diego. Soon Dr. Dwyer and Helen Smolke, a nurse from Holy Ghost, developed a medical clinic there as well.

A battered woman who came to take refuge at Casa Juan Diego dramatically revealed to us the importance of Casa Maria's food distribution. She had five children, two from a previous marriage who were nine and ten years old, and three preschoolers from her current marriage. She was as thin as a needle. We learned that the abusive alcoholic husband only bought beer and milk. The only food our guest and her children had was what was given to them at Casa Maria. That food distribution included only the basics—rice, pinto beans, vegetables, fruits, and bread. We prayed it would help people survive, or in so many cases, help them to be able to use their money to pay the rent.

By 1988, we were able to pay off our mortgage for the new main building. Casa Juan Diego had burned down about every three years since its foundation in 1980. The next fire was due in 1988. We decided to schedule our problems in order to control them. In the February 1988 issue of the *Houston Catholic Worker*, we announced that the third fire would take place on February 17 at 7:00 p.m. But this would be a different kind of fire, a fire created by the burning of the mortgage.

The Mass of thanksgiving and the "mortgage burning" was scheduled for Ash Wednesday. It seemed the best date, not only because Casa Juan Diego had risen from the ashes twice, but also because we needed to be reminded that all things are going to return to ashes someday, including the new building. We were very grateful for a safe building with decent plumbing and wiring, but at the same time we needed reminding that a new building or house does not a House of Hospitality make. What happens in a building is more important than the structure itself. To preserve a House of Hospitality one must work at it, one's heart must burn—that is where the fire is needed—burn with the love of the poor and of the refugees and immigrants.

Many friends of Casa Juan Diego attended the Mass, celebrating in joy. There was a tense moment when during the burning of the mortgage the fire alarms went off. Thank God it was just the burning of the paper that caused the alarms.

Some time later a woman called who told Mark she had been referred by the diocese to talk to us about donations of property. She wanted to give property away to give thanks to God for what the Catholic Church had done for her children. She was not Catholic, but when her children were failing in school, she had gone to Fr. Marcel Knutson, a local diocesan priest and pastor of a parish with a thriving school. He accepted the children in his parish school, where they did well in the elementary grades and went on to succeed in high school and university.

The property, on the east side of Houston, included seven apartments on two lots. It served us well, providing transitional housing for women and children who needed time to prepare for their future. Volunteer groups like the Knights of Columbus helped with repairs several times. We made sure that a fire escape was added to the building, for it had a second floor. At times, we had a sufficient number of Catholic Workers to have someone to live at the apartments, which we called Casa Marcel in honor of Fr. Marcel. At other times, the families lived their on their own. It was difficult to supervise because it was on the other side of town.

Some years later, we received a visit from the Missionaries of Charity, Mother Teresa's sisters, who had been in Houston for several years and had been unable to find a permanent place. They looked at various sites, but after we took them to Casa Marcel, they knew that this would be a perfect place for them to be established in Houston. We donated the apartments to them to continue their work of contemplation and service to the poor.

As the large new concrete building went up at 4818 Rose Street and we were beginning our work in southwest Houston, we kept hearing stories of violence against immigrants at the United States–Mexico border: men beaten and robbed, women raped, people drowned. We wondered what we could do. The need was clear. There were so many stories of people stranded in Mexico who had no place to go after fleeing war and the fruits of war in Central America. There were horror stories of mothers who were homeless and at the mercy of coyotes who raped them.

Anita, a young Guatemalan woman, had stumbled into Casa Juan Diego into the middle of two hundred women going through our clothing donations. She was pregnant. Anita appeared distraught and upset, if not terrorized. She presented a letter from a pastor in the Rio Grande Valley. It read:

> To Whom It May Concern:
> Anita is a Guatemalan who needs help very badly. Will you extend a hand to her and help her out? Let's remember that whatever we do for the poor we are doing it actually for Christ. I hope Anita will receive very good help from you. I will pray to God to reward you greatly for this act of charity shown to her.
> Fr. Benjamin Orozco R., OFM

Clearly something awful had happened—violence of some kind. She was presented to the women staff, especially to the native Spanish-speaking staff so they could arrange hospitality for her and put her at ease. She was a native speaker of an indigenous language of Guatemala, but could speak Spanish.

Anita had recently left Guatemala with two young mothers to come to the United States for the same reasons most people come, to avoid war and being killed, to avoid malnutrition and starvation for their children. She left the children behind with their grandmother and sold everything to pay her way and the way of two other mothers. The two other women were her friends—or so she thought—until she came to the border of Mexico and the United States. They abandoned her after finding work and never contacted her again, though they had promised to assist her with work and transportation in the United States. Immigration officials in Mexico took what little money she had left after helping her friends.

At the river, a man with a car offered to help Anita. He said he would not charge. She was so grateful. But the man was a coyote. Coyotes do not work for free. As soon as they crossed the river, he took his pay out in the flesh. He raped her and passed her on to another coyote who also raped her. This went on with a number of coyotes, and by the time she came to the United States, she wanted desperately to return to Central America—or to die. Anita said that the best thing that ever happened to her was being picked up by U.S. Border Patrol. The immigration officers lectured her about breaking the law by entering the United States illegally. She willingly confessed all, longing with all of the feeling she could still muster up to return to her mother and children in Guatemala after such an awful experience. Sympathizing, they allowed her to leave on her own recognizance, and Fr. Orozco sent her to us.

By the time she reached Houston, clad in a raincoat, Anita was a basket case. She remained distraught after her arrival at Casa Juan Diego and would periodically sob uncontrollably. Sometimes she would leave and go elsewhere in Texas; we would receive calls to come and get her. We were able to arrange housing for Anita with a Guatemalan family and someone for her to talk to, prior to her returning home.

Anita represents the problems of many at the border, not only with coyotes, but also with the Mexican immigration officials or police. Her story is not just the story of one woman, but of many. Refugees had nowhere to go once they got to the river. Their stories made us want to do violence, even though we are pacifists. We decided that we should take our ax and our plowshares and open a house in Matamoros, Mexico, to provide a place for these women and other immigrants and refugees to stay.

We began to explore possibilities and opened the first House of Hospitality for refugees and immigrants in Mexico in 1987. Like Casa Juan Diego in Houston, it was the result of dreaming and praying first, and planning and organizing second. Experience had taught us that we needed a strong support group if we were to undertake such a project so far away in a foreign land. We began with the Church. Bishop Fiorenza was very gracious in responding to our request for a letter to the Bishop of Matamoros telling about our work in Houston. Bishop Fitzpatrick of Brownsville also wrote a letter.

Bishop Sabás Magaña of Matamoros was very receptive and open to the idea of the House of Hospitality for refugees and the homeless. He immediately introduced us to the vicar general and arranged for us to meet one of the pastors. Finding the bishop was very interesting. We simply entered a little gate next to the cathedral, went up some narrow stairs, and there he was in a small office. We waited while a poor, elderly woman saw the bishop to ask about baptismal documents. We were impressed by his availability to the people.

We met with the bishop of Matamoros a number of times to confirm our intent and his. The pastors we met were also receptive to the idea of a House of Hospitality, but it took some doing for us to explain the Catholic Worker movement and how we function. (It's difficult enough in English.) The pastors knew that since refugees and immigrants were in a strange land, they went to the Catholic Church to seek help, and they wanted to respond. How to do it on a practical level was the question. To our satisfaction, the bishop from Matamoros insisted that the Catholic Worker House be staffed by local people.

Fortunately, we met a family who was interested in working with us. We actually met them during our search for a duffel bag a guest of our house in Houston had left there on his way north when he stayed with them for a couple of days. He gave us the address and asked us to pick up his belongings. That family helped us start the house. We rented a small house for 70,000 pesos ($30 at the time), and the local staff began receiving guests. Refugees began coming immediately, referred by local churches. The parish in which the house was located, Nuestra Señora de Lourdes, adopted the project. Fr. Oscar Lozano was most helpful. The parish leadership soon thought of building a House of Hospitality on the grounds of the parish mission, San Felipe, to serve refugees and homeless from the whole area. It echoed Peter Maurin's idea that each parish have a House of Hospitality on parish property.

From the beginning, all concerned with the house were committed to providing temporary housing and meals for the refugees, as well as for homeless Mexican people in the area and for those who might be deported back to Mexico from the United States. The parish was made up of seventy small communities. The communities took turns providing meals and meeting the needs of the guests. They agreed not to become involved in taking people across the border.

We built the house with donations from the Houston community, a very simple structure with one section for women, another for men, a kitchen area, and a separate room for the *encargados*, the people who would be responsible for the house. We were surprised to find that a couple of years after Casa Juan Diego in Matamoros began, there was an article about it on the front page of the *New York Times*. Thousands of refugees have passed through the house over the years, as well as people who had been deported. We continue to underwrite the cost of the house to this day.

Since that time, Catholic parishes and dioceses have gradually developed houses in various parts of Mexico, especially on the routes where the majority of immigrants have traveled. Those arriving hungry, thirsty, and exhausted now have a place to safely rest for a few days. Houses along the Mexican side of the U.S. border also receive people deported from the United States. As the raids and deportations in the United States have multiplied in recent years, these houses receive large numbers of people who have been deported without a penny and no way to get home. Some who are deported have not lived in Mexico since they were small children and do not know their way around at all.

In the meantime, the House of Hospitality we had constructed in Houston was becoming very crowded. Some nights, in addition to fifty on beds, there were close to forty more men sleeping on the dining-room floor of our big house on Rose Street. Some slept on the cushions from the sofas in the dining area, others on the sofas without cushions. There were over 150 people in the various houses of Casa Juan Diego. The women and children lived on the second floor, and since there were not so many of them, they usually all had beds to sleep in. It was always a little uncomfortable and challenging having the men and the women in the same building. They were all suffering, most were lonely after a terrible journey away from their homes, and all needed to pull their lives together. Some of the women were battered. It was not a good time to begin a new, flirtatious relationship. But, of course, given the human condition, these relationships inevitably arose. In order to allow the women space downstairs during the day, Mark insisted that the men go out during the day to look for work except on Sundays, and we and the other Catholic Workers were always working with people on their plan for the future in order to move them on before more people arrived. We built a separate small dining room so that the women and children could eat peacefully, without having to struggle to find room at the tables filled with men.

We knew that we had to do something about the crowded conditions at Casa Juan Diego. We also knew that we had to do something about keeping our guests off the streets. Msgr. Jack Davis must have realized what was going to happen when he remembered Casa Juan Diego in his will. His legacy was an answer to our prayers. Father Jack knew Casa Juan Diego well. He used to bring his pickup full of clothes, always insisting on helping unload the clothing himself. The only thing he ever asked was that we put his sister in Pearland, Texas, on the mailing list for the newspaper. Father Jack did not give us compliments on our work. He was all business. He decided to wait to tell us what he thought about this work in his last will and testament. When the check from his will was brought to us and we opened it, our knees became wobbly. It was a large sum of money.

At the same time that the check came from Fr. Davis's estate, several properties became available in the neighborhood. We bought an old warehouse on the corner of Durham and Floyd, one block from the Rose Street building. It was a large building containing 5,700 square feet. The money left by Father Jack Davis was more than adequate to make a down payment on the building. We were able to add a little more from the Christmas money and soon, with contributions, were able to pay off the building. This was our new home for men. We established the Padre Jack Davis Co-op in that building and invited our newspaper readers to come there to pick up workers for yard work, simple carpentry, and painting.

In order to separate the men's and women's buildings, we closed down for a week—the only time Casa Juan Diego has closed voluntarily since 1980. Since 1991, the Rose Street building has been the House of

Hospitality for women and children and the receiving center for donations of clothing and food.

When a Catholic counseling agency, which had been given the use of a large house and property on Rose Street (four blocks down from our main building), decided to move to the suburbs, the foundation that owned the building offered to lend it to us for hospitality to poor families. We were pleased, although we were already very busy. We accepted the loan of the house and a large family came right at that time asking for a place to stay. We moved them in, and all went well until the plumbing stopped working. We discovered that the building was not connected to the city's sewer system. We were grateful that the foundation fixed the plumbing. They donated the building to us in 2002.

After the family moved out, the 4416 Rose property served us well for various purposes, including a center for teenage immigrant boys who had nowhere to go. For this reason, the house was called Casa Don Bosco. The youths, along with Catholic Workers, developed a project for the construction of simple, pine coffins, which went on for several years. More recently, the building has been used to house the sick and injured.

The Sisters of Charity asked us if we needed more help. We did. We were aware that several houses with apartments a block away from the Rose Street and Floyd Street houses had become available. They would be very useful for transitional housing for mothers and children, those who needed more time. The Sisters helped us to buy them.

Then there was another problem—the Guatemala-Mexico border.

Carlos, one of the *ayudantes* of Casa Juan Diego, told us that if we wanted to help immigrants and refugees, we must go to Tecún Umán, Guatemala. It was to this border town that all Central Americans, even South Americans, who were picked up in Mexico were deported. He spoke of women offering their services for twenty-five cents at the Park of the Desolate Ones (given this name by refugees and immigrants) on the south side of the river. We put Carlos off at first, but he insisted. He knew we had a house in Mexico and might be able to help on this other border further to the south.

If the immigrants and refugees coming from Central America got across the Suchiate, the river that separates Mexico and Guatemala, on the Mexican side they met thieves—with and without uniforms—and often gang members, all of whom took any money and anything of value they had with them. Both groups were cruel. Some immigrants attempting to enter Mexico had even their clothes taken and were deported in their underwear. Large numbers were deported. In fact, at that time, all those deported from Mexico, no matter what their country of origin, were deported to Tecún Umán. Half of the population of the city was made up of refugees and migrants coming or going or simply stuck there, homeless.

Our experience in starting a house in Matamoros stood us in good stead. To address the problems at the Suchiate, we first went to the north side of the river to visit Bishop Arizmendi of Tapachula, Mexico. He was very hospitable and friendly and explained that a parish in Tapachula was already giving some hospitality.

We discovered that the south side of the river, Tecún Umán, was under the auspices of Bishop Alvaro Ramazzini of San Marcos, Guatemala. He too said, "Come." He told us that the pastor of the parish in Tecún Umán, *El Señor de las Tres Caídas* ("The Three Falls of Jesus"), would pick us up on the Mexican side of the river when we arrived for the first time and drive us across.

To reach Bishop Ramazzini we had to travel up the mountains to San Marcos. A Scalabrini priest was able to take us up the mountainous roads to the bishop's house—and what a trip it was. Fr. Albino, apparently a former Brazilian racecar driver, broke all records in getting there. What a person of faith, passing on curves, driving quickly up hills and mountains with no fear of oncoming vehicles! We figured that if we survived, it would be a sign from heaven that there would be a center for immigrants in Guatemala. Louise fought carsickness in the back seat all the way; fortunately, she was wearing "Sea-Bands" on her wrists, which helped a lot. Mark almost wore a hole in the floorboard as he kept pressing brakes that weren't there.

Bishop Ramazzini welcomed us with a nice meal. We would have enjoyed the food even more if we had not had headaches from the journey and shell shock from the trip up the mountains. The bishop drives those mountains day and night to visit the people of his diocese, many of whom are indigenous and very poor. Bishop Ramazzini was very much in favor of a center for women and promised to talk with Fr. Jesús of Tecún Umán.

Coming down the mountains, a little slower this time, we visited Malacatán, a town not far from Tecún, where Fr. Albino showed us a newly constructed clinic-hospital for children. Upon leaving the clinic, we noticed that one bar after another was full of heavily made-up women sitting at tables. They did not appear to be Guatemalan. The signs on the bars said, "Women available." The women in these "bars," we discovered, were Central American refugees and immigrants stranded south of the Suchiate. It was 11:00 a.m.

We returned to share with Fr. Jesús, who had picked us up at the airport the night before. He had a parish of 10,000 people, a new parish school, and 36 mission stations to attend to. He had recently started the school, staffed by five Mexican religious sisters, which serves 500 Guatemalan children, preparing them for careers in order to avoid a life of poverty. He was so busy that to expect his involvement in another project would be totally unreasonable—that is, if you are reasonable people.

We talked for a long time. Fr. Jesús thought that maybe Fr. Albino could open a little office for immigrants somewhere far from the parish. The turning point came when we described the blocks-long lines of *campesino* men who on Market Day lined up outside the bars (described above) filled with immigrant women. Now! Not only were the women working the bars his parishioners (and part of the floating population of 10,000 in Tecún Umán), but the men frequenting the women were also his parishioners, part of the Guatemalan population with deep roots in the area, whom he loved and had served for sixteen years in his parish.

Fr. Jesús made a decision to support a house to receive women and became a leader for a center for homeless immigrants. He took responsibility for construction of the center and provided land donated to the parish. On our next visit to San Marcos, the architects presented elegant plans for a building that would cost $350,000, presented with a three-dimensional model. We smiled, of course, and said we had only a fraction of that amount ($50,000). The bishop said that it would be built for that fraction—and it happened. Fr. Jesús asked a group of religious sisters, the Oblates of the Redeemer, to run the house. Their charism is to work with marginalized women, including prostitutes, giving them hope and love.

The center, which holds forty women and has a separate staff house for four, was dedicated in 1995 with a great fiesta and hundreds of parishioners participating. Bishop Arizmendi of Tapachula, Mexico, and ten priests of the diocese joined Bishop Ramazzini in celebrating the Mass. The sisters from the parish school led the schoolchildren's choir; children and sisters played guitars. The women of the parish council prepared a chicken dinner for all with a delicious, cold *orchata* to drink. It seemed that the house in Tecún Umán was another part of the fulfill-ment of Peter Maurin's dream of having parish houses of hospitality.

The enthusiasm about the new house for women encouraged more thought and enthusiasm about a more extensive program for the thou-sands of immigrants and refugees in Tecún Umán. Soon the Scalabrini Fathers, whose charism is to work with migrants, began plans to set up a center in Tecún Umán, also on land donated by the parish. Generous friends of Casa Juan Diego donated $25,000 to help them start the proj-ect, which grew into a large center for immigrants in Tecún Umán.

While we were traveling to Guatemala to encourage the beginning of Houses of Hospitality for immigrants and refugees there, we contin-ued our work in Houston. When a property became available on the opposite corner of Rose Street from what was now the women and chil-dren's building near the clinic, we believed it prudent to purchase it, in the interest of protecting the women's House of Hospitality. That house became another refuge for sick and wounded immigrants, whose num-bers were growing in our houses.

We had always been conscious that a key component of Peter Maurin's program was agriculture. We did not have a farm, but we were blessed with enough space to develop two large gardens. The enthusiasm of Catholic Workers and volunteers from the community made sure they were started. Special preparation of the soil was required in Houston; we were told that in its natural state the soil could only grow okra. The gar-dens not only provide food for the table, but also are the creation of many hands, allowing the participation of our guests. There are fruit trees as well as many vegetables growing in the gardens. They remind us that the garden is a very important symbol in biblical literature, from the Garden of Eden, the garden of delight, to the Agony in the Garden. They also remind us of Peter Maurin's maxim that we should earn our bread by the sweat of our brow, not by the sweat of someone else's brow. We collect hats from the donated clothing to protect the gardeners from the sun, as Houston's heat is fierce. We were disappointed that the statue of St. Francis was stolen from one of the gardens, but thought that perhaps someone needed it. To steal the new one they'll need dynamite.

When the neighbors complained about the men at our Floyd Street house, believing that all the men on the streets in the neighborhood look-ing for work came from Casa Juan Diego, it was suggested to us that we should not be in the center of the city, but should move everything out into the country. We did not accept that suggestion, because ours was an ideal location, just a couple of miles from downtown Houston, where immigrants arriving in the city could find us. The realtor who had generously helped us with all of our properties made this suggestion. We never could have managed our properties without her. Neighbors had criticized her for selling us the warehouse property, especially those neighbors who owned adjoining property and were unable to sell it. When an old restaurant building became available in the same square block as our women's and children's House of Hospitality, she convinced us to purchase it and sell the converted warehouse. It was a very good plan and has worked out well. Friends helped us to build an addition to the old restaurant building to provide a large room in the new men's center where we could celebrate Mass for all of our guests on Wednesdays and have a place for food and clothing distribution.

We still had one old building on Rose Street next to the women's building, which we had also acquired in the 1980s. We used it for the medical and dental clinics at Casa Juan Diego, but it was falling apart. The holes in the floor grew larger; it was a challenge not to step into them as clinics took place. One hole was so big that a person's foot could fall into it. Temporarily, a large piece of plywood was placed over the largest holes.

Friends of the Houston Catholic Worker came to tell us they wanted to help us with a new building for the clinic. They involved their parish, St. Cecilia's, in gathering funds. The Sisters of Charity, who have always helped, provided the remainder. It took a long time, perhaps three years, to get the building started, but it was finally finished. Some of the volunteer doctors missed the old one. They felt that they had really been on the frontier when they came each week or month to the raggedy old building.

We are fortunate to now have a beautiful dental clinic in that new building, open when volunteer dentists and dental hygienists are able to come. Daily people come to the door with swollen mouths and terrible toothaches, seeking help. We often have to have a raffle to determine which patients can be seen. Two dental surgeons are also willing to receive patients in their offices if our dentists determine that they need to see them. Some of the clinic staff still tell stories about how the sloping floor in the old building caused the dental chair to slide across the room as they were working.

Doctors who volunteered at our southwest Houston house saw the new clinic and hoped for more space for their Casa Maria clinic. In 2008, we built an addition for the family living there so the clinic could have three examining rooms, with more space for the medicine dispensary and for interviews to take medical histories.

After giving the Marcel apartments to the Missionaries of Charity, Casa Juan Diego still has ten buildings in Houston. We do not plan to acquire any more.

6

OH, FREEDOM!

Frequently we have been asked: How can Casa Juan Diego possibly function and grow, with so many people in need arriving to be served? How can all of us keep going, day after day?

The answer is freedom. Freedom is the source of strength. It is exhilarating, energizing, and empowering. The freedom of the Gospel is quite different from rugged individualism or doing whatever we want. It involves a revolution of the heart that cannot be suffocated by the forces of comfort, possession, pleasure, egotism, and narcissism. It is the dynamite of commitment and passion. It is the freedom to serve in the context of the Mystical Body of Christ.

The Catholic Worker movement has inspired many by its example of freedom to live the Gospel radically. It inspires us. As had so many saints before them, Peter and Dorothy—with the dynamism of the Gospel—broke through everyday patterns of life and those reigning philosophies that limit the possibilities of living the Gospel. These habits and patterns of our lives quickly transform into wings of lead if they are not in dialogue with our loving freedom.

In her diaries, Dorothy Day quoted Peter Maurin on freedom and the responsibility that comes with it:

> Peter's greatest message for us, greater even than his message of poverty, was man's freedom and responsibility. It was a timeless problem. It was a problem a better social order would help to make easier to solve, but it is a problem which will always remain with us "until the day dawns and the shadows rise and the Desire of the everlasting hills shall come...."
>
> A great and terrible thought setting us free, and also making us realize our responsibility.[1]

We have the freedom and responsibility to respond to those most in need. That, of course, can be overwhelming at times. When friends of Casa Juan Diego complain that we are doing too much and should stop this marathon, that we are doing violence to ourselves, Mark reminds us of a retreat he made with Fr. Bernard Basset before we were married. Fr. Basset was a famous English Jesuit retreat master and author. Before the retreat, Mark was not only doing his own work, but also that of several others. He was providing pastoral care for two floors of a six-floor hospital in addition to his other duties. The other four floors were being neglected by his colleagues, and he was called upon to care for them as well:

"I presented the problem," Mark said, "knowing full well that being the good psychologist that Fr. Basset was, he would condemn his colleagues and forbid me to do the others' work, that he would say, 'That's their responsibility!'"

He did not. Indeed, he did not!

"Fr. Basset listened attentively to my woes, but as soon as I finished, he shot out of his chair, shouting, 'The washing of the feet! The washing of the feet! It is all answered in the washing of the feet!'"

In other words, get your mind off those others and onto the feet of those you serve. Which meant freedom! Lighten up and do all the work. We had complained a lot, but it had accomplished nothing. We discovered that freedom shrivels self-pity and reduces complaints to ashes.

For us, the freedom of the "washing of the feet" approach brings healing to the lives of the poor, but just as important, it brings healing to the "foot washers." We understand why some in the early Church thought of it as a sacrament. The washing of the feet does not take away exhaustion, that drained feeling, or tension headaches, but it cures bitterness. At times, it brings a joy and an experience of grace and the supernatural not found in reading theological texts. We don't abandon prayer and reading for foot washing, however. The Scriptures are the basis of our work. We also find that theological articles, the writings of Dorothy Day and Peter Maurin, and the work of those who influenced them help us realize the freedom of the Gospel.

We are foot washers and problem solvers rather than hand holders. This approach helps us to not succumb to favoritism for one guest over another for reasons of emotional attachment. We try to respond according to the need of the person who comes to us. Clearly, someone whose whole life is spent caring for a paralyzed person needs more material help than others, although all may need some help. Constant vigilance is required to avoid preferential treatment and to keep one's patience in the face of many demands and even hostility. The washing of the feet can be accomplished for both likable and unlikable people; problems can be solved for both those who appear to be beautiful and those who appear to be ugly.

We have discovered that the paradox of freedom is the paradox of the Gospel: The way to save your life is to give your life. Gain by giving. Be a go-giver, as Peter Maurin said, instead of a go-getter. Taking the risk of freedom—being receptive to God's grace using the model of Mary's *fiat*—makes us truly free. What we do may not be understood, some may not agree, and some may be convinced we do very little work and should do more. That is a risk of freedom. We are free to make our humble attempts to follow Jesus and serve him in our brothers and sisters, but there are always dangers. We could become lazy or grouchy.

Those of us who supported the civil rights movement in the sixties know the spiritual "Oh, Freedom." The song came from the terrible time of slavery in the United States, when African Americans had no freedom and were abused. The song can also give us insight into all kinds of slavery and the wonder of freedom in the middle of adversity:

Oh, freedom,
Oh, freedom,
Oh, freedom over me!
And before I'd be a slave
I'll be buried in my grave.
And go home to my Lord and be free.

As those who sang the song knew, it is through the Gospel that we find true freedom, in spite of what surrounds us. The question becomes, How, in the middle of very difficult circumstances, can we use our God-given free will?

Our attempts to listen to the Spirit and respond creatively have brought us to serve a community of people often invisible to most of society. Late one evening in May 1989, for example, we were reflecting on recent days at Casa Juan Diego. The dining room looked like a disaster area. There were men spread out all over the place, including the entrance and the men's dormitory hallway. There were more men on the floor than in the beds. The upstairs rooms were full of women and children. During the past three months, many hundreds of refugees had come to Casa Juan Diego because of a court decision allowing them to travel after applying for political asylum. In addition. there had been unusually freezing cold weather in the Rio Grande Valley area and a huge number of refugees had nowhere to go.

Looking more closely, we could see that Casa Juan Diego was not a disaster area. The expressions on the men's faces gave a different picture, a beautiful one. They had suffered much on their journey, were poorly clothed, and maybe hadn't yet showered, but their weather-beaten faces were at peace.

Walking through the bodies, we thought of the many stories that would come from people who had left mothers and fathers or wives and children to seek refuge and peace. These people had taken great risks to come here to sleep on the floor of Casa Juan Diego's dining room.

They had come for various reasons: to get a decent job, to be able to support their families with some dignity, to avoid being killed by their country's army, to avoid being forcibly recruited by the army or the guerrillas, to keep their children from being malnourished.

With the guests asleep, it was especially peaceful because there were no questions. How can I find my relatives? Can you get me a job with one of your friends or relatives? How much does it cost to go to Los Angeles? How can I become legal? How can I get permission to work in the United States? I worked today, but I wasn't paid. I need pants. I need shoes. I need a ride. I need medicine. I need ID. When are you sending a bus to Miami or Los Angeles? (We don't charter buses!) Our work is much easier and much more beautiful when everyone is asleep. It makes it easier to reflect on our freedom.

The freedom celebrated in the song, the freedom of the Gospel, is so different from practicing hedonism and seeking power over others and creating wealth for oneself and stockholders on the backs of poor workers. When some people say, *Oh, freedom*, they mean:

Oh, the *freedom* of free trade, free sex, the free market.
Oh, the *freedom* to not pay workers a just wage, even though their children are ill and undersized from not having enough food.
Oh, the *freedom* to charge exorbitant interest on loans and credit cards.

Oh, the *freedom* to charge rates on electricity higher than people can pay.

Oh, the *freedom* to build walls to keep others out.

Oh, the *freedom* to drop cluster bombs and not worry about civilian casualties.

This concept of freedom keeps people from doing the right thing.

The freedom of the Gospel is not about buying ourselves things, nor about building bigger banks to hold our money, nor about arming ourselves to the teeth to protect it. It is not about determinism, the fatalism that the "invisible hand of the market" should control our lives without any restraint or concern for workers. It is not about massive imprisonment of poor citizens and poor undocumented workers.

The freedom we have to do good, to create a world where it is easier for others to be good, is quite different. Catholics do not have to wait for orders from Rome to begin washing others' feet, to be "go-givers rather than go-getters." We do not have to act in the bureaucratic way that has become a model or be afraid of doing something different. We are free to love our enemies. We are free to develop alternatives to an economy that takes away the dignity and meaning of work. We are free to help the stranger in a strange land. We are free to overcome our self-centeredness and go the extra mile. We are free to give up all and follow Jesus.

Friend of Dorothy Day and Peter Maurin, Benedictine Father Virgil Michel said, "The freedom to do good is almost overwhelming." *OH, FREEDOM!*

When the refugees were pouring into Houston in 1980, we were free to choose, to serve, or to say *"Non serviam."* How could we have the audacity to start something like Casa Juan Diego without any funding or staff? *OH, FREEDOM!*

How could Archbishop Romero, known as a "safe conservative," find the insight and courage to stand with those being tortured and killed, going to jails and morgues to be with his people under attack? He might be tortured or killed himself. He said he was responding to Christ in the poor. *OH, FREEDOM!*

Where do immigrants, faced with a desperate situation in a global economy that gives little value to any worker, find the courage to begin a trip known to be the most dangerous journey in the world, crossing several countries by foot and by freight train to try to reach a place where they can work and support their families? *OH, FREEDOM!*

When the hospitals of Houston and when families started calling us about a place to stay for those who were undocumented, or paralyzed, or shot in the back, or seriously ill, or HIV-positive, or blinded from uncontrolled diabetes, at first we said, no, we don't do that, we can't do that, how could we do that? But we had the freedom to find a way to help. *OH, FREEDOM!*

In 1987, a call came from Richmond, Virginia: "We received your name from Bishop Sullivan's office and understand that you are the only place in the United States that will house this Salvadoran refugee who had a head injury and doesn't know where he is. Will you take him?" *OH, FREEDOM!*

Each day we are free to respond to Jesus in the poor, and also, if we can, protect those who need protection. It was going to be a peaceful July evening. That is, until the phone rang with a call from the men's house. A large golf club was recently donated to the poor of Casa Juan Diego (just what we needed). An angry man was standing in the center of the meeting room swinging the fancy club and threatening to kill anyone who came close to him. If anyone moved, he swung. Mark was asked to come and disarm him. *OH, FREEDOM!* He headed immediately for the men's house, praying as he went that he could resolve the problem nonviolently and without the police. He promised the usual as he ran—ten minutes of prayer every day for a week in thanksgiving for a successful outcome.

As he slowly opened the door to the men's house, he saw dozens of frightened men glued to the walls with José, in the center, poised, ready to strike. Mark headed directly for José and embraced him and the golf club like a brother, not only because we loved him as a brother, but also because it keeps the swings and punches short. He noticed immediately that this man did not live in the house. "These guys are not treating me right, *Señor Marcos*," he cried out in Spanish, breaking down in tears in Mark's arms. We wept, too, in thanksgiving that no one was hurt. You could hear the sighs of relief as stiffened bodies along the walls relaxed. Then we took the man to his home in the neighborhood. *OH, FREEDOM!*

Another day we received a call from a church group regarding a battered woman who would soon have to leave a shelter that only allowed a thirty-day stay. She was asking for assistance with rent, but they could not help her because they had federal funds, and the grants were very strict. They had to prove that she had a formal job. Babysitting night and day did not count. We, though, were free to help her. *OH*, the *FREEDOM* we have without bureaucracy.

A hospital called to ask us to pay the return fare to her country for a pregnant woman who was ill. Easy, thanks to generous people! *OH, FREEDOM!*

When the sheriff's deputy called to ask if we could take a woman he found in the street who was seriously mentally ill, we were hesitant to accept her because we knew it would be difficult for us and for our other guests. She was very frightened, hearing voices that terrified her. The deputy had only two options—send her to Casa Juan Diego or to the Immigration Service, which would deport her to the Mexican border, hundreds of miles from her home. He hated to have her deported in such a condition. But we were free to try to find help for her. *OH, FREEDOM!*

When she arrived, we began to talk with her in a comforting manner. She told us about the voices she was hearing. We called the Houston Police Department and asked for an officer trained in mental health. The officer who came spoke Spanish and, between us, we convinced her to go to the hospital. There she signed her first name and was accepted. Two weeks later, we received a call from her nephew who was a student at the University of Houston. He asked in amazement how we had found her and how she got to the hospital. We explained and apologized if the family was upset about the hospitalization, but we believed it had been the right thing to do. The nephew said, "Oh, no, we are so grateful. She had been successfully working as a live-in maid in Houston. The very scary Halloween decorations had pushed her over the edge. The whole family is grateful to you."

Marina came to us with her two children. She told us that the journey to the United States was terrifying and that she had never experienced such desolation and pain. It was a real Way of the Cross, but it was not as awful as finding herself alone and isolated on the street in the poor *barrios* of Houston. Marina gives new significance to the meaning of hospitality. People who call hospitality Band-Aid work have not worked with poor immigrant women. To take a homeless woman off the street who has no papers, no relatives, no resources, and no entitlements, and to give her time to recuperate emotionally, empowers her and gives her freedom. To address her medical needs and those of her children, to get the children settled in school, to help her learn some English, to arrange a job, and to rent an apartment: all of this is empowerment. It is accomplished through no-strings-attached hospitality and *FREEDOM!*

A Spanish-speaking mother and her children were living in an unheated garage in the winter in Houston. (Yes, there are cold days in Houston in the winter.) Will we house them? *OH, FREEDOM!*

There was a call from the bus station. A family of six was stranded because they lost all their money and papers to Mexican immigration officials. Would we come and get them and give them a place to stay? *OH, FREEDOM!*

Ben Taub Hospital called to see if we could accept Mauricio back. Mauricio had been with us for a year after suffering a stroke and being partially paralyzed. Then he fell and broke his leg and shoulder. He also had cancer. He was from El Salvador and no agency would take him in, because he could not prove he was legal, although he had been here a long time. Could he come back to Casa Juan Diego? *OH, FREEDOM!*

A Sister of Charity from St. Anthony's Center called to say there was a family of eight there from Guatemala who just got off the train. Would we come and get them and take them in? *OH, FREEDOM!*

Susana was tricked into coming to the United States. She was promised a job here, taking care of children or working in a supermarket. She had never been separated from her family before, but when she heard of this job, she agreed to come. She left her girls with her mother and father. She walked for such a long time to get to Houston. She swam across the river. She spent nights in the desert, wet from the river and very cold. When she arrived, a man put her to work in a *cantina*. They wanted her to work almost naked and didn't allow her to use the telephone. They wanted her to take care of clients and made her dance with them. They made her drink alcohol and be with the men. She said the men grabbed her legs and her body. She could not leave to go anywhere. At dawn on a Monday, she escaped from that place with the help of three men, "clients" who were drunk. The inebriated men ran a red light, and they all ended up at the police station. There the police told Susana of Casa Juan Diego. Would we take her in until she could arrange to go back home? *OH, FREEDOM!*

Maria de Guadalupe had to leave Guatemala. Her children had little to eat, their clothes were almost rags, and there was no money for the school supplies, uniforms, or shoes required by the Guatemalan public schools. Her husband was abusive to her and the children, and used his earnings for alcohol. Maria decided that she would to go the United States to work as a live-in maid. She sold what little she had, took the children to their grandmother, and headed north. Her money didn't last long at the Guatemala-Mexico border. She crossed the Suchiate River into Mexico several times, but was turned back each time by Mexican immigration authorities after they robbed her of everything. She was returned to Tecún Umán, Guatemala, a depressed place where thousands of desperate, homeless immigrants milled around, with no money, no job prospects, and nowhere to go. At that time there was no house for immigrants and refugees there. Maria was fortunate to finally cross the river and make her way north. It took nearly a month to cross Mexico, as she took part-time jobs at low pay to survive. She walked, took the bus, and at times, the train.

When she arrived in northern Mexico, two very nice men offered her a trip to the Rio Grande at Matamoros, across from Brownsville, Texas. However, Maria paid an awful price for this help, because they both violated her and then left her alone. She was beside herself, but knew she had to continue her journey because of the children. She approached the Rio Grande with great fear and trepidation. Maria crossed the river safely and made her way north. She walked five days, mostly at night, sleeping in the outdoors with wild animals and drinking from the watering troughs of Texas steer. She had no food until she received help from a parish near Corpus Christi, Texas. She came to Houston and knocked at the door of Casa Juan Diego. Louise answered the door. In telling her story, Maria burst into tears: "I think I'm pregnant." What do you say to such a person who is poor, has nothing, and is pregnant? Louise said what she always says: "*Bienvenida*, welcome to Casa Juan Diego." That is our freedom, to be able to say yes to the stranger in a strange land. We were able to arrange a good job, so Maria could send money to her children for their food and schooling. She began to raise her youngest child in Houston. *OH, FREEDOM!*

We are free to intervene in situations of violence in order to protect people. Sometimes we or other Catholic Workers have stood between people who were attacking each other. Sometimes we or other Catholic Workers have held a person back from throwing a knife. There was a serious fight between two men in the entrance area of one of Casa Juan Diego's buildings. Police were called. In the meantime, Mark went between the two men to break up the fight. After the police intervened, they saw the blood on Mark's hands and shouted at him, "AIDS! AIDS!" As he went to wash his hands, a young Catholic Worker wryly stated, "It's too late, Mark! It's too late!" To date, none of our staff nor we have contracted AIDS or tuberculosis, which occasionally has shown up among our guests.

Sometimes freedom is the freedom to say no to pressures from the culture, as in the situation of Marta. "You must have an abortion—you must have an abortion—right now," insisted the doctor at the emergency room in July of 1999. "Your child will be born deformed if you don't. You have nine-day measles. You could wait until you can have the amniocentesis test in two more months, but by then it will be very late for an abortion. You had better have it now." Marta was very upset. This was an awful decision for her and her husband to make. She wanted to wait. She had never been married before. She had never been pregnant before. She was thirty-six-years old and had always wanted a child. She absolutely refused to have an abortion. "Maybe later," she murmured. Marta wanted a choice.

Marta's measles affected all of Casa Juan Diego and the hundred guests living there. All had been exposed to the disease, including the other pregnant women and the newborns, whose immune systems are not fully developed. Were we going to have an epidemic? Were we going to be quarantined? Were we going to be shut down? What was the next thing to do? We did the obvious: We isolated Marta and her husband in another of our houses. We called the Health Department. The Health Department recommended that, first, we isolate the person with measles, and second, we call on Monday for further instructions. In a few days, the Health Department came to inoculate everyone and to take blood from Marta to see if she really had measles. We insisted that all present guests be inoculated, as well as all new arrivals. We waited for further outbreaks. We prayed! Ted, a visitor, came by the first night of the measles scare. Noticing that some of the women were pregnant, Ted told the story of his cousin, who gave birth after having measles in the early months of her pregnancy—some thirty years ago. The child was still living—blind, deaf, mute, and unable to walk. The child required total nursing care.

When a young doctor friend visited, we broached the subject of Marta and her insistence on not having an abortion, talking about the dilemma and how we wanted to support Marta in her decision for life. He blurted out, "I guess if 'those people' are pro-life, what does that make me? Pro-death?" Like many, the doctor was uncomfortable with the pro-life movement, feeling that there was not much love there. We said we didn't know whether there was much love in the pro-choice movement, either. We responded to the doctor by approaching the abortion issue from the point of view of the seamless garment philosophy, the consistent ethic of life. We didn't convince him. In fact, it seemed that we lost a friend.

Some days after Marta's blood test, we received the results. "No," said the nurse from the Health Department. "Marta never even had measles." Good news for Marta, her husband, and that little being with three months of life! Everyone felt free. *OH, FREEDOM!*

When Catholic Workers Andy and Blossom Wright (who spent eight years at Casa Juan Diego) decided to get married, they refused to be imprisoned in very expensive wedding arrangements. Their priority was the celebration of the sacrament. Andy found his wedding suit in the clothing donations of the men's house, and Blossom her dress at the Salvation Army. The reception was a potluck dinner, and Andy's father played the accordion to provide the music. *OH, FREEDOM!*

When Andy and Blossom became pregnant with their first child, they were shocked when they went to get prenatal care. The doctors insisted that Blossom immediately have an amniocentesis to find out if the baby was "defective." After all, the doctors said, the baby might have Down syndrome. Andy and Blossom were incensed and determined not to have the test. Andy said, "My cousin has Down syndrome and he is a great guy, beloved by all the family." *OH, FREEDOM!*

After Casa Juan Diego had existed for a number of years, we had the idea to ask people to consider not buying so many clothes and instead to donate that money to be used for the poor or by the church. It was inspired by the massive amounts of clothing we sometimes receive as donations, an indication of how many clothes a person can buy, while others go without. While we were glad to distribute the clothing, it became a challenge to organize so much. Clothing, as far as we know, is meant to preserve modesty and to provide warmth for our bodies. Our acquisitive society pressures us to buy more to be in fashion. We began a campaign through our newspaper called "No Clothes for a Year." We had many humorous reactions to the title, but the meaning was clear. With the money saved by not buying new clothes for one year, many people could be helped. Because we knew how hard it is for people to give up shopping, we made up buttons that people could wear saying, "Don't Make Fun of My Clothes!" A surprising number of people participated and donated money for the poor. *OH, FREEDOM!* They said it made them feel quite free. Perhaps they would agree with Dorothy Day and St. John of the Cross, who suggested that the virtue of detachment meant that we must travel lightly through the dark night.

Nicholas Berdyaev, studied by Dorothy Day and Peter Maurin, was known as a philosopher of freedom. Critics contend that religion, especially organized religion and the institutional church, interferes with freedom. Berdyaev pointed out that those who fear loss of freedom by making the leap of faith might not have reflected on how "unfree" they currently are, blindly obeying the commands of their environment and social relations. He noted that even if these people believe they are rugged individualists, most also feel that it is necessary to obey fashion trends and buy the products society insists on—though it may mean the destruction of the environment and the impoverishment of many workers through the methods of production. Consumerism, peer pressure, slavishness to style, and addiction to the latest technological gadgets have a way of defining and imprisoning a person and inhibiting all thought of the creative possibilities of one's destiny—the opposite of human freedom.[2]

Peer pressure, even bullying, are present not just in clothing styles and technology, but in intellectual fashion or fads. Some people take fads as their creed without much analysis and might give unquestioning obedience to their leaders until the leaders are finally discredited. Most would not have dared to question Freud's ideas, for example, during his century of popularity, while now he is discredited and ridiculed. In the university, a place for the free exchange of ideas, a professor who questions ideas that are popular but not truthful or helpful may not be on the job for very long.

The Church can actually help us see things on a deeper level in order to become free from things that enslave us, from sin, and from the negative passions that can overcome us, illustrated so well in the traditional definition of capital sins. The Church can help us understand that anger directed at God or at some poor scapegoat is often misplaced. A closer look also often reveals that some of the most serious problems in our world are the result of the misuse of freedom.

Berdyaev, along with the CW founders, emphasized that Christianity does not depend on constant miracles, but very much on the creative, even daring, activity of Christians in the world, working together with God's grace. Living out the Gospel is not necessarily doing amazing things and creating fantastic programs; it is responding to the needs of our brothers and sisters in a world in which sometimes darkness, cruelty, and wrongful exercise of power seem to be the norm.

Fads even affect theologians. In his encyclical *Veritatis Splendor* (*The Splendor of Truth*), John Paul II addressed some of the methods offered by professors of moral theology that, he believed, were being affected by intellectual fads, such as proportionalism in resolving ethical questions. The first third of the encyclical reflects on the quandary and challenge facing the Gospel story of the rich young man whom Jesus asked to give all his wealth to the poor and follow him. As Catholic Workers, we thought that was one of the most important sections of the encyclical, one that could help us all understand our freedom.

In the face of the great suffering of so many people and the possibility of doing only a little to help, it is sometimes easy to become discouraged. In a Christmas sermon, theologian Hans Urs von Balthasar reflected on these realities:

> I only need to open my eyes and ears, and I shall hear the cry of those unjustly oppressed growing louder every day, along with the clamor of those who are resolved to gain power at any price, through hatred and annihilation. These are the superpowers of darkness; in the face of them all our courage drains away, and we lose all belief in the mission that resides in our hearts, that mission that was once so bright, joyous and peace bringing; we lose all hope of really finding the poor Child wrapped in swaddling clothes. What can my pitiful mission achieve, this drop of water in the white-hot furnace? What is the point of my efforts, my dedication, my sacrifice, my pleading to God for a world that is resolved to perish?

Balthasar continues his reflection, answering the question himself with the words of the Gospel: "Be not afraid, for behold, I bring you Good News of a great joy." He then reminds Christians that in suffering and discouragement we are not alone: "Rejoice then, for God himself has passed this way!"³ As we see with Our Lord living the Way of the Cross, free will is not taken away by suffering.

Peter Maurin analyzed and critiqued the problems of his times; he pointed out the errors and evils of society. In responding to the drama of the split between the Gospel and the everyday lives of people, his recommendation for action was to proclaim: "It is better to announce than denounce." *OH, FREEDOM!*

Peter believed that each person is called to do something special with their lives, that each Catholic has a vocation to respond to the call of Jesus to give up all and follow him. For Peter Maurin, following Jesus meant the freedom to try to create a world different from one in which vast numbers of poor people labor for long hours for a pittance under difficult conditions to allow others to live at a luxurious level. Dorothy wrote:

> Peter made you feel a sense of his mission as soon as you met him. He did not begin by tearing down, or by painting so intense a picture of misery and injustice that you burned to change the world. Instead, he aroused in you a sense of your own capacities for work, for accomplishment. He made you feel that you and all men had great and generous hearts with which to love God. But it was seeing Christ in others, loving the Christ you saw in others. Greater than this, it was having faith in the Christ in others without being able to see Him.⁴

But Peter saw through the pitfalls of the social order. He pointed out the errors and evils of society. As Dorothy said of him,

> It was the state of the world which filled him with these vast desires. Man was placed here with talents, to play his part, and on every side he saw the children of this world wiser in their generation than the children of light. They built enormous industrial plants, bridges, pipe lines, skyscrapers, with imagination and vision they made their blue prints, and with reckless and daredevil financing made them actual in steel and concrete. Wheels turned and engines throbbed and the great pulse of the mechanical and physical world beat strong and steady while men's pulses sickened and grew weaker and died. Man fed himself into the machine.⁵

Peter could say the same today in the light of our technological society, with all the potential and real misuse of that technology.

The freedom of the children of God allows a positive, creative response to what God has in mind for us for our lives in the world. This is not the freedom of chaos or libertinism. Emmanuel Mounier, one of those who inspired the Catholic Worker movement, called this our destiny. In a chapter on freedom in his book *Personalism*, Mounier addresses the question of the many different ways that freedom is defined and perceived, pointing out that freedom is much more than choice. It is not choosing that which is not good or which is mediocre and calling that freedom. As he put it, "A sort of philosophic myopia tends to see the center and pivot of freedom in the act of choice, whereas it lies in progressive liberation to choose the good. What would be the value of freedom merely to choose between the plague and cholera?"[6] In one of his most memorable statements, Mounier said that we are not freed merely by detaching ourselves from the bonds that paralyze us, but by attaching ourselves to our destiny.[7] The understanding that Mounier and Maurin had of our destiny was quite different from the Puritan-influenced idea of Manifest Destiny, which claims that the United States has a providential role in history that allows it to dominate other countries, an idea adopted by politicians and other Americans over the centuries.

Taking personal responsibility involves the freedom to act. We were asked to participate in a Catholic radio program on the issues around voting in an upcoming election. It became clear as we talked with others on the radio program that voting, while perhaps having some slight influence, is a very small contribution by comparison to giving one's talents, one's life, to do something for others. *OH FREEDOM!*

Theologians, philosophers, and the Church help us to understand the crucial and difficult questions about means and ends in attempting to fulfill our destiny. We cannot base our freedom on something that makes others less free. We have to be careful in this "land of the free and home of the brave" that we do not make that mistake. One danger in this area is the absolute belief in capitalism and the free market as the best way to control our destiny. If we accept that our very lives must be controlled by an outside factor, we are not free. Certainly, those who labor many hours each day, repeatedly doing the same thing for very little money, are not free. It must be hard for those who cannot afford to buy food to be told that an exciting example of the freedom of our economic system is having so many different cereals to choose from in the supermarket.

Where rugged individualism is celebrated in the day-to-day work-week, we sometimes get the impression that, to get ahead, it is all right to trample on people, leaving behind individuals who were just stepping-stones to our success. This is true for countries as well. It cannot be right for a powerful nation to seek what is only for its own gain rather than seek peace and prosperity for all. Foreign policy and economic policy can be rugged individualism at its best—or worst.

One day, when we were picking up donations at the Marek brothers' loading dock, one of their workers asked us, "Who do you work for?" We didn't know what to say. We didn't know how to answer. Who do Mark and Louise really work for? Who do all the Catholic Workers at Casa Juan Diego really work for? Over the years, several people who worked for agencies or citizens in need have demanded to speak to our supervisors when they were dissatisfied with our answers to their questions. We didn't know what to say. Do we work for the mayor by providing hospitality to Houston's many homeless immigrants and refugees, feeding many hungry families each week, or helping troubled and battered women who have nowhere to turn? Did we work for the Holy Father—at that time, John Paul II, who in the 1980s told his audience in San Antonio to welcome people from the South? Did we work for the bishop, who encouraged us in our work and encouraged others to encourage us? Did we work for the pastors who bailed us out when we were broke? Did we work for those who send support regularly and whom we rarely see or have never met? We concluded that we worked freely for Christ, especially Christ in the poor—inadequate and ineffective as our work often is. We work—

> For Amilcar, who cannot return to Latin America because he is a marked man for working with the poor.
>
> For Raul, who beat his wife and, when interrupted and made to stop, kept repeating, "But she is my wife!" as if that gave him permission. We used our freedom and unceremoniously "unpermitted" him.
>
> For Eusebio, who fled Guatemala with the army in hot pursuit and who would be dead if he hadn't escaped.

For José, whose best friend was killed when he fell under the train they were traveling on.

For Francisca, who took a freight train going the wrong direction, and was found unconscious from lack of food or drink outside of a Houston restaurant with her traumatized three-year-old daughter.

For Pedro, who lost his leg when he jumped from a train.

For Julia, who watched her children die of worms in the brain (*lombrices*) in her country.

For Ana, who comes for food each week for her kids because her husband makes only the minimum wage and cannot do more than pay the rent and utilities.

For the families of the deported from the immigration raids, who have lost their breadwinners.

OH, FREEDOM!

We thought, maybe we work for each other. Louise says she works for Mark. Mark says he works for Louise. The work certainly has added an interesting dimension to our marriage.

Actually, no one gives us orders. So many people desperately ask for help. We are free to respond as we can with God's grace to the great needs that surround us. We can do little in responding to great need, to pain, and to tragedy, but we can be there and do what we can for each one, trusting that the Lord will transform our small efforts as he transformed the few loaves and fishes brought to him into food for an immense crowd.

The inspiration for freedom in the Church comes from the example of the saints. The great commandments are a guide for our lives, and philosophical concepts are crucially important in decision making. (For example, the end does not justify the means, hence the importance of choosing what ends we will work toward and with what means.). But the real inspiration for freedom comes from saints rather than rules. Confessor to popes, Don Divo Barsotti said:

> Witnesses are needed to make sure that there is a living reality—the living reality created by the saints. Without the saints the Church becomes a despotic power (I say this with a shiver), as in the frightening image of Dostoevsky's Grand

Inquisitor. Only holiness justifies the Church's teaching; otherwise all the documents and statements of the Magisterium become empty words. There are men and women who are evident signs of a reality that is not of this world. That differentness is thrust upon one; it is like finding oneself in front of a miracle. This is not because they are not subject to nature (they are wretches, like all others); but nature cannot explain this. Salvation is not an assent to a generic moral code, or to the values of peace, of humanism, but to the person of Christ and to one's own person. It is a passionate love for Christ that moves the people who meet the saints.[8]

We try to follow the model of the saints. Some ask us about burnout in this work. We suffered burnout years ago. We survived it probably because we like what we do. The great thing about Casa Juan Diego is that no matter how bad you feel, you know that your work and effort just might be worth it. We may go to bed exhausted and with eyes and head aching, but we know that the dawn will bring a new day, a new perspective, and a new head and eyes—resurrection, we might say. The work of Casa Juan Diego might kill us, but at least we will die happy, contented, free, and hopefully with our boots on.

7

GOD WILL SAY,
"WHERE ARE THE OTHERS?"

An old fairy tale from Russia tells the story of a young girl who was lost. She couldn't find her mother. Villagers who wanted to help asked the child, "What does your mother look like? Tell us, so that we can help you find her." The little girl answered, "My mother is the most beautiful woman in the world." The villagers were very happy with her reply. The mother would be easy to find. So they went far and wide with the little girl, searching for her. Each time they found a very beautiful woman, she would say, "No, that is not my mother." and they were disappointed. Finally, the villagers came across a wrinkled, weather-beaten woman with a scarf on her head. The little girl ran to her with great joy. Beaming, she turned to those who had been helping for so long and said, "See, I told you she was the most beautiful woman in the world!"[1] We at Casa Juan Diego identify with this story. So often people who come to us appear dirty from a journey, or bent and lined with age, suffering, worry, and work that is too hard for them.

When our guests have had a chance to shower and put on clean clothes, when they know that they have a place to stay for a time, their appearance changes. They are more beautiful or handsome. But, as in the story of the little girl and her mother, the beauty is often on the inside. Sometimes it takes a little while for them to speak and share their stories, and sometimes it takes time for others to get to see their beauty. We are so busy with suffering people that sometimes we cannot or do not take the time to see the beauty in each one. But when we do—even with people who do not fit into middle-class values, people who do very irritating things, people whose self-esteem has been very damaged by life experiences—the beauty shines through, even if it is the humiliated and disfigured face of the suffering Christ. We find the real person as we come to know them.

Most of the people who come to us are also searching for someone—a mother, a sister, a brother, a wife or husband, or a friend. Often they are searching for escape from impossible situations. They trust in God—in fact, each one who tells us the story of a horrendous journey to get here speaks of how God was with them. But now they may also need a person to help them along their way. Finding these others or assisting guests in finding them is very much a part of the work of Casa Juan Diego. The most joyful events occur when the new immigrant or refugee finds the person he or she seeks, no matter how that person looks on the outside.

Dorothy Day wrote in the "Aims and Purposes of the Catholic Worker Movement" (published in 1940 in the *Catholic Worker*): "We cannot live alone. We cannot go to Heaven alone. Otherwise, as Péguy said, God will say to us, 'Where are the others?'"

We can understand this on several levels. For Charles Péguy and Dorothy and Peter, it meant to share the life of faith with others. It meant living in such a way that one could help others get to heaven. It meant helping to create a new heaven *and* a new earth, where justice dwells, "giving reason for the faith that is in us." For Dorothy and Peter it also meant performing the fourteen corporal and spiritual Works of Mercy: feeding the hungry, giving drink to the thirsty, clothing the naked, receiving those who sought refuge in Houses of Hospitality, visiting the prisoner, burying the dead…instead of the works of war.

We can take the question "Where are the others?" very literally. "Where are they?" is the question that has so often been asked at Casa Juan Diego. Even before immigrants have had a chance to shower and eat, they ask how they can find their relatives. Where are the others? Where is my wife? Where is my sister? Where is my brother? Where is my father? Where is my cousin? Where is my friend? Our work is our response to the question "Where are the others?"

We have often not had the answer. A world of danger and darkness faces those who travel so far on their own. Sometimes immigrants disappear in the desert or drown in one of the rivers separating countries. Sometimes they are killed by a train. Sometimes they are killed by coyotes because their families did not come up with thousands of dollars in extra fees charged after their arrival in the United States. Casa Juan Diego receives letters, phone calls, and e-mails from families searching for their loved ones, even years after they have disappeared. For example, one letter asked, "Do you know Jorge Mendez, who was murdered on the streets of Washington, DC?" Families are left to wonder forever what happened to their loved ones, sometimes fearing that they have simply abandoned their families.

Hans Urs von Balthasar once said that "in order that he shall find God, the Christian is placed on the streets of the world, sent to his manacled and poor brethren, to all who suffer, hunger and thirst; to all who are naked, sick and in prison."[2] God seems to have placed us here at Casa Juan Diego in the middle of immigrants and refugees on pilgrimage. So many of them have suffered violence, hunger, thirst, and sickness, or in have been in detention or coyote prisons.

On the other hand, part of Casa Juan Diego from its earliest history, there are beautiful stories of safe arrivals and actual reunions. It has always been a joy when we have been able to help answer the question "Where are the others?" These occasions are small miracles.

From the beginning of the journey, the immigrant begins to lose his or her identity. He has no family to turn to; she doesn't speak the language of the dominant culture; he frequently does not have an ID or legal papers. Migrants are also almost impossible to find in the prison bureaucracy if the U.S. Border Patrol or the Immigration Customs and Enforcement Agency has detained them. Detainees usually do not have money to make phone calls. Families try to find them, but cannot locate the numbers of detention centers and county jails. Families, or the detainees themselves, frequently do not know where their relatives are held. Casa Juan Diego receives calls from various parts of Texas and even Central America from families trying to locate loved ones who have come to the United States. Usually neither the detainees nor the families know that in order to locate relatives, it is important to know their "A" number, their alien number in the United States, which is given to them when the Border Patrol or ICE (Immigration and Customs Enforcement) picks them up. Sometimes a birth date helps.

When guests arrive at Casa Juan Diego, the fortunate ones come with an address or telephone number of a relative or friend. The first attempt to reach the person by phone is very tense. Is it the correct number and the correct relative? It may be a call to New York, Washington, or Los Angeles, or even to Cleveland, Ohio. When we see the immigrant's face light up and hear them say, "This is Maria. I'm at Casa Juan Diego in Houston," we know we are on the right track.

When Marilú, a pregnant refugee from El Salvador arrived in the early 1980s, she said she had an uncle in Houston. That's all—no address or phone. Nothing. But her uncle did have a relative in the state of Vera Cruz, Mexico. We could reach the relative if we called a teacher who knew someone who worked at a store, who knew a neighbor of the relative, who could visit her and try to find one of the old letters the uncle had written to a certain person, and whose return address might be on one of the old envelopes. The process that evening was unbelievable. We were like Houston Rocket fans cheering at each minor success in making contact. Although we spoke to various people in Mexico for Marilú, ultimately we were disappointed. We did not find the address.

The following morning we took Marilú to a clinic because, she said, a law enforcement person had beaten her up in Kingsville, Texas. She was still suffering and was worried about losing her baby. When she called to say that she was finished at the clinic, we drove by to pick her up, but when we arrived—late—she was not there. The person who went with her to also be treated at the clinic said that she had left with a strange man in a car. We were upset for obvious reasons. She wasn't there as she had said she would be, and we know what happens to young women who are forced or enticed into cars of strange men in a city like Houston. We returned both saddened and angry—knowing that we would be getting a desperate call sometime during the day and praying that nothing would happen.

Something did happen! At about 5:00 p.m., a small pickup drove up and in it was Marilú smiling away, waving her arms, and bouncing up and down. The person driving the pickup was not a man, but a woman. It was her aunt. How in God's name did she find her aunt among two million people? Miracles happen to those who believe, and Casa Juan Diego believes.

A young boy arrived from El Salvador in search of his mother. He insisted that she was in Houston somewhere. He was only thirteen. Casa Juan Diego had many guests at the time and he was so young. We asked for help from the Spanish television stations. Within minutes after Carlos told his story on Spanish TV, his sister called from San Marcos, Texas, and arranged to come to get him at Casa Juan Diego.

Ann Ball was not only an author loved by many for her books on the saints and Catholic history and culture, but also a friend of Casa Juan Diego. Since the early 1980s, Ann had prepared the altar for the Mass of the Day of the Dead each year at Casa Juan Diego. Each year she also organized an Easter egg hunt for the children. We had known Ann for some years when Raúl, another thirteen-year-old, arrived at Casa Juan Diego alone after a long and difficult journey across several countries. We didn't know what to do. Raúl could stay at the men's house for a little while, but that was not a good long-term solution for a young boy. At about the same time that Raúl came, Ann dropped in to visit and Raúl found an adoptive mother. As we talked with her, we shared our concerns. Ann's heart went out to this young boy alone in the United States. She began asking about Raúl, whose family was in El Salvador. We weren't sure about the details, but we thought the lawyers who helped us earlier had told us that one could adopt an immigrant child if the adoption took place before his or her fourteenth birthday. Quickly, Ann made the decision to take Raúl into her home and look into the legal questions later. Raúl became her adopted son.

We have gone to the bus station many times trying to find people. One of our earliest bus-station experiences during the civil war in El Salvador was with a teenager who fled the violence of the war. A priest called to say we would find Juan at the bus station around the witching hour. Juan was there, hiding behind the lockers. It was after midnight and Juan was desperate. Like everyone else, he had lost family and friends in the war. He did not talk much about the right- and the leftwing forces in Central America. He talked about death. The guns came from Eastern and Western powers. The bodies came from El Salvador. Juan displayed signs of clinical depression. He was very lethargic, he hardly responded, and he did not eat. He couldn't have been more than fifteen years old. Juan came to Houston, or rather was sent here in hopes that someone would find his relatives to alleviate his despair.

Juan pulled from his pocket with great respect a piece of paper with the words "Casa Juan Diego" written on it. Many people arrive with such pieces of paper in their pockets. Fortunately, Juan had another slip of paper. The second paper is called the "good news" at Casa Juan Diego. It had the name and address of a brother who lives in Houston. The "good news" was confirmed. The street did exist on the map. It was located off Cavalcade Street on the north side of Houston.

The next morning we went searching for Juan's brother. We had the address memorized since we didn't want to take any chances on losing the piece of paper. Juan was still depressed, although he said he had slept well. As we drove from the house, we told him that we had to pick up our son first, who had a violin audition at Rice University, and that he would accompany us to find his brother. As we began to speak about our son, Juan listened intently. When Mark mentioned our son was also fifteen, Juan's expression changed, and for the first time a large broad smile appeared that wiped the depression from his face.

All of us headed up Route 45 to Cavalcade Street to find Juan's brother. We found the address immediately but as frequently occurs, there were apartments in front and back, above and below, all squeezed together to house a few more people to make a few more dollars from the new immigrants. We entered the complex. A woman hanging drywall asked angrily in English and Spanish who we were and what did we want. After we told her who we were, she went inside and sent out one of the workers to check on us and this teenager. The worker looked us over, especially Juan. He hesitated momentarily and then embraced Juan. It was his brother, the lost brother who had been missing but now had been found. It was one of those "I am your brother, Joseph" scenes. Juan's smiling face made up for the long hours of work: payment in full.

The "bad news" comes those times when we are not able to find the street, or, worse yet, we find it but the relative no longer lives there. One of the saddest things to deal with is when refugees have lost the U.S. addresses and phone numbers of their relatives. Sometimes people lose all their papers, identification, and money when crossing the river, in addition to the addresses. Frequently, they have lost all of them to immigration officials and police in countries on their way. This loss means not having a home or refuge in the United States. It means having no family. It often means a loss of employment, because relatives usually find jobs for family members, especially if they are good workers.

When this occurs, we encourage guests to use our phone to call their relatives in Central America or elsewhere, not counting the cost. It is not easy. Often, there is only one phone in the village and people have to leave a message or make an appointment to call again. Another problem is that people can't stop talking once their relatives answer, inflating our phone bill. In recent years, we have been buying phone cards for new guests. They come with a limit.

Others try to find Casa Juan Diego in a taxi. Sometimes the cab drivers pretend they cannot find the house and drive around and around in order to raise the fare. This is especially true when people have come in at the bus station in downtown Houston, which is only a couple of miles from Casa Juan Diego. When they arrive, the cab driver sometimes demands more money than the person has, and someone has to pay the fare. Taxi drivers sometimes threaten to call Immigration. We do not like this taxi arrangement, because in some cases we have had to bail out the person for the taxi fare.

One night before everyone was in bed, a taxi pulled up. The driver said he had a Spanish-speaking teenager he had driven twenty miles from Katy, and the fare was $57.00. Apparently a coyote had just put him in the taxi and given the driver our address. We didn't like this and didn't want to pay. The driver took things into his own hands, namely the neck of the young man, threw him into the taxi, and said, "I know what to do with these kinds of guys." Visions of the young Honduran floating head-down in the Buffalo Bayou changed our mind. We paid. We were glad the young man had found us.

Another night, very late, the phone rang at 4:00 a.m. A religious sister from Brownsville was calling to say that a young woman just out of a Rio Grande Valley hospital and unable to walk was in a taxi in southwest Houston and couldn't find her husband. The address was wrong. "What should she do?" She should come to Casa Juan Diego, but please God, with a different taxi driver. It was not the same driver. In fact, he was a most polite, cordial individual who had been trying to locate her address for three hours.

Some of the stories we remember best center around the Mass, so much a part of the faith and culture of many of our guests, although not all are Catholic. During our Wednesday evening liturgies, we celebrate the arrival of our guests. Like those present at any Mass, different guests relate on different levels. Some have life-changing experiences at Casa Juan Diego. Some may have never had the opportunity to make their first communion or have been away from the Church for many years. One young man from Cuba was very excited when he assisted at our Mass. It was the first time he had been to Mass in his life. The same was true of another man from Honduras. After Mass, a few guests have asked how they can arrange to make their first communion or be baptized.

In our early years, we received a young man who had just arrived in Houston, and he insisted that we find his sister. He had her address: *Main Street, Houston, U.S.A.* No number. We failed, of course, as Main Street in Houston is a very long street. We suggested that, while waiting to find her, he might accompany us to the Spanish Mass at St. Anne's Church, along with other guests of the house. Amazingly enough, during the Kiss of Peace at St. Anne's he recognized his sister. He had found her! It pays to go to Mass!

Sometimes friends and relatives cannot be found when a person is disoriented or has lost his or her memory. Melvin and Miguel came to us from the hospital with shaved heads and tons of Dilantin to prevent seizures after their brain surgeries. They had stitches and deep furrows in their heads. Both had serious head injuries and didn't know who they were, where they had come from, or if they had any friends. The hospital told us that we must take them because they were "unfunded"—which means that they were undocumented immigrants and no agency, no institution, and no other service would take them. They did not quality for any kind of government aid. Melvin and Miguel were homeless.

Melvin and Miguel came to us with nothing and we asked nothing of them, except that they take their medicine and stay off the street, as we are near a busy thoroughfare. After a few weeks, Melvin began to come around and remembered his name and an address. We were able to connect him with family.

Miguel was more difficult. His memory didn't return. He did not seem to improve, and we had visions of having Miguel with us the rest of our days. He took special interest, however, in our weekly liturgies at Casa Juan Diego, especially in the Spanish songs. One evening at Mass, we noticed Miguel listening intently and becoming very quiet during the singing of the liturgical songs we had learned while in Central America and Mexico. All of a sudden, he jumped up and said, "I know who I am! I know who I am! I sang those songs while I was a seminarian in Guatemala!" We were so pleased, and we asked if he could remember where he had lived. He said he did and could take us there. We accompanied him to the small apartment where his friends lived. Fortunately, they were at home—but filled with disbelief because the friend they thought was dead had appeared. It was a joyful reunion.

We will never forget the smile of Silveriano, one of those smiles that go right through you. Silveriano came to us from a Houston hospital, as do many immigrants. He really worried us. He had suffered serious head injuries and was like a zombie for several weeks, not talking, only sleeping day and night. We pushed him to keep his follow-up appointments (we take guests by the hand if we are worried they might not get to their appointments on their own). Most hospitals give no follow-up care to the uninsured poor after emergency treatment; fortunately, the county hospital sometimes does. The details of medical care keep us busier and more worried than anything else we do; there are always a hundred details to remember every day. If we miss one, it is very hard for people outside to understand. Worrying over Silveriano must have worked, because one day he came out of his room all cleaned up and with a smile as broad as his face. He announced that he was going to his sister in Comanche, Texas. We had not known about the sister: he had just remembered.

Sometimes it seems that the Lord has sent someone to help us find people. Three times during the early years of the Houston Catholic Worker, Mark was wandering, lost, through the Ben Taub Hospital Emergency room recovery area, looking for one of our guests who was seriously injured or ill, to see if they were among the living or the dead. Each time, unexpectedly, an unknown person stepped forward and asked, "Who are you looking for, Mark?" The angel would find the person, give the pertinent information, the prognosis, and then disappear into the milieu of people dressed in blue and green scrubs.

The encounter with the family is not always what has been expected. Carmen had received word in El Salvador from her brother in the United States that her mother was very ill and dying. She desperately wanted to come to the United States to see her one last time. Carmen's brother sent money for her to make the journey, and she began the long and difficult trip. Things didn't go too badly until she had a serious fall in south Texas and hurt her knee. The group she was with abandoned her because she could not walk, and they could not carry her. Left to the loneliness of south Texas brush and wild animals, including snakes and coyotes, she slowly and painfully crawled for hours to the highway, dragging her useless leg. After some hours, some compassionate Texans picked her up and brought her to Houston where they called Casa Juan Diego.

Pain was written all over Carmen's face. She looked all of her seventy-plus years. We wept with her as we slowly, very slowly, helped her into the van. We arranged medical care for her and called her relatives. Within a day or two, she was on crutches and ready to travel to see her dying mother. Minus the pain, Carmen's appearance changed markedly. It turned out she wasn't seventy, but forty. We put her on a plane the same day we went to Ohio to bury Mark's mother. Carmen called later to give us the disappointing news. When she arrived at her brother's house, she discovered that her journey had been for naught—her mother had died before she left El Salvador. The family had been afraid to tell Carmen that earlier because she had a bad heart. She called to thank us. It wasn't necessary; seeing her on her feet and looking thirty years younger was compensation enough.

We were stymied with Isabel, who was five to eight months pregnant (she didn't know which) and had a one-year-old with her when she came to the door of Casa Juan Diego. She also seemed to have mental problems. We could get very little information from her, even after she stayed with us for several weeks. We began to think that she wasn't mentally ill at all, just a lot smarter than we were. She handled us and our questions perfectly. This meant, of course, that she was a survivor and might do very well without us. However, she did tell us that she was hospitalized in a psychiatric facility for some time after each pregnancy—this was her fourth. Little by little, we were able to piece together enough information to find the address of Isabel's brother on the North Side of Houston. It was the first we knew anything about her family. We felt the trip to find the address was a leap in the dark; we thought for sure that we were going to be disappointed. It was early Saturday morning when we drove to the North Side. Isabel's brother was there, hung over, but there, and after washing the sleep from his eyes, he was most friendly and cooperative. In fact, it became apparent that the family had been searching for her for two months and had gone to the police and hospitals looking for her.

When people do not know where else to turn to find people, addresses, or phone numbers, Casa Juan Diego is a source of information. The telephone rings all day long. It is difficult to locate things in the telephone book if you do not speak the language. People call, for example, to ask how to find the parish of San Gerónimo in Houston (which at this time has three Spanish Masses, all well attended). We are glad to give them the information, knowing that searching the directory under "San Gerónimo" will not help them find "St. Jerome's Church."

One of the calls requesting information was from a Catholic family. A young immigrant woman was raped by the coyote who brought her to the United States and was now pregnant. They had found her, or she had found them. The caller had taken her into her home. The young woman had decided to place the child for adoption through Catholic Charities, where many families apply to adopt a child. During her stay with the family, however, the caller's son grew to know the young woman. They became engaged and decided to keep the child. The caller was not asking for a place for her to stay, but for a clinic that could provide prenatal care at a reasonable cost. This young woman had found exactly the people she was looking for, even though she had never met them.

The coyotes hired to bring people here often create the lost. Margarita, a Salvadoran, arrived just in time for the Way of the Cross one Good Friday evening. She had found her temporary destination. She joined us in singing as we processed through the streets to the simple altars set up at our various houses throughout the neighborhood. From station to station, immigrants carried the large, heavy cross we use each year, as they took turns reading their meditations on Christ suffering in history and the Christ who suffers so much today in his refugee and immigrant people.

Later that evening at the women's meeting, Margarita told the story of the journey she and her husband had just made. She told how they came from the border wandering for five days in the brush. The coyote had abandoned them after she and her husband had paid him in full, before they got to Houston. They were exhausted after days of walking, thirst, hunger, and swollen feet—and nights of worrying about snakes and coyotes (the animal type). They had been lucky to find one family that gave them a meal. Margarita and her husband were grateful to have found Houston and Casa Juan Diego.

We really didn't know what to do to help Epimelio, a young man from Guatemala, when he arrived at our house. He could not hear or speak, or at least very little. He could write a little and we were able to find out what village he came from in Guatemala. The other Catholic Workers all tried to help him, but we had no long-term solution. Fortunately, that summer, seminarian Miguel Alvizures from the Archdiocese of Galveston-Houston was helping at Casa Juan Diego. Miguel was originally from Guatemala, from the department of San Marcos. (In Guatemala, there are specific regional areas within the country, something like counties or states in the United States, and these regional areas are called departments.) When we discovered that Miguel was going home for a visit, we talked with him about Epimelio, and he agreed to try to find his family, although he knew it would be very difficult because there were so many little villages in the mountainous area in which they lived.

Miguel later wrote in the *Houston Catholic Worker*:

We have no idea how he managed to get to Houston from Guatemala, but one day Epimelio was at Casa Juan Diego's door and the doorkeeper took him in. All he had with him was a birth certificate from which we knew the name of his parents, that he was from a rural place in the department of San Marcos, Guatemala, and that he was eighteen years of age. He also had a letter in English which said that he was looking for his parents.

I went to San Marcos to try to find his parents on a trip I thought was going to take two days, but it actually took a whole week. I found myself going up and down the mountains of San Marcos following people's directions to find Epimelio's family. They told me to follow a road close to the top of the volcano, but when I got to the place, I found out that nobody knew about Epimelio or his family. Some people then advised me to look in another place, but I had to walk many miles because of the lack of roads, only to hear the people of the village say that they didn't know anybody with such names or descriptions.

Finally, I found a little village where people knew about Epimelio. They were amazed to know that he was in Houston. They knew his family and told me that I was about two hours from the place.

Epimelio's father was at his own father's funeral, but when he heard about me bringing news of his son, he came quickly to his home. He told me that he had another son who was living in the United States on the East coast and thought that he might take Epimelio to live with him.

Back in Houston, I told everything to Mark and the people of Casa Juan Diego. I also brought a picture to Epimelio from his parents. His face turned serious to the point of crying when he saw the picture. Then he smiled and asked by signs how they were doing. I tried to tell him that they were doing fine and happy to know of him.

Mark asked me if I wanted to go with Epimelio by bus to meet his brother, which I was glad to do.

Epimelio's brother told me he didn't know how to pay us for what we did for him. I told him that he was already paying us because I remembered the words Mark usually tells the people he helps that any time they help anybody else, they are repaying us.

There is great joy at Casa Juan Diego when the lost are found. It is hard, though, to think of all those who have not been found. It is hard to continue to get calls and e-mails from people who cannot find relatives who started on the journey to the United States; sometimes the calls and e-mails are from those who have not found relatives ten years later or more and still wonder every day.

During the early years, we often drove refugees to the bus station or to the airport so that they could join relatives in another state. That kind of travel has slowed considerably with the changes following 9/11. Nowadays guests at Casa Juan Diego rarely have the paperwork needed to fly. Also, in the past few years, Immigration has been boarding Greyhound buses looking for people without papers. Earlier, though, this was frequently the way we helped people travel.

After some tense experiences, we realized that we should tell the refugee an earlier time than a plane ticket actually said. If the plane was leaving at 11:00 a.m., people who had never flown before might jump in the shower at almost 10:30 a.m. to prepare for the trip, or might arrive very late after going to an inexpensive beauty parlor or after buying something for the trip from the little money they had been able to earn. There are two airports in Houston; one is closer than the other. Whether we could possibly arrive on time would depend on which airport it was and how many minutes we had.

So often the poor, and especially migrants, are invisible. In this prosperous country, they are hard to find, even though they exist in large numbers. Groups from the suburbs sometimes want to help Casa Juan Diego, but do not see the poor where they live. More than a hundred families in one parish in Spring, Texas, for example, have participated for a number of years in making lunches. Each lunch contains two sandwiches and a piece of fruit, which parishioners take turns bringing to Casa Juan Diego. These lunches provide a noonday meal for immigrant workers who live in our houses. We also distribute the lunches to day laborers waiting for work on nearby streets (perhaps their only meal). And we save a few lunches for our guests who may have to go to the hospital and wait long hours. These parishioners have found a way to help the poor even though they do not see them near their homes.

As the immigrant population has spread across the United States in the past decades, immigrants themselves have been almost invisible to many—except for their employers in meat processing plants, on farms, in construction; in plumbing businesses where they are assistants to do the dirty digging when needed; and in the companies that cut down huge trees. Somehow, those who need farm workers, yard workers, maids, and nannies are able to find them.

Immigrants are not the only ones who are hard to find or out of the public view. The poor, the unemployed, and the sick with no one to care for them—even though all of these may be citizens—are brushed aside and often feel alone as if no one cares for them.

No matter what great teachers and saints say about the presence of the Lord in the poor, there are still people who insist that those who struggle just to make a living and survive are not worth anything: they are ugly, they are parasites. Immigrants and refugees, especially, are the subject of xenophobia and hatred. The beauty of their persons and the tragedy of their situation are missed by the critics, who might say, Why bother finding these people?

At Casa Juan Diego, we hardly have time to go seeking the lost, since overwhelming numbers of the poor, the sick, and the injured come to our doors. Somehow, they find us. Our challenge is to help in a small way.

We pray that when we meet the Lord he will not have to ask us, Where are the others?

8

"LOVE IN ACTION IS A HARSH AND DREADFUL THING"

Dorothy Day said that if she hadn't read Dostoevsky, she would not have been able to live with the problems of the people who came to the Catholic Worker house. She wrote in the *Catholic Worker* in May 1973: "I do not think I could have carried on with a loving heart all these years without Dostoevsky's understanding of poverty, suffering, and drunkenness." She quoted one of his sentences so often that she sometimes received credit for it instead of him. Our experiences have confirmed the meaning of this sentence, which is from *The Brothers Karamazov*: "Love in action is a harsh and dreadful thing compared to love in dreams."

This is the context of the line: In *The Brothers Karamazov*, a woman wanted the monk Fr. Zosima to tell her how she could have proof of God and be convinced of immortality. Father Zosima responded, "By the experience of active love. … In as far as you advance in love, you will grow surer of the reality of God and of the immortality of your soul." The woman asked what the monk meant by active love. She already loved humanity, she said. Often she dreamed of a life of service to the unfortunate that filled her with warmth. She could nurse the afflicted; she would be ready to kiss their wounds. But sometimes she wondered how she would react if she were not repaid in gratitude for her service. What if the person was rude and demanding or even complained to the "authorities" (as we've discovered can happen). What then? She could not bear ingratitude. She had to have immediate gratitude as a repayment for any love she gave, especially in good works. "I expect my payment at once—that is praise, and the repayment of love with love. Otherwise," she said, with both insight and fear, "I am incapable of loving anyone."

Fr. Zosima answered,

"Love in action is a harsh and dreadful thing compared to love in dreams. Love in dreams is greedy for immediate action, rapidly performed and in the sight of all. Men will even give their lives if only the ordeal does not last long but is soon over, with all looking and applauding as though on the stage. Active love is labor and fortitude, and for some people, too, perhaps a complete science. But I predict that just when you see with horror that in spite of all your efforts you are getting further from your goal instead of nearer to it—at that very moment you will reach and behold clearly the miraculous power of the Lord who has been all the time loving and mysteriously guiding you."[1]

The Lord comes to us in the disguise of the poor. The face of Jesus, however, is not always visible in the poor. For us, it is like the Eucharist. We see the bread, but know through the eyes of faith that Jesus is present. The face we see is frequently one of suffering, despair, pain, helplessness, and loneliness, or even, at times, the face of anger, greed, or selfishness. We don't love and serve the poor because they are better people or more lovable than others—although, to tell the truth, they are sometimes more interesting than the bourgeoisie!

We can romanticize working with the poor. But what do you do when the face of Christ spits on you or curses you? Or quotes Dorothy Day back at you? Or doesn't say, "Thank you. You all are really great"? What do you do when the poor person gets drunk and wants to fight, or wants to steal everything that isn't nailed down—and not only wants to, but does? The work becomes hard, endless, and frustrating unless we pray and meditate, and go to our spiritual roots. In the heat of the day, when there are lines of people waiting in the hope that we can solve their problems, it is easy to lose the perspective of "the washing of the feet." Our work is unlovely. We're not Dorothy Day or Mother Teresa, and even if we were, the work would still be unlovely.

Things can go so wrong. The problems are so serious, with trained and committed people so few and good resources so rare, that our work is a constant challenge and sometimes we go from one crisis to another. Hospitality is the hardest thing we do. Babies are born around the clock. People have to find a place to move to. When those who come for help are refused something because we cannot or do not offer it, they may call, say, St. Joseph's parish to say we are not nice enough. True, if we can't stand the heat, we should move out of the kitchen. Fortunately, the heat of God's love and that of the immigrants can counteract any pain.

The challenge of hospitality is not just the problem of beds or floor space, but dealing with various needs and difficulties of guests. Out of ten guests, nine may be a treat to serve. The tenth is sometimes a problem. When you receive people with hospitality, you house their virtues and their vices, their health and their sicknesses, their skills and their lack of skills, their good habits and their bad, their good traits and their bad. There are peaceful people and a few who are violent. There are people who never drink and those who get drunk every Saturday night. There are people who are cooperative and a few who respond only to threats. The vast majority of our guests are a joy. But there are a very few who have been through too much or who have learned to manipulate others in order to survive. Some guests are never happy and do not appreciate what is done for them.

Because we have an open-door policy on receiving refugees, new immigrants, and Spanish-speaking pregnant or battered women, we open ourselves to problems. On any given day, often with over a hundred guests in our houses, something is bound to go wrong. Someone will not get enough to eat or the right thing to eat, or they will not have the right clothing at the right time. Catholic Workers run to answer the door, take guests where they need to be, or give out bus cards and directions, at the same time trying to make sure that the medicine prescribed by doctors is available from the pharmacy; that the food is put away when it arrives for the kitchen; that rice, beans, fruit, vegetables, and bread are put in order for the distribution for several hundred people the next day; that meals are prepared; that sandwiches are distributed to those waiting for them; that rooms are ready for new guests; that new guests are hospitably received; that the bumps and scrapes of children who fall and hurt themselves are washed and given a Band-Aid or are referred to the hospital as necessary. Then the seriously injured or ill person arrives at the door, and everything stops to respond to another crisis.

Giving food and clothing opens us to criticism from the very people who receive them. We try to have an orderly line for distribution of food and clothing, but there have been times when our efforts are ignored. Once we had some dressers and chests of drawers to give away—a very valuable commodity for poor families. Several mothers saw us coming and literally tackled us to ask about them. We didn't respond, "Thank you, Jesus," or, "You all have the face of Jesus," but, "You all ought to try out for the Dallas Cowboys." We didn't really say that, but it crossed our minds.

In our early years, one woman returned in her late-model car to throw the simple food we had given her all over the floor of Casa Juan Diego, shouting, "We were sent here by welfare to receive good food, not this garbage." She left with a threat: "I am going to report you to the welfare department and have you sued." This woman spoke English, was a citizen of the United States, and was obviously used to better things. The welfare department had referred her to us until she could get her food stamps. She probably threatened us with Immigration, too, the most popular threat at Casa Juan Diego from those who are angry. Regarding the lawsuit, the woman was true to her word. A lawyer called. He had to repeat several times that the woman wanted to sue us because she was unhappy with the food she had received. After we explained our operation in the most guilt-inducing way we could muster, the lawyer was ashamed and apologized profusely.

This woman continued to come to Casa Juan Diego for food for weeks afterward. She was still welcome. Problem people are allowed to return for food and clothing as long as they don't rob us, don't show up drunk, don't try to beat up anyone, and don't try to take advantage of our guests.

We never know who will arrive at the door. One evening a very large woman—nearly three hundred pounds and drunk—came shouting and cursing, all in perfect English, about a person who should have stayed longer at Casa Juan Diego, but was gone. She demanded to know why the man she had sent to Casa Juan Diego was not living there. As Mark wrote in the August 1991 *Houston Catholic Worker*:

> Since the individual was near the door, we knew that the solution was to move that person outside the door and lock it, so that everyone inside could get some sleep. It was already late. As we began edging her toward the door, swinging was added to the repertoire of cursing, screaming, and insults.
>
> Come on—you wanna fight, I'll fight you, was the refrain. Not wanting to be like the former president who said, "I forgot to duck," I ducked. A staff member who stayed only a few days (he tired quickly of climbing over refugees sleeping on

the floor to get to his room each night) came to support us and said we reminded him of Muhammad Ali—"Float like a butterfly, sting like a bee." I was thinking fast. How to solve this confrontation? Ironically, our pacifism held—but then it is easier to be a pacifist if you're outweighed by a hundred pounds and haven't boxed since school days.

We were able to move the confrontation out of the house and away from the front of the house, dodging left jabs, rights to the head, and upper cuts. Finally, we arrived at the street with our guest flailing and cursing. There was a man waiting on the street—and now both were going to start cursing and swinging, or so I thought. Instead, the man was very embarrassed and quietly said, "Come on, Matilda, stop that nonsense and get in the car!" He didn't push it, as he didn't want to be the object of his wife's wrath and blows either.

When Matilda noticed someone taking down the license plate number, she stopped swinging and headed down the street, obviously afraid of getting her husband in trouble. We thanked the Lord and went to bed.

We are very protective of our women's house, but on rare occasions, a woman guest sabotages security herself. One day Mark and a visitor were walking along the side of our women's House of Hospitality when they saw a man climbing on the roof over the door, very close to an open window on the second story. A woman was talking to him from the window. Unbelievably, the young woman, who had a child, had shouted out the second-story window to a group of vagrants, asking them to get an ice cream for her from the ice cream truck that had just appeared, and then to climb up the outside of the building to bring it to her. One man tried to oblige her until Mark intervened.

Difficult times have not necessarily come at convenient times. Usually, they have occurred when everyone is supposed to be asleep. It was very late one night and it was very bad news: the unpleasant noise of four drunken young men. Their shouts, cries, and running around would disturb the entire household unless someone intervened. Men do not often get drunk at Casa Juan Diego, but when they do, it is most difficult. Mark wrote the story of that episode in the *Houston Catholic Worker*:

These four young men were not strangers to me. I had accepted them into the house the day before, read the rules to them and helped them make their beds. I went to their room where they were all hilariously drunk. They offered me a drink, but I was not thirsty. Since drinking is forbidden here (because it leads to serious fights), I reminded them of this and went about collecting all the beer cans, both empty and full, whether on the floor or in their hands. They did not appreciate this. I was not in a very appreciative mood either. My feelings were of anger, not of fear, although pacifism came more easily as I got older.

The young men vacillated between being silly and hostile. I did not vacillate, not out of principle so much as because it was late. I was tired and they were drunk and I had to deal with it. I took the cans to the trash and returned to find that they had uncovered another set of beer cans—tall ones at that. I repeated the collection ceremony and reminded them that drinking was not allowed. They protested through their beer and their tears. My temptation was to let them drink themselves into a stupor and go to sleep, and save myself a lot of trouble.

Upon returning from the trash a second time I found them crawling into the window of one of the other houses. They were still in their underwear. I tried to get them back into their room in order to contain the noise and fights, hoping they had had enough beer to be somewhat settled. They continued, however, to vacillate between hostility and being silly, wrestling with each other on the beds and, occasionally fighting seriously, and were not about to sleep. I was the only sleepy one. Finally, one of them started for the store in his underwear to buy food, although we suspected he probably wanted more beer. I invited them all to eat at their home (for one more night), since we had just received a large donation of *burritos*, a good ready-to-eat food. After quickly eating the *burritos* they returned to their room with me and within a short time were asleep. Upon leaving them I was very sad. I just hoped and prayed they wouldn't succumb to alcoholism, that international curse that knows no barriers.

Holidays are the best of times and the worst of times at Casa Juan Diego. The celebration of Jesus' birth is sometimes seen as an opportunity to drink excessively. In 1989, when someone asked us, "How was your Christmas?" we could only answer, Great, but…

We were overwhelmed with the generosity of people that Christmas, like so many Christmases. Casa Juan Diego could survive many months because of this generosity. People brought valuable things like turkeys, coffee, sugar, disposable diapers, aluminum foil, toilet tissue, hand and dish soap, and clothing. We began Christmas Eve with our guests with our traditional ceremony that comes from northern Mexico. We all sang a beautiful, simple lullaby to the Child Jesus (taught to Louise by people from Mexico), as immigrant children from the house rocked *el Niño Dios* (the Infant Jesus) back and forth in a blanket until the song was finished. One of the refugees from Guatemala told the Christmas story—which drew as much interest from the adults as from the children.

Two refugees told their story about their departures from their countries and how, time after time during their journey to the United States, there was "no room at the inn" until they came to the inn that is Casa Juan Diego. Especially moving was the story of the guest who had just escaped the recent war in El Salvador. Thanks to the Red Cross in his country, his wounds had been treated, and he survived. Instead of being dead in El Salvador, he was alive for Christmas at Casa Juan Diego.

Since we had invited those with whom we share our food and clothing each week at the distribution, the room was crowded, Some of the women had brought tamales and hot chocolate to help us celebrate. The mood was great as we celebrated the feast of "No Room in the Inn," but that mood changed after the liturgy and cookies when we heard rumors of guests breaking whiskey bottles in room six. The rumors turned out to be true. Christmas Eve became a small riot.

We love drunks but not their drunkenness, and the two emotions became mixed up as we confronted the men, who knew very well that they could not drink while in Casa Juan Diego. Not even on Christmas! We had explained to them when we received them as guests in our inn that they couldn't drink in the house or outside of it—in bars, in stores, in churches, or anywhere—and still stay at Casa Juan Diego. Drinking was tantamount to renouncing your bed—even if it was a mattress on the floor.

So what could you do on Christmas Eve? Tell them that there was no room in the inn, like people told the Holy Family? But what could we do with men drunk enough to curse and make insults and fight with all those around?

Our usual routine in these situations is to arrange for the drinker to stay the night at a cheap motel in our area to give him time to sleep it off and have time the next day to make other living arrangements. Moving the inebriated person out allows everyone else to get some sleep. But this time the motels were closed because their pipes had frozen during this unusually cold winter in Houston, and they had no water. We decided to let the men stay—even after another broken whiskey bottle—since we try not to put people on the street without a plan. However, we ran out of plans and patience when they went from breaking whiskey bottles to breaking windows. We were feeling strangled by our own value system. At this point, however, the drunks developed their own plan. They became very mobile, worried that the police would come for them, and they ran off. We boarded up the windows and finally went to bed. Of the five, none was a refugee, and the worst spoke perfect English, which told us something. The next day volunteers from a parish came in to cook the Christmas dinner to make a beautiful celebration.

One of the joys of Casa Juan Diego is that many alcoholics who come to live with us stay on the wagon for a long time, even a year, if they become an *ayudante*. The sad part is that after they leave us, we may find one or two of them inebriated and rather unkempt on the street.

Visitors comment about how beautiful it must be to help so many people and how we must feel great doing it. "Do you feel good?" they ask. Some have suggested that the value of the work depends on "feeling" the love we profess. One young man went so far as to say that anything we do or anyone does to help a person in desperate need is worthless if we don't have warm feelings toward the person in that moment. We, however, have always been taught that love is an act of the will. Once the first stage of the warm feelings has passed, love continues. We were recently reassured in this belief when reading the section "Passions in the Moral Life" in the *Catechism of the Catholic Church* (no. 1768): "Strong feelings are not decisive for the morality or the holiness of persons." How reassuring—because we do not always have strong, joyful feelings when there is a crisis. We and the other Catholic Workers here do not say that we love getting up at 2:00 a.m. to take someone to the hospital or to deal with a person drunk on whiskey. We get out of bed to respond to a crisis or to take a person to the hospital if we need to, but we are not always overflowing with loving emotions at that very moment.

The response we receive to our efforts to help confounds us. One day a police officer wanted to arrest Mark for polluting the environment at our men's house. Mark could not figure out what he was talking about until the officer forced him almost at gunpoint to go outside with him. There he pointed to some small balloons lying outside the fence under the trees in a park area behind the house. The policeman said they were colostomy bags that someone had tossed over the fence to discard them—and he insisted that they be cleaned up immediately, which was done without protest. We had a guest at that time who used colostomy bags—we even purchased them for him. It never occurred to us that he had found a new way of disposing of them by simply tossing them over the fence. We care for many sick and wounded people, but nothing like this had ever happened before and has not happened since. We cleaned them up ourselves and then spoke to the guest.

Some things can be done only by an act of the will. For example, there is much "people traffic" in Casa Juan Diego. All day people come through for food, clothing, furniture, and hospitality, often passing through a large gathering area where donations are placed for the next distribution. On more than one occasion, someone has donated a toilet and placed it in a corner. We know—now—that we have to move fast with toilets, because someone will use them even though they are not connected. According to what people have sometimes left in those toilets, they really needed to use one. Someone has to clean them out after the fact, and since we could not ask anyone else to, it has to be us.

The "harsh and dreadful" aspects of the work are not necessarily related to individual persons, but often to old buildings.

One Christmas a church group came to serve dinner at our men's House of Hospitality. What we did not tell the volunteers from the parish was that shortly before they arrived, all the plumbing had stopped working. As the men kept mopping and mopping, those church volunteer cooks and servers must have thought that immigrants are very clean. We knew, however, that as soon as the meal was served, we had to close the house.

Here we were, knee-deep in raw sewage. Nothing worked, nothing flowed. "Back up" took on a new meaning: it no longer meant reinforcements; it meant that which went down kept coming back up. It was not a pleasant sight. Doc from the plumber's kept saying we could still use the toilets and not worry—but it would taken a troop of psychiatrists to make us feel good about his therapeutic approach. What he did not say is that it is like a balloon that you squeeze: the air goes to another part. The same with the plumbing. What went down in one area just came back up in another.

We knew we couldn't keep people in our men's house. It was a fright. We had to do something with our fifty guests. As soon as everyone finished eating, we started to find places to take the men where they could stay for several days while the plumbing was fixed. The first shelter we headed for was the Open Door Mission. We had called ahead and, without hesitating. they said that they would accept twelve men because they knew us and because they knew it was only for several days. The plumber would have things fixed by then.

Next, we headed to the Salvation Army with twelve more guests. We knew that it was a nice place. We called ahead, and they said, "Y'all come!" We walked in with the twelve, but as soon as the door closed behind us, three enormous men screamed, "Up against the wall, up against the wall!" and "Take off your hats!" Even we wanted to dive for the floor—though we have been doing this work for years and don't scare easily. You have never seen such frightened men as the twelve from Casa Juan Diego. We thought no one would stay, but fortunately, they trusted us and stayed. There was really nowhere else to go. We explained that the Salvation Army deals with some of the toughest street people in Houston, so they have to be strict. We reminded them that some men who don't get what they want from Casa Juan Diego say that they are going to come back to kill us. There are some tough guys out there. We gave the Salvation Army a check to keep the men for three days, which is how long it was supposed to take to fix the plumbing.

We had more men to place, so we offered to help with transportation for those who had family or friends in other cities. As we gathered at the bus station, additional people who were stranded there joined us and made an awful crowd—so much so that the sheriff's deputies were about to arrest us for creating a riot. We were able to get a dozen or so on the bus. We headed back to the men's house to care for those who remained.

What to do with the rest? We thought about a cheap motel, but as we were heading to the motel, a group of our guests was returning from the Open Door. "Those guys are going to kill us," they said. It was too late to explain that the Open Door also deals with some tough people and thus has to be strict. So there were more men for the motel, which again accepted us and our money. It was a delightful negotiation, which took place in English, Spanish, and Vietnamese. We put four men to a room and gave them extra blankets and several days' supply of food, because we knew the plumber would have everything fixed by then.

We returned to Casa Juan Diego men's house to see how things were going. We became like St. Peter of Alcántara (mentor of St. Teresa of Avila) who never looked up for years so that he could stay recollected. We didn't look up because we didn't want to see any homeless men we couldn't help. We could not face them.

Meanwhile the plumbers brought a big mechanical snake, which (one would think) could open up anything. It didn't. They called a supervisor who said they would send a crew to fix it on Monday. On Monday, they sent another team with the same snake to open the sewer. It didn't work. After several days of phone calls and pestering on our part, the plumber sent a team to dig. When it came to digging, the personnel changed and the language changed. Everyone was now Spanish-speaking. This had happened before, so we expected to use our Spanish: the language changes when the job gets tough.

First, we had to write a $900 check for the plumbing company before a shovel hit the ground. After digging awhile, they announced the bad news that the city line we were connected to was broken, and the city would have to fix it. After more time passed, the city came out. But they said it was the plumber's fault. The next day the plumbing company sent another crew to investigate, only to say it was the city's fault. The city returned with a crew to investigate, and again said it was the plumber's fault. The next day the plumbers again sent a crew that again said it was the city's fault. And then the city again sent a crew to investigate and again said it was the plumber's fault.

After days of exchanging blaming, one of the city's sewer men told us that the "supervisor of all supervisors" was coming tomorrow. He came and said that plumbers must fix it. They finally did. The three or four days had turned into two weeks. Finally, we could stop looking down and again greet new guests.

Dostoevsky's Fr. Zosima taught us that active love is the key to faith, but that those one helps may not always respond with gratitude and may even attack those who help. When people arrive at Casa Juan Diego, they are ecstatic with delight and gratitude in finding an oasis of peace and protection. They cannot thank us enough. They would kiss our hands if we allowed it. But for those who cannot handle dependency, this can change quickly, and within a short time they begin to see us as the enemy. Sometimes the reality of being dependent triggers a hostile reaction and even rage. Some guests have reported us to powerful people, but whatever "powers that be" they have been able to find have never offered to house them. A few guests who have had many failures in their lives or problem relationships with their parents place their frustrations or anger on those with whom they find hospitality. The broken person cries out, sometimes in rage: "Heal me! Fix my problems!" (or worse). We Catholic Workers can help, but we are not God and we cannot solve all the problems. We sometimes lose patience with quarrels involving guests; involving undisciplined, difficult children; or involving intoxicated, threatening men.

Those who are most in need, most wounded, are the ones who seek shelter, not the strong immigrant families who are working hard and supporting themselves. Those families, as hard as they work, may still need help. They are the ones who come to our food distribution and to our clinic; they do not come for shelter.

Guests do not meet all the expectations of some other guests, to put it mildly, and conflicts begin. A few may attack other guests, whom it is our responsibility to protect. At times we have had to stand between people who were threatening to hit each other or had already done so. We have had to restrain people who had just thrown a knife and were trying to find another one to throw. We didn't expect this to happen among the women as well, but it has, on several occasions. The conflicts have varied causes. Language differences among Spanish-speaking countries have set people off. What is a perfectly good word in one country may be a terrible insult in another.

Sometimes we feel that we wouldn't do this work for any amount of money. It helps that we give our work as a gift, but the work itself brings us to our knees. It seems that the Lord wants us to be broken like our guests, to realize that the seed and the Spirit bloom only in ploughed, cultivated, and broken soil, not in the hard, smooth ground. Only faith can underwrite this work day after day, night after night, year after year, with no future except today's challenges. We don't have much of a choice, either: go to our knees or collapse. We believe, or we die.

There have been tragedies in the houses. One man, who was not an immigrant, came to Casa Juan Diego and presented himself as one. He was given a bed at the men's house and hanged himself there. We don't know what despair and depression drove him to suicide. It was only later that we discovered his wife and family had been looking for him for some time. John, a bright young Catholic Worker and recent Notre Dame graduate, came to tell us what happened. When he got up early that morning, the *ayudantes* took him to see the body, still hanging in the men's house. Soon the whole situation was complicated by the presence of hundreds of people arriving for the weekly food distribution. The police were everywhere, but because they were doing an investigation, it was hours before they cut the body down. It was a difficult time for us all.

The Lord asks us to care for the "least ones." Immigrants are the least ones of today. They are ignored or despised by many Christians. We at Casa Juan Diego cannot abandon the most broken ones because a few respond in frustration or anger, or cannot handle their depression. We share in their crucifixion and hope in the resurrection. Without faith, our work would be considered masochistic. As one social worker from a Houston hospital screamed at us for complaining when they were sending yet another person, "You just have a martyr complex." Love and faith make it possible, even though it is not always easy. Life is stronger than death. Love is stronger than fear and frustration, and we must love our enemies, even those who tell the world we are terrible people.

Some people who know our religious roots and our faith approach have asked us if there is a place that does this work without religion, without a basis in faith. We have to answer that we do not know of such a place where people keep offering hospitality and the Works of Mercy year after year without that kind of basis. For Dorothy Day and Peter Maurin, their faith was the key, the foundation, of the Catholic Worker. Marc Ellis remembered that, during his time at the Catholic Worker, he asked Dorothy this kind of question: "I asked her whether, as Camus asked in *The Plague*, a person could be a saint without God. It seemed that she had trouble answering the question, finally answering that without faith the Worker life was impossible."[2]

We have to say, though, that any harshness and dreadfulness directed toward us—including people who call Immigration asking that they close us down—are small indeed in comparison with that inflicted on our guests and so many undocumented potential guests of Casa Juan Diego in our society.

9

ESCAPING VIOLENCE, ONLY TO FIND IT AGAIN

One night we heard the faint sobs of someone crying. The sounds and voices of the night are so different from the sounds and voices of the day at Casa Juan Diego. No longer do we hear the voices of dozens of women and children asking for food and clothing or the noisy clangs of pans in the kitchen, where cooking begins early in the morning and ends late at night. No longer are guests trailing after us, asking us to help them with a bus ticket to Dallas, to cash a check, to mail a letter, to talk to someone about a job, to stay for another week, or to try to find another relative.

But it was night, and that night we heard the quiet, muffled sound of a young Salvadoran teenager crying himself to sleep. He was one of many young Salvadorans crying themselves to sleep in Houston and other cities. They were crying for the same reason: they were alone in the United States. Their families had sent them here so the army or guerillas couldn't force them to kill or be killed. The young Salvadorans could not find even distant relatives and were often in trouble with the Immigration Service. But to send them back to their villages would have created very serious problems for them and their families. It was 1984.

We next heard the cries of a newborn babe who wasn't on a sleep schedule yet. The baby seemed to be protesting. It was in the land of exile, the United States, where the child's pregnant mother had brought him in her womb to escape death in El Salvador. The father was killed shortly after the child was conceived in El Salvador. The baby did not have a good future there, where the ravages of war had worsened the problem of malnutrition and had destroyed the school system. Men were not the only ones who died in the war: children and mothers died as well. Finally, the child drifted off to sleep to the quiet rhythm of the mother's humming, interrupted periodically by her own tears. *Blessed is the fruit of thy womb.*

A few days later, Sara arrived. She had been made a widow by the war in El Salvador when her husband, a member of the armed forces, was killed. Sara knew that if she was going to avoid being a victim as well, she must leave her country. After raising a significant amount of money, she was able to hire a coyote to bring her north. During the trip, he raped her. Sara made it to the United States and was able to begin a new life in what she hoped would be the Promised Land, but she was not alone. There was new life in Sara's womb. She was pregnant with the coyote's child. Sara went to Alabama to live with her new baby. She didn't blame the child. It was not the child's fault, she said.

Soon afterward, a group of thirteen relatives arrived from El Salvador. The husband of one woman had been killed in the massacres. (There were three massacres of peasants by the armed forces in El Salvador in the early eighties: at El Mozote in 1980, at the Sumpul River in 1981, and at El Calabozo in 1982.) A second woman had lost her husband a year before; a third, more recently. One had left the army because his superiors had warned soldiers what would be expected of them in order to crush the opposition in the conflict. The soldier felt he could not murder innocent civilians as he was being ordered to do.

Most of the first refugees we received when we opened Casa Juan Diego were from El Salvador and Guatemala, where a kind of government-sponsored terrorism reigned through death squads; these governments were supported with advice, weapons, and funds from the U.S. government. The violence and repression in both countries was overwhelming. Anyone who even looked at certain people the wrong way could be jailed, tortured, or killed. Church workers, CCD teachers, and catechists were prime targets. Many thousands of catechists had already been killed. We knew people who could not go to Mass in those countries because in certain areas it was considered subversive.

One Salvadoran priest went to Archbishop Oscar Romero to ask permission to leave. The violence was so terrible he felt he would probably be killed like the others. The archbishop said, no, you must stay with your people. The priest, unable to face the terror, left anyway. By the time he visited us at Casa Juan Diego and told his story, he was married and living in the United States.

No one was untouched by the wars. It seemed that there was not a person in El Salvador who had not had a relative killed in the conflict or a relative missing an arm or leg because of bombings and land mines. More than 10 percent of the population of El Salvador was displaced. If a similar situation occurred in the United States, thirty million people would be displaced outside the country.

We had not thought about refugees from Nicaragua, where the situation was different. Antonio Somoza, a cruel dictator, had been deposed, but some considered the situation under the "Sandinistas" (followers of Sandino, an early Nicaraguan revolutionary) as less than ideal and fled. Nicaraguan adults and families came because they hated the Sandinistas and blamed them for all of the ills of the country, including food shortages, unemployment, forced conscription, and the lack of freedom.

We weren't sure about receiving Nicaraguans. The United States was funding, arming, and training guerrillas called Contras, who were fighting against the Sandinista government. We could not agree with what our government was doing. The refugees from Nicaragua, however, were also people, and we received them—not because of their political beliefs, but because they were homeless.

One of our first guests from Nicaragua was a young lad, a new refugee who had just been released from the county hospital with no place to go. He had been repeatedly stabbed when he was attacked and robbed on the street in Houston. His many surgeries were not yet healed, and his wounds were still draining. He had an index card in his hand with Casa Juan Diego written on it, given to him by the hospital social worker. We gave him a shy welcome; meanwhile, all of his needs immediately flashed before us. A young man who had just escaped from El Salvador after losing two brothers came forth and was very solicitous, offering his small pallet and volunteering to care for him. He now had a new brother.

The numbers of Nicaraguans were not as great as the representation from other Central American countries—we had many more Salvadorans and then Guatemalans. The irony was that a few years after we had been in operation, some Nicaraguans protested against Casa Juan Diego in Houston for not housing their countrymen. They picketed the house, said we were Communists, and called press conferences (to which nobody came) to denounce us. These protesters would have identified themselves as Somocistas, followers of the deposed dictator Somoza, in opposition to their present government of Sandinistas. When they realized that we had always accepted Nicaraguans, they stopped their protests. In fact. there were Nicaraguans in the house as they protested.

One evening at Casa Juan Diego, we had some excitement: an important Sandinista priest from the government in Managua was going to visit. We had not invited him, but someone wanted to bring him. We have had many visitors from all sides of the political spectrum at Casa Juan Diego without problems, so it didn't make much difference, except that it was unusual to have a priest-politician visit. However, that evening, the aura of excitement was replaced by fear. Some of the guests became very upset when they learned that the priest-politician was coming. They were afraid that he was coming to get them for not allowing their fourteen-year-old son to join the military in Nicaragua. Their son had already been conscripted when they fled. They preferred to leave their country rather than comply with forced recruitment. The family hid in the far corners of the building during the visit.

So many risked their lives on the terrible journey to escape the violence in their countries. Often they were young men, teenagers, who came to the United States to avoid being forcibly recruited by the army. And on the other side, refugees from guerilla recruitment also arrived. Rogelio came to the United States from El Salvador to avoid being forced into the army to fight in a war he did not understand and to avoid killing his brothers and cousins, who had been conscripted by the guerillas, the "other side." We gave him a bed, a pair of shoes, and clothes from the clothing room, and we scheduled him to see the volunteer doctor in our clinic because of dehydration and his swollen, bruised feet.

The refugees fleeing wars seemed to set aside the violence they had seen or participated in as they came into an environment of peace—or perhaps it was natural common sense, wisdom, and self-protection that they were exercising. Even those on opposing sides of wars did not argue politics in our houses. Usually, the people who came were not extreme rightists or leftists. Only Nicaraguans expressed their feelings about where they were on the left-right spectrum because of the support of the U.S. government. But refugees were and are people fleeing their homelands ravaged by war and what goes with it: women, men, mothers, fathers, teenagers, and children—all sickened by violence, tragedy, poverty, and the carnage that was taking place in their countries. They were people who wanted to stay alive in the middle of tragedies and trauma.

Maria Concepción was eighteen when she arrived at Casa Juan Diego from El Salvador with her four preschool children. After arriving in the United States, her husband had abandoned her. She stayed with us for a while and then somehow got a job and an apartment. We worried about her and went to visit. We found the children alone in the evening in an old terrible, decrepit apartment that looked almost like it had been abandoned. It appeared that the job the mother had obtained was in one of the disreputable *cantinas* in Houston. What to do? We moved the family back with us and tried to find an alternative to handing them over to Child Protective Services. Upon returning to Casa Juan Diego, the children ate as if they had not eaten for some time. The young mother obviously could not survive alone in a strange land. Her husband's family had been received as refugees in Canada, she said, and would welcome her and the children. The question was how to get them there. We asked help of a religious sister at a Catholic Worker house in Detroit that would serve as a way station on their journey, while arrangements were made for entrance into Canada. We bought plane tickets both for the five of them and for our own family, having enlisted our now-teenaged children to help with the little ones and the luggage for the journey. It was quite a trip. We rejoiced upon uniting one family.

During the time that we were in El Salvador, Catholic priests and laypeople were deported, jailed, or killed because their government feared Communism. The same was true of Guatemala. Organizing people to seek justice had brought only persecution and violence. The majority of the people had nothing to do with either Communism or liberation theology. They did have a concern for the poor. They spoke of cooperatives and land reform. Christian base communities, unions, student groups, and other popular organizations became targets because they opposed the governments in the hope of improving society. Visitors told us that Archbishop Romero had said you can talk about many things in Latin America, but if you touch the land, *"Exige sus mártires"* ("It will call forth its martyrs"). The question was how the *campesinos*—the peasants, the people—could possibly make economic progress on any level when they were up against military dictators and the giant of the United States. In our December 1983 paper, we wrote:

> Becoming dupes of Communism could be a real danger in Latin America. Communists believe absolutely that truth is rel-

ative. It can be used for any end. For them deception and lies can be the truth, if they promote Communistic truth or lies. Communists speak glowingly of liberty and justice until power is achieved, after which the Communistic truth changes.

The other danger in Latin America is becoming dupes of those who believe absolutely anything can be done in the name of making money. For these people, the truth serves profits, not vice versa. For them nothing must stand in the way of the path of making more money.

Both groups are masters of deceit.

They have manipulated public opinion to believe that people concerned about human rights and seeking above-starvation wages—even church people—are subversive, and these can be murdered to stop the spread of this "atheistic menace," whereas the real motive is wealth and power.

They are made nervous with talk about above-starvation wages and labor unions because any money given to poor workers diminishes, though slightly, the enormous gain available. For them the only good human rights leader or good labor leader is a dead one.

The diplomatic pitfall of those who believe in democracy is supporting anti-Communist groups merely because they are anti-Communist. Some anti-Communist groups in Latin America have been as satanic and oppressive as the government of the Stalinist era in Russia, destroying a whole generation of democratic leaders in El Salvador and Guatemala, for example, in the name of stopping Communism.

"Stopping Communism" has been a shibboleth that has opened the door to the murder of thousands of people concerned about human rights and human dignity including many who were trying to implement Catholic social teaching.

After Archbishop Romero was assassinated, Auxiliary Bishop Arturo Rivera y Damas became the new archbishop of San Salvador. Not long after his installation, Archbishop Rivera y Damas called the government's attacks on the people a war of extermination and genocide against a defenseless civilian population. The carnage prompted him to remark: "The guns are from outside the country, the dead are from inside."

It appeared that there were several small guerrilla groups in El Salvador who were not terribly strong and were not able to overcome their differences in order to work together. But in 1980, after the assassination in March of Archbishop Romero, they came together as the FMLN (*Frente Farabundo Martí para la Liberación Nacional*) and began major military offensives in response to the government repression and terror.

Throughout the 1980s, as some in the United States were speaking about the right of oppressed peoples to rise up against their governments, we talked with the many refugees from Central America who were our guests. Though we had initially sympathized with the guerillas, we doubted the effectiveness of counterviolence. We heard more and more about atrocities by the death squads, but we also heard negatives about the guerrillas. In the later years of the war, older gnarled men arrived at Casa Juan Diego to take refuge, saying, "Our very life is our work on the land, but the guerrillas told us that if we picked the coffee they would cut off our hands."

At the same time, the war in Guatemala, funded by the United States, targeted the indigenous people of the country. This had roots back in the U.S. intervention in the 1950s to protect the Chiquita banana company. Friends and new refugees told us the most terrible stories of whole villages being killed because someone might have been helping guerrillas. And as is the case in this kind of civil war, if guerrillas asked for help, the people were threatened with violence if they did not assist.

It was hard to hear the stories from Guatemala. The government violence against civilians in the name of repressing Communism, especially against the indigenous people in the countryside, was appalling. An eyewitness, Maryknoll priest William Donnelly, told his story at our Mass one Wednesday evening. It was then published in the *Houston Catholic Worker* in the May–June 1990 issue:

> How many martyrs are there now in Guatemala? We will know only on Judgment Day. I'll never forget my friend, Gabriel. He was an Indian catechist. His village was in the sieges of war, but Gabriel stayed with his people, animating them to persevere in their courage and faith in God.
>
> One Sunday night Gabriel was conducting a prayer service when a group of armed men arrived at the little chapel. They ordered all the men outside. "Since you are all praying, kneel

down," they said. Gabriel, rapidly sensing what was about to happen pleaded, "Don't kill them, they are all fathers of families. Kill me. I'm the leader." "Very well," the armed men scoffed, and then proceeded to shoot all the men, saving Gabriel for the last. The women, still inside, said that the men made no outcry when they were being killed, only encouraging one another to die like Jesus because they had done no wrong. The terrified women and children later fled to Mexico.

Repeat that story thousands of times and there you have the story of Guatemala. Young Guatemalan soldiers dying, leaving families saddened forever. Guerrillas dying, leaving families fearful of saying they even knew them. And between the two groups the people, sinking ever deeper into poverty and despair.

More than 100,000 people have been killed since the CIA-directed coup that overthrew the government in 1954. There are some 45,000 disappeared people and the number is rising. Every day the newspapers recount stories of victims of assassination squads, politically motivated murders, whose bodies, mutilated through torture, have been found in trash dumps, city streets and lonely country roads.

How many people did I meet who had to stay at their little shacks, toughing out illness because they had nothing to spend on a doctor's fee or the medicine someone might recommend. A prominent example of racism has been the theft of the land of the indigenous through trickery and paper work that left them amazed and which continues right up to the present day. And how many people, great people, have been eliminated because they sought to obtain a better life for their brothers and sisters.

The guerrillas were working the people and getting many to join their cause. It was getting easier for them since the military governments in turn were becoming more brutal and repressive against the popular people's movements who were independent of the guerrillas and working for social change through peaceful action.

The military began accusing the Church, especially the Catholic Church, as being one of the principal causes of the people's unrest. The priest belongs in the sacristy, they said. By working for the betterment of the people and discussing God's plan for a just and free society for all, the priests and indeed the Church was seen to be "paving the way for Communism." This proved to be the most tragic misunderstanding of reality. Thousands of catechists were persecuted and many killed. Thirteen priests and other religious personnel were murdered. All of us lived in fear. Spies were so feared that one only spoke in confidence to very trusted family and friends. Even today, no matter where they may be, Guatemalans are loath to touch on the subject of what is happening in their country.

As the war reached its worst point in 1982, hundreds of people were killed in my parish and many thousands in the whole country. The guerrillas assassinated a number of people marked by them for death. Somewhere along the line the military made the fatal decision that in order to stop the guerrilla advance among the civilian population, whole communities where there was suspected guerilla support, if not active participation, would have to be eliminated. About 400 villages were wiped out, several of them in my parish. The army killed all—men, women, and children. Thousands of Guatemalans, the majority indigenous, since they were the majority of those being killed, fled then to Mexico.

Exactly as Father Donnelly had described them, the Guatemalans who came to Casa Juan Diego were quiet in the middle of other refugees and spoke little about what was going on in their country unless we spoke to them privately. When we had a quiet moment, we asked Lupe why she came. She came because the government was recruiting people in the country to be a part of what they called "civil patrols." That meant forced participation in army tactics against their neighbors. It was a strategy to involve the people themselves in the repression. Lupe told us, "I had to avoid being involved in a civil patrol in Guatemala. If I refused, I would be killed. If I participated, I would have been forced by the government to kill my friends and neighbors. So I fled."

Lupe and so many of our guests who have come over the years to Casa Juan Diego have told us of their terrible journeys to the United States. They fled the violence of war or economic injustice in their country only to face robbers, thieves, corrupt police officers, wild animals, snakes, thorns, the violence of the coyotes who contracted to bring them here, and the possibility of imprisonment and deportation.

There is joy in arriving at an oasis of peace, but the memory of the violence they left, and of the cruelty of the journey, will never leave the immigrants. The moment they jump onto a train to come north, they experience violence again—the violence of the train tracks where lie the arms, legs, and even heads of victims. A common way to cross Mexico is to sneak aboard the tops of freight trains. On the long rides, migrants often fall asleep and fall off the trains. Or as they attempt to get on as the train starts moving, some do not succeed, and the train pulls them under its wheels. Thieves also hop the trains to violate the women, or to rob and kill the men. Those arriving told us how the thieves throw other migrants off the top of the train if they do not give up the money they had put together for the trip—sometimes by mortgaging a little home.

The men are almost always robbed. Men and women hide the little money they have for the journey as best they can, but the robbers, either gang members or immigration officials or police in different countries (or at least men dressed as police), know how to obtain information from people and get their money from them. One guest described how a friend had been strung up on a rope as if to be lynched and lost consciousness in this process. Women are fair game to violent men, even if accompanied and protected by husbands, brothers, or friends. With pistols to their heads, husbands, brothers, or friends have to listen and weep helplessly as the women are raped. This trauma is difficult to overcome.

Besides the gangs, thieves, and officials, another source of violence against the vulnerable is the coyotes, those paid to guide people through the challenging journey across countries without documents. Some people come alone, and a few, amazingly, make the whole trip on their own. The majority have to contract with someone who knows the way and can avoid checkpoints and the authorities who would deport them. Some of these "guides" hold captive the people they are supposed to be helping, while they pressure the families for more and more money— more than the original agreement. In recent years, our guests have told us how the coyotes get immigrants' relatives on the telephone and then begin to beat the immigrants so their loved ones will hear their cries and come up with more money. Men have arrived shaking with fear of the coyotes; women tell of repeated rapes.

In recent years, as enforcement of the border has grown tougher, it appears that almost the only coyotes who can get people through are gang members and drug dealers. They have made a lucrative but incredibly cruel business out of transporting desperate people looking for a way to feed their families.

It was not always difficult for Central Americans to cross Mexico. In fact, for Mexican immigrants coming into the United States, there were not even border checkpoints until the early twentieth century. Since the time Central American refugees and immigrants started fleeing to the United States, however, they have faced not only the presence of our Border Patrol, but also Mexican immigration officers, who—pressured by the United States—make life very difficult for them as they attempt to cross Mexico. A Mexican immigration official told us in the mid-1980s that Mexico was receiving $50 to $100 a head from the U.S. government for each person they deported. The political pressure from the north continues to be strong for Mexico to not allow Central Americans to finish their journey.

In addition to corrupt Mexican police or immigration officials, gangs prey on the migrants. The thugs who rob and rape our guests on their journey through Central America and especially the south of Mexico are from gangs that also terrorize the population in Central America, especially the youth, and that operate in the United States as well. Join or be killed is what the young people who live in the area are told. Once you are in, if you leave the gang, you and your family will be killed. Along with the violence of war and the economics of the global market, the gangs are a major reason that people leave their countries and try to get to the United States—so our guests and those who come for help from the community in Houston tell us. Young men have arrived in Houston in wheelchairs, having survived being shot trying to leave a gang.

Very few people in the United States have been given asylum (and at this point none in Houston) because of persecution by gangs, who operate on a level of cruelty that is hard to accept or imagine. People who work with refugees in various countries trace the roots and development of these highly organized gangs to two events—both the fruit of Central American wars. A large number of the teenagers who left El Salvador during the civil war went to Los Angeles, so many that Los Angeles had the largest Salvadoran population next to San Salvador. There the refugee youth were confronted by well-established gangs. Out of self-defense they felt they had to develop their own gangs—which they did. When they were arrested later for criminal activity, they were deported, and the gangs were transplanted to Central America.

The other significant factor about the gangs is less well known. The United States government funded and trained a Contra army in Honduras and Nicaragua to fight the Sandinista government in Nicaragua with guerrilla techniques. They were not a part of the Honduran army nor the Nicaraguan army. Poor to begin with, they had left their regular jobs to become Contras. Now they had nothing except experience and training in violence and cruelty, but without the discipline of the regular military. Some of those who receive and work with immigrants in the south of Mexico believe that, when the Nicaraguan war ended, many of those men, who now had no jobs, became members of the gangs when they were first forming.

One family from El Salvador started out on the treacherous trip to the United States because their son had been killed by a gang. They decided to come by boat on the Pacific side, and left the country with their remaining son. The mother, Lucia, recounted that when the Mexican police boarded their son's boat, it sank, taking their second son to his death. Having mortgaged their house to make the journey, the couple continued on to the United States to earn money to send back to their daughter-in-law and two small grandchildren. Once they were in Brownsville, the coyote demanded more money but when the money came, the coyote murdered the husband and escaped. The survivor, Lucia, stayed with us for a few days. Here is her story:

> Gangs of delinquents in El Salvador killed my first son, Ignacio, who was 23 years old. It was this painful circumstance that made my husband and I and our other son emigrate to the United States. This same gang of robbers was looking for my family in order to kill us. In order to leave El Salvador, I had to take out a loan of 6,000 colones ($500) on my little house.
>
> Mexican policemen caught up with us in the middle of the river between Mexico and Guatemala, stopping our passenger

boat. They arrived in a smaller boat and told us all the undocumented had to move onto their boat. Then they began to insult us, beating all of the men with their guns. The police hit our son in the face with a gun and blood ran out of his mouth. They hit my husband on the back and took all the money we had with us. They did the same to the entire group; we were nineteen people of different countries. The Guatemalans had four big duffle bags of clothing and when the police stood up, with the weight of the clothing and of all the people, the boat sank.

Ten people drowned, among them my second son, Gonzalo, 22 years old, leaving three orphans who are my grandchildren.

In spite of the death of our other son, my husband and I decided we still had to continue our journey. When we arrived at Matamoros at the end of November, since we were completely out of money, I had to beg, going with a man on all the buses, singing, singing, in order to collect money for food and to continue our journey. We didn't know at the time that there was a house of refuge in Matamoros.

We crossed the Rio Grande on November 29. Arriving in Brownsville we met up with a coyote who offered to take us to Houston for $800. As we didn't have this money, he took us to his home so that from there my husband could communicate by telephone with his family so they would send money to pay for the trip. His family asked him to wait a few days so that they could get the money together. It wasn't until Monday that my husband's brothers sent him $1,000.

Every day the coyote had taken my husband to Western Union to check on the arrival of the money, but each time in the evening he brought him back. It was only this last time on the Monday that he received the money that he did not bring him back. The coyote came home alone.

I thought Immigration must have picked up my husband and returned him to Matamoros. I searched that night and all day Tuesday and didn't find him. It wasn't until Wednesday that I went to the Sheriff. It was he who told me [the coyote] had shot my husband to death on Monday between midnight and the morning. The Sheriff himself, knowing that I had nowhere to go, took me to Casa Romero (Ozanam Center) operated by the St. Vincent de Paul Society of Brownsville. If we had known this house existed, my husband would not have died.

At the morgue they told me I should not look at my husband's body because it was so disfigured from the bullets in his head. I never saw him again.

I could not leave the area until I knew what they were going to do with my husband's body. I waited until his family was able to pay so that his remains were returned to El Salvador, where his mother received him. Now I find myself alone without my husband and without the only two sons I had. In the pain and trauma of the death of my husband, I lost the baby I was carrying. I have four grandchildren as a remembrance of my sons. For this reason, I gathered my courage. I don't know from where it came, except from God our Father.

I could not retrace my steps and flee back. My grandchildren, my mother, my aunt who are now my family depend on me and I am their only hope.

We offered Lucia more time to rest and asked her about going for counseling after all the tragedy. We knew it would be important. She indignantly said, "I have suffered much, but I'm not crazy. I have spent a few weeks recovering. Now I'm going to work in the oranges in Florida so my daughter-in-law in El Salvador will not lose her house. She and the children are all I have left."

When a group of students visits Casa Juan Diego from a university, we usually seek out a guest who is willing to tell the story of his or her journey from Central America or Mexico in order to share the reality of the suffering faced on that trip. In 2008, a group was visiting from the University of Notre Dame's "Urban Plunge," a seminar they offer on the Church and social action. We asked Consuelo if she felt she could share her story. "Oh no," she said, as her eyes welled up with tears. "It would be much too hard. It is easier for the men who tell their stories before the Wednesday evening Mass. It is too hard to talk about the terrible things that happen to us women." Consuelo had been raped by coyotes and was now seven months pregnant, trying to decide whether to give up the baby for adoption or to keep it. She was leaning toward keeping the child, even though she was also in contact with Catholic Charities regarding adoption.

For immigrants who are not assaulted, the journey across Mexico and then the southwest United States is a lonely one, through unpopulated areas where people can get lost or starve, be bitten by snakes (rattlesnakes are common in Texas), or die in the desert from overexposure to the sun. The trip from their homes is often a *via crucis*, a Way of the Cross, as they face the violence of hunger, thirst, and thieves. The Way of the Cross began for many the same way as it did for Jesus—with a death sentence. The future refugee was put on "the list" of a death squad or a gang, perhaps because he or she was a union leader trying to obtain better wages and working conditions.

The journey of the migrant is one of suffering that includes stations along the way: two of the most dramatic stations are at the Suchiate River, which is the border of Guatemala and Mexico and is where violence has been at an extreme level for decades, and at the Rio Grande, where violence overflows on both sides.

The Rio Grande is treacherous. Some people, having been warned about it, find it at low tide and wonder why it is considered a great river and so difficult to cross. Others, caught in its unexpected currents, drown. When the lucky ones emerge, first they come upon river thieves, waiting to rob them, and then the U.S. Border Patrol, waiting to deport them.

Immigrants who die in the river or in the beastly hot desert don't complete the Way of the Cross. No one ever finds out what happens to them. They become reminders of the journey's difficulty. Those who survive face being hunted down in Texas, Arizona, or California as they enter, or in the areas before the last checkpoint, which is about a hundred miles into Texas for those whose goal is Houston.

Immigrants sometimes hope for a resurrection, for new life, for a new existence after they cross the border. They usually do not find it. Little do they know how hard it will be, how little milk and honey there is on the other side, how little gold paves the streets of the United States. Little do they know how hard it will be to find work and get their papers. Little do they know how unwelcome they will be. The families on the road from Central America or Mexico will undergo the experience of Mary and Joseph. There will be no room in the inn. No one will welcome them to their empty stables. We at Casa Juan Diego have tried to be the inn where they *are* received, at least for a little while.

Refugees and immigrants suffer violence before they leave their homeland and on their journey to the United States, and then they suffer the violence of rejection by people who see them as modern-day lepers. While our work at Casa Juan Diego is filled with joy and hope, the tragedies that migrants face are sometimes overwhelming. Over the years, people have poured into our houses with each story worse than the last until we can hardly stand it. "Tell us what you need. Do not tell us your story," we are almost driven to say. As T. S. Eliot said in the first of his *Four Quartets*: "Human kind / cannot bear very much reality."

After immigrants finally arrive in Houston, violence is the daily fare for some of them. Not able to open bank accounts, they have to carry the money they earn on their persons. Smart thieves soon discover this. Thieves sometimes observe when they leave work and where they cash their checks at a small store, and then rob the immigrants at gunpoint or knifepoint. Sending money through wire services like Western Union is also a dangerous venture. So many have been robbed of the money they meant to send or what they just received from families or friends. Without identification, some immigrants have allowed strangers who do have ID to receive the money for them. Unfortunately, sometimes the stranger flees before handing it over.

Once, two men who had been assaulted and robbed arrived at Casa Juan Diego. One had his leg broken badly and the other had his kneecap shattered. The one with the broken kneecap had tried to resist and then negotiate with the robber, but the robber spoke only English. Both men returned home to their respective countries with our help, permanently scarred and without money for their families.

Pedro told us about his problem: He couldn't work and thus couldn't pay the rent for the one-room apartment where he and his wife live. We knew his place because we had given the furniture for the apartment and moved their few belongings. Pedro said that he was waiting for a bus at Shepherd and Washington in front of an abandoned building when a man came out of the building and put a knife in his back. He took Pedro's wallet with all the money he had—just $23.00—then stabbed him. As Pedro was telling this, he took off his shirt and showed where he had been stitched up at the hospital. Fortunately, his internal organs were not touched. It is not unusual for our men to be surgically opened from the chest cavity to below the navel to check if internal organs have been hit after a stabbing, usually related to being robbed.

Once, one of our most reliable Honduran Catholic Workers was shot from the street at our men's house. We had just given him an award for the Immigrant of the Year for his work. He was hospitalized for days, but fortunately recovered.

How often have we seen the bloodied, black-and-blue faces of the robbed immigrant? How often have we seen people with busted jaws and broken teeth, eyes swollen shut, like Jesus beaten by the Roman soldiers? How often have we seen people with no feet because they were cut off when they jumped off a train, or with legs totally paralyzed by a gunshot in the back? Their number is legion. We saw the movie *The Passion of the Christ* and read critical reviews of it. Some called the level of violence in the movie obscene. All these years, the poor, the immigrants, and the refugees have experienced their own "Passion of the Christ," but no movie reviewer or reporter has ever called the violence they suffer obscene.

It is ironic that, by the late 1980s, the United States had given El Salvador $3.3 billion in aid to build a democracy, but instead an oppressive government was built, bent on protecting the interests of landowners, the military, and businesses rather than the interests of the people. We often forget that U.S. taxpayers were paying the way for these groups without their knowledge. Without their knowledge, U.S. taxpayers were financing death squads and underwriting the oppression of the poor. Without their knowledge, U.S. taxpayers were forcing immigrants to leave their country to seek refuge here.

The guerillas conducted a major offensive late in the war in El Salvador to try to end it. Alfredo arrived at Casa Juan Diego in 1989, weeping as he told us about dogs eating the people who had been killed during the recent battles and then left on the streets.

In 1989, six Jesuits and two women were murdered at the University of Central America in El Salvador. All of us at Casa Juan Diego were devastated by the news. We had heard that everything was in place for an explosion, but hoped against hope that more violence could be avoided.

We had to try to do something when the Jesuits were so blatantly killed, so we organized a demonstration in Houston against U.S. sponsorship of the war in El Salvador. There was a very good response, especially for Houston, which was not noted for large attendance at demonstrations. Because it was one of those very rare occasions when the temperature dropped to 10 degrees in Houston, we were surprised that over fifty people came to protest this policy of the United States in El Salvador, including a good number of priests, but also including clergy from other denominations. Even though we are from up North, we had already spent many years in Texas. We bundled up against the cold, but had forgotten about our feet. We had no boots or warm socks and our feet froze. All who attended were moved by the sense of solidarity with the others who had come to make their voices heard together. Others who tried to come did not arrive because they had accidents—many roads were icy in Houston that day.

With the killing of the Jesuits, the people of the United States had had enough and support for the war waned. Eventually a peace accord was signed and the FMLN became a political party. But the Salvadoran people, devastated by war, continued to come to the United States and to Casa Juan Diego.

We still hear stories of the wars in Central America and their effect on the people who lived through those times. Our guests are now of another generation, but the memory of the death squads, the terror, and the massacres lives on in the families, as told to children by their parents and grandparents. Other Salvadorans tell us how, later in the war, their mothers would hide them under the beds if they heard the guerrillas were near, because they knew they would want to take the children to become guerillas.

A young Salvadoran came to Casa Juan Diego in 2007 to ask our help. We tried to help him, but he was always disappearing. At first, he was vague about what might be his problem. He hinted that he had encephalitis and asked us to buy the long list of medicines that had been prescribed at the hospital. He had been told that if he did not take the medication, he would die, but he was only given prescriptions, not the medication itself. After discovering that the medicines were prohibitively expensive, we bought just a few. We took him into our men's house, but he only stayed one night and took off. When he finally confessed that his problem was AIDS, we were able to get him help, for funding for AIDS treatment is readily available in the United States, even for the undocumented. We tried moving him into one of our houses for the sick and wounded, but he stayed only a day or two, even though he badly needed help. We learned through our conversations with him that he had not regularly lived in a home since he was seven years old. The guerrillas in El Salvador had kidnapped him from his mother's house and taken him to the mountains to live as a guerrilla during the war. It was hard for him to adapt to living in a home. He said that, when he was taken from his home, he was busy during the day; it was at night that he missed his mother.

On occasion even people from war-torn countries on other continents have found their way to Casa Juan Diego. The Immigration Service called one day to ask if we could accept a mother and child from Bosnia. They were going to keep the husband at the detention center in Houston, but the mother was free to leave with her child on her own recognizance if we could accept her. We said yes, as we always do when Immigration calls. We knew there were three languages in Bosnia. We hoped she spoke Croatian, because Mark knew some Croatian priests in Youngstown, Ohio, but when she arrived with her five-year-old daughter, we found that our new guest, who was very agitated, only spoke Albanian.

Our Bosnian guest was afraid to stay at Casa Juan Diego, clinging, ironically, to the Border Patrol agent who had brought her. He, in the meantime, looked very uncomfortable in the entrance of Casa Juan Diego and only wanted to get out of there as soon as possible. She had a piece of paper that had the name of Catholic Charities on it and she wanted to go there. She begged the agent, without using words, in a sign language both he and we could understand, to take her there. We didn't know how to explain that Catholic Charities only keeps children, unaccompanied minors, who have been detained by the Immigration Service, not families that included adults. Luckily, a Catholic Worker turned out to be excellent at drawing stick figures. As she explained in this form of art that the child would have to be separated from her if she went to Catholic Charities, the new guest began to wail. Then our CW showed her in stick figures that if she stayed with us, they could be together. The woman was then glad to stay and allowed the Border Patrol agent to leave. Fortunately, she had a telephone number for her brother-in-law in New York who spoke English, and in a couple of weeks, he was able to come and get her.

Several refugees from wars in Africa also made their way to Casa Juan Diego, telling of their harrowing experiences. They came respectively from the Democratic Republic of the Congo, from Cameroon, and from Mozambique. Depending on what country had colonized theirs, they spoke French, Portuguese, or English. We can communicate with Portuguese speakers because it's close to Spanish. Louise was able to recall some French from high school and found others more fluent to help.

163

When one French-speaking guest needed to take a translator to her asylum interview with the U.S. government, a French-speaking volunteer at Casa Juan Diego accompanied her. The translator was upset for weeks afterward about the attitude of the interviewer. The terrible asylum interview almost equaled some of the refugee's frightening experiences in her war-torn country.

In addition to the violence in the streets, immigrants and refugees suffer increased domestic violence in the United States. We didn't start out to work with battered women, but since this phenomenon cuts through all social, racial, cultural, and economic barriers, it was inevitable that there would be battered immigrant or refugee women among those who came to take refuge with us, and also inevitable that some of these women would be accompanied by the husband or boyfriend who was the batterer. When we were able to obtain another large building for a men's House of Hospitality in 1991 and to free up the large building on Rose Street for just women and children, we were able to receive more battered women and more pregnant or homeless immigrant women who were already living in Houston, but who were still very much a part of the immigrant community. What we discovered as we talked with them is that the phenomenon of domestic violence increases as people are uprooted from their families and communities in their countries. The dignity of the husbands is undermined as they have difficulty finding work and respect here, while there is no one to support the women here when they most need the help of families and friends. Although some had been hit or beaten in their own countries, many women told us that the violence increased when they came to the United States, and they were unfamiliar with people or resources here. We have been able to provide some of that support.

Dorothy Day, always opposed to violence and war, wrote in the April 1948 *Catholic Worker* about Peter Maurin's description of his own experience in the military: the discipline for killing and the loss of individual dignity. She contended that Christians who justified war were perhaps unaware of the psychological damage done to those who have military training and experience, not to mention those who are victims of violence and betrayal by their neighbors. She said that they used the idea of a holy war to justify a defense of Jesus Christ by bombs, a blood-soaked earth, quick death, hate. A hate that always exists in war despite the unreal and pedantic distinctions of theologians whose love of refinements is equaled only by their ignorance of psychology, of what happens to a man to get him prepared to murder.

In spite of peace accords in the mid-1990s, violence and poverty still wrack Central American countries, and immigrants still continue to come. The people of Central America are still as poor, if not poorer, than ever. And the wealthy still own the land.

Social movements in Central America had at first given people hope, people who had been ground down to mere survival level for so long. But the repression was devastating. In El Salvador, 75,000 people were dead and 1.5 million refugees had fled the country. In Guatemala, it is estimated that 200,000 (mostly Mayans) were dead or disappeared in the 36-year war.

In 1996, peace accords were signed to end the war in Guatemala. Bishop Alvaro Ramazzini, with whom we worked to provide houses for migrants, played a key role in the negotiations. In the two years that followed, church leaders in Guatemala led an investigation into the atrocities during the war and developed an interdiocesan project called Recovery of the Historic Moment (REHMI), a project of interviewing and listening to the people in order to heal the wounds of violence, to help communities deal with their fears and anger caused by the conflict, and to bring reconciliation to a country whose social fabric was torn apart by the violence.

Bishop Juan Gerardi Conedera chaired an investigation with the Human Rights Office of the Archdiocese of Guatemala, in which 7,000 victims of violence during the war were interviewed as part of the REHMI project. His report, *Guatemala: Never Again*, was published in 1998. It is a 1,400-page, four-volume work detailing devastating human rights abuses during the many years of war, 90 percent of which were attributed to agents of the government and less than 5 percent to the guerillas. Two days after the report was presented, Bishop Gerardi was bludgeoned to death. A popular version of the report was developed and distributed throughout communities in Guatemala. Bishop Ramazzini asked Catholic schools to teach the report as part of their history curriculum.

For us, the tragedy is compounded many times by the role of the United States in supporting the repressive dictators in these conflicts. While these things were happening, as in South American countries like Chile, we knew that the financial support, encouragement, and military training came from our own country, all in the name of stopping Communism.

The United Nations sponsored a truth report on Guatemala's vicious 36-year civil war, which called the government's tactics "genocide." Tom Roberts wrote that the UN report, entitled *Guatemala: Memory of Silence,*

> held the United States responsible for supporting brutal military dictators, for using the Central Intelligence Agency to aid the Guatemalan military and for training Guatemalan army officials in counterinsurgency tactics that resulted in widespread torture and death.
>
> The 3,500-page report, published in nine volumes and titled "Guatemala: Memory of Silence," was compiled by the Commission for Historical Clarification. The report was mandated by the Guatemalan peace process that culminated in the Accord of Oslo, signed in Norway in June 1994.
>
> A widely dispersed 60-page document containing conclusions and recommendations places the overwhelming blame for decades of torture and particularly the systematic elimination of Mayan villages on the government and the military and its agents.
>
> The report vindicates the religious and human rights groups whose characterizations of the terror and torture were largely dismissed over the years in official U.S. circles.[1]

Bishop Ramazzini said on several occasions that even in the aftermath of the conflict, there is still much fear because the methods of repression were so savage and cruel. People never knew who was behind things or who they were talking to. He sees the polarization of Guatemalan society as one of the worst effects of the war. The bishop himself has received death threats several times because of his stand for the poor.

Violence as a fact of life is a legacy of the war in Guatemala. In addition to mob justice and gang violence, the drug cartels from Mexico found it easy to spill over into Guatemala and create havoc. The situation became so bad that, in 2009, Cardinal Rodolfo Quezada Toruño, archbishop of Guatemala City, called on Christians to participate in a peace walk on January 10 in the capital. Over 10,000 people participated, protesting the murders, rapes, abductions, and drug-related violence of the war.

Robert White was the U.S. ambassador to El Salvador in 1980, the year Archbishop Romero was assassinated, the year the four American churchwomen were killed, and the year we made the decision to start Casa Juan Diego. In that year, Ambassador White wrote to Washington that any economic reform would be totally ineffective because of the situation of extreme violence on the part of the government. Margaret O'Brien Steinfels wrote about what faced the ambassador:

> Nineteen eighty was a pivotal year for El Salvador.... When White arrived early in March, his assignment was to encourage the growth of a political center and to discourage the flagrant human-rights abuses of the military and the death squads (usually the military in civilian dress), which were driving moderates and leftists into political alliances with the guerrillas. This was the assessment he made in a report that month to Washington: "If the systematic violation of human rights in the countryside does not cease, all the agrarian and banking reforms in the world will not help. Sometime over the course of the next six months, the civilian members of the junta and Colonel Majano will have to insist on the ouster of those in the army and security forces who permit and encourage torturing and killing innocent civilians in a brutal effort to end political action. The extreme right will keep on trying to convince the conservative officers to return to their natural alliance with the rich."[2]

Ambassador White's words were prophetic. However, not only was his advice not heeded, but he was also removed as ambassador to El Salvador, fired by Alexander Haig, as he said, because he opposed a military solution in that country. A decade of suffering for the Salvadoran people followed.

In January 2007, statements in the press by those who fought in El Salvador about the uselessness of that U.S.–supported conflict made the stories of so many refugees who have passed through our doors present to us again. Reported in the *Washington Post*, Salvadoran government soldier Jose Wilfredo Salgado's spoke about his experience as a soldier:

> "We soldiers were tricked—they told us the threat was communism," he said. "But I look back and realize those were not communists out there that we were fighting—we were just poor country people killing poor country people.... We gave our blood, we killed our friends and, in the end, things are still bad. Look at all this poverty, and look how the wealth is concentrated in just a few hands.[3]

Salgado admitted collecting baby skulls as trophies from civilian massacres and then using them as candleholders or good-luck charms. Any means, including the massacre of entire villages, was used by the governments in El Salvador and Guatemala, with training and encouragement from the CIA's School of the Americas in Atlanta, and with the encouragement of our own government—all in the name of stopping Communism. In Nicaragua and Honduras, it was the "contras," the guerrillas, that we sponsored, who carried out their activities by anything but pure means.

In 2007, the Salvadoran Catholic Church published a book in 2007 entitled *Testigos de la fe en El Salvador* ("Witnesses to the Faith in El Salvador")[4] to record the stories of ten Salvadoran martyrs who are not as well known as Oscar Romero or Rutilio Grande, and to keep their memories alive in the Salvadoran people. The first account of the ten priest-martyrs (the book includes one seminarian and one bishop killed in 1993) is that of Fr. Alfonso Navarro, who was killed when we lived in El Salvador.

Training for killing, torture, and war wounds the whole society, not only in Central America, but in other countries where the United States has sponsored wars as well. The violence has long-lasting effects on people. During the Cold War between the United States and the Soviet Union, people lived their lives in the shadow and fear of Communism and nuclear war. That fear has now been transferred to terrorism, allowing all kinds of public policy decisions to be made that inhibit freedom. When we live in fear, we are not free.

Loving our enemies is one of the hard sayings of the Gospel, but one of the most important. Loving our enemies could not have worse results than the tragedies of war.

10

THEIR BONES WILL
RISE AGAIN

"Them Bones," a spiritual based on the Book of Ezekiel about the Lord bringing dry bones to life, has special meaning for Casa Juan Diego. Many who come to us have lost their limbs, have been paralyzed in work accidents, have been shot in the back or in the head, or have had their bones crushed on the terrible journey to the United States. Their bones are now useless.

Our lives are steeped in the mystery of suffering and death.

During our time in El Salvador, we saw people involved in social movements jailed, tortured, and killed by death squads. Already in 1977, tortured bodies began to appear in the streets and in garbage dumps; with the years, their numbers multiplied. Who remembers these people? Where are their twisted bones today? So many tried to escape the violence by coming to the United States, but lost their limbs on the journey.

Immigrants have often told us about the bodies they saw left behind—those cut in two or decapitated by trains, those shot, or those thrown off the trains by gang members in the south of Mexico.

We looked around the room after Mass at Casa Juan Diego one Wednesday night—one man had a cast on his leg, one had casts on both wrists and was unable to bathe himself or go to the bathroom alone, two others had casts on their arms. Another was in a wheelchair. We wondered what it might be like to stack up all of the lost limbs and broken bones of the immigrants who had walked or traveled on freight trains to the United States, had work accidents after they arrived, were shot, or were run over by cars. We thought of what an enormous pile of bones that would be, and then we thought of the spiritual about the dry bones coming to life. Based on a passage from the Book of Ezekiel in the Bible, the song (which has many versions) goes like this:

Them bones, them bones, them dry bones,
Them bones, them bones, them dry bones,
Them bones, them bones, them dry bones,
Oh, hear the word of the Lord!

The foot bone connected to the ankle bone,
The ankle bone connected to the leg bone,
The leg bone connected to the knee bone,
Oh, hear the word of the Lord!

The knee bone connected to the thigh bone,
The thigh bone connected to the hip bone,
The hip bone connected to the back bone,
Oh, hear the word of the Lord!

The back bone connected to the shoulder bone,
The shoulder bone connected to the neck bone,
The neck bone connected to the head bone,
Oh, hear the word of the Lord!

This song, known by schoolchildren in the United States, is unforgettable. The version they learn in school, however, does not even hint at the part of the story where the Spirit of the Lord breathed life into the great multitude of dry bones and put flesh on them, raising them to their feet and to life. In fact, the public school version omits the last line of each verse, often replacing it with something like, "Oh mercy how they scare!" We didn't realize this until young Catholic Workers told us they knew the song, but had never heard the last line.

Ezekiel's vision of the bones coming to life is a prefiguring of the resurrection of the body. We reflect on the Church's teaching that, as Christ rose from the dead, so will our souls be reunited with our resurrected, incorruptible bodies on the Last Day. Judgment Day will be a great day for Casa Juan Diego, the day when all these bones will come together, and these bodies will be raised, an exceedingly great host of the poorest and the wounded.

Injured, sick, and lost immigrants and refugees continually arrive at our doors or call us on the telephone. Sometimes their bones are broken or gone, and sometimes they are alone because of mental illness. The passage from St. Matthew's Gospel in chapter 25 impels us to respond to the Lord in the poorest, the abandoned, the injured, the sick, and the homeless.

One of the main means of travel for immigrants is by freight train. Groups gather to wait for the trains in Mexico and later in the United States. When the trains start up, they run to jump on. Some do not make it; the powerful wind current created by the train sucks them underneath.

When train accidents happen in the south of Mexico, which they frequently do, the immigrants never make it to the United States, but when they occur at the border, the immigrants might end up at Casa Juan Diego. Some of our guests have had their legs or feet cut off by trains on their journey north or damaged so badly they had to be amputated. Sometimes we have been able to purchase prostheses even though they are very expensive. They make it possible for those who have lost legs, arms, or eyes to walk again or be presentable again in society.

Ernesto wrote about his journey after he crossed into Mexico from Guatemala (*Houston Catholic Worker* 1995):

> We continued until we boarded the freight train, which the immigrants call the iron beast. In the train station of Ciudad Hidalgo I asked others who were there waiting for the train, "Hey, *compa'*, what's happening? When does the train leave?" They told me, laughing, the train has no hour or day. You just have to wait until night. Fortunately, we began to see movement in the train that would leave for Tapachula and then Tonalá, Chiapas, at approximately 2:00 a.m. In the early morning the train left, and with it hundreds of migrants. I didn't know where they all came from. They came out from all sides like ants. We came about fifteen in each car. When I looked out on the sides of the train, I felt like it was a carnival of people.
>
> When we came close to Tapachula on this stretch, the assailants started to come out, from car to car of the train, assaulting the people. If you don't give them anything, they throw you off the train. I saw many people thrown off the train and saw the men put their hands all over the women and even rape them.

When one sees these things, one feels impotent in not being able to do anything, since they are up to 30 gangsters and delinquents. The only thing one can do is ask God to protect us.

We got on the train enthusiastically, not knowing what was awaiting us. Upon arriving in Tlaxcala, there was an Immigration and army check point and we all jumped off the train. I jumped off and then I saw my friend, the guy from the Port of La Libertad, who was walking along the side of the train, and he didn't jump. Then he jumped and when he fell, the wheels of the train cut his two feet. When we picked him up he cried out, "My feet! The train took them off!"

Seeing this, I went running to a telephone to call the ambulance. The press arrived first. We did not want the press. At this moment we needed an ambulance to help my friend. When the police and the ambulance arrived, the others left and told me, "Let's go, because Immigration will come."

"No," I told them, "If they deport me, it doesn't matter, but I will not leave my *compadre* alone.

They took him to a hospital to recuperate. I had to sign so they could amputate his foot. Later, the *Grupo Beta* took charge of sending him back to El Salvador. After this, I was afraid to continue on the train.

The freight trains affect the lives of countless people. An immigrant woman who came to Casa Juan Diego witnessed the bloody sight of a train consuming her friend:

The train was coming and we went to take it. We began the race behind the train to get up on it. I was ahead and he behind, and I succeeded in getting up the stairs of one of the cars. I went up as high as I could so that he could get on the same car. He tried once, but couldn't make it, and the train was picking up speed. In his desperation, he began to run in the opposite direction of the train and tried to grab the stairs of the third car, where I had already gotten on. I was able to see that he couldn't catch hold of the stairs and he hit himself on the corner of the car and one leg slipped under the train and it was cut off. I was so sad I wanted to cry. I didn't get off because the train was already going very fast. I was able to see the blood, and my friend picking the blood up with his hands.

The Rio Grande, a milestone on the journey of immigrants, has become a graveyard for countless people who tried to cross and were swept away by the waters. The Rio Bravo—the name of the Rio Grande on the Mexican side—may look shallow and narrow, but where the refugees and immigrants cross, it is deep enough to drown in, especially if there has been heavy rain and the current is strong. Each year, the Rio Grande seizes hundreds fleeing war, poverty, and violence—people who will not be seen or heard from again.

One day in 1984, a young woman from Guatemala came in and said she must talk with us. She had a problem. The clothes on her back, which were all she had, were hardly dry when she arrived on the doorsteps of Casa Juan Diego. Maria was eighteen years old. Her lifelong friend from her *colonia* did not make it. Juan could not swim. He escaped from the problems and oppression in his own country, but could not escape the waters that divide us. The coyote did not attempt to save Juan; in fact, he threatened to kill Maria if she breathed a word of Juan's death to anyone. Juan's father kept writing to Maria to ask about his only son, having received her address from her family. Someone had to tell him about his son's burial in the cemetery that is the Rio Grande. She asked our help: "How do I tell his family?"

One Wednesday evening before Mass, a young man wept as he told his story of losing his best friend to the Rio Grande. Several young men had saved the young man, but they could not save his friend, who had said he knew how to swim. A few weeks later, a Honduran mother of three children told how her husband had been swept up by the Rio Grande—and lost forever. He was trying to cross with his five-year-old son. Three youths saved the son, but they could not save the father. A passerby took the five-year-old back across the river to Mexican immigration, who, through the Honduran consulate, put an ad in a Honduran newspaper. Through this ad, the mother and child were reunited and brought to Casa Juan Diego.

A woman called to ask if anyone knew the names or homeland of three young men who had recently drowned in the Rio Grande, swollen with floodwaters because of recent rains. Could we see if the immigrants and refugees at dinner knew them? The guests reported that they knew the name of only one, but that the three were from Honduras. The caller felt better, since her missing brother was from Guatemala.

Julio Cesar jumped from a train in Odem, Texas, but slipped and fell under the wheels, losing a leg. He awoke in a hospital in Corpus Christi and didn't remember a thing. Because he was undocumented, Julio could not receive disability or any government aid, and would be homeless upon discharge because he did not have proof of legality. But his hospital social worker had previously sent us guests when he worked in Victoria—and so called us now. We picked Julio Cesar up at the bus station and took him to meet Francisco, who had lost both legs to a train in Houston. Both were depressed when they arrived at Casa Juan Diego, but as their legs healed, they hoped for prostheses, which we promised to purchase for them. They turned out to be very expensive, but we had made a promise that we had to keep.

A young man named Angel jumped into a train car in Laredo to continue his journey into the United States so that he could work and send money to his wife and children, only to have iron pipes crush his foot. The Immigration Service called and asked if we could accept Angel and pay for his bus fare to Houston. We made our usual disclaimer that we have no locked doors and cannot be responsible for returning the person to Immigration; they assured us this was not a problem because they were releasing Angel on his own recognizance. We agreed and picked Angel up at the bus station late that night. The doctors in Houston hoped to save his leg and inserted a metal halo to help the bones grow back together. Angel hoped that it would heal. But after trying for weeks and months, the doctors abandoned the idea and cut off his leg.

Meanwhile, Angel participated in the activities of Casa Juan Diego. He played the guitar with us each week at Mass and attended a nearby fundamentalist church. He was very discouraged when his leg had to be amputated. When his leg healed enough, we raised the money to purchase a prosthesis. One day Angel struggled to walk on crutches, clearly handicapped; the next day, with his prosthesis, he walked across the parking lot as if nothing was wrong. Seeing him walk with his new leg filled us with joy, and Angel was given new hope.

During the 1980s, the Immigration Service called from Laredo regarding another train victim. They had a young man whose leg had been severed at mid-thigh. Would we accept him and could we pay his bus fare? We said yes and sent the fare. As soon as Oscar's wound was treated, he was put on the bus. We picked him up at the bus station at 5:30 a.m. On the way back to Casa Juan Diego, we asked how he was feeling, and he admitted he didn't feel well in spite of the painkillers. He grimaced in pain when he said, "*Es un poco fresco*"—the wound is very fresh. Fortunately, a volunteer doctor at our clinic that morning evaluated him and sent him to the hospital, where he spent two weeks because of an infection in the wound. Oscar was very ill and had a long recovery, but once he received a new leg, he was a different person. He was able to walk, albeit with difficulty because his amputation was well above the knee, but he could walk without crutches. With his prosthesis, he could begin to work and send money back to his family. Oscar told us later that he had lost his leg because, while riding the train, he had stepped out to the edge of the car to urinate, and his leg was pulled under. He removed his belt, and another fellow about to hop the train helped him to apply it as a tourniquet to slow the bleeding until he could get to the hospital.

When Luis approached Casa Juan Diego, we could not figure out his problem. He appeared drunk as he stumbled from parked car to parked car, seeking support so as not to fall. When he got past the cars, he moved to hugging the walls of our building. When we went outside to figure out what was going on and to catch him after he fell, we found that Luis was very sober. He had lost his legs below the knee from a train accident. The artificial legs he was given weren't strong enough to carry his weight and had become more and more useless and wobbly. He obviously needed new legs, but when he went to a prosthetics company, they told him that the legs would cost $2,500 each. We helped.

One of the most memorable stories is about the time Daniel came to the door and demanded to see Mark or Louise. Because he didn't get an immediate response, he became loud and vociferous. Finally, Mark came out and asked Daniel to settle down and explain his behavior. He said, "*Señor Marcos*, relax. I lost my arm in a train accident and you purchased a new arm for me. I wanted to give you the first hug with my new arm." Although Daniel was not ugly, many would have thought him so before his new prosthesis covered where his arm had been severed at the shoulder.

Situations like Jorge's always frighten us. Jorge arrived with two colostomy bags instead of a stomach. Some of the young Catholic Workers wanted to put him to bed and prevent him from moving, since he was obviously very ill. Casa Juan Diego has two houses for sick and injured men; the men we usually send there are not just temporarily ill, but probably permanently unable to work. The staff insisted that Jorge go to the sick men's house at once. The guest rebelled and demanded that he be allowed to help with the work in the house and not just sit around. He was not an invalid, he said, and insisted on going to work as a member of our co-op, which he did. He is one of our best workers, colostomy bags and all.

Others who come to us—some of whom have lived in the United States for a while—have lost an eye to disease. Sometimes early medical intervention might have prevented the loss, but the immigrants did not know how to get it until it was too late. At times, however, we can solve problems. In 2006, a hospital called to ask us to pay for home care for Roberto, who was blind. We agreed. As we got to know him, we asked how he became blind. He had no idea—suddenly he had completely lost his sight. He could not get an eligibility card for the county clinics and hospitals because he had no identification, not even from Guatemala. Through the archdiocesan clinic, we were able to get medical help for him. The doctors discovered that he had lost his sight because of cataracts. They were removed and Roberto could see again.

We have also received immigrants who have lost limbs or their sight because of untreated diabetes. They couldn't afford a doctor or sort through the bureaucracy in order to get help from a public clinic.

A few times, bones have miraculously healed themselves, even in this world. In 1992, Julio lost the sight in one of his eyes when he fell through a loose trap door and hit his head on the edge of a bathtub. The dust had not settled before his employer's lawyer arrived at the hospital with a form for Julio to sign, giving up all rights to compensation except for $500 the man offered him for the accident. Julio signed against his will. Not coming from a litigious society like ours, he sadly said, "*Lo que no es de uno, no es de uno*" ("What doesn't belong to a person, doesn't belong to them"). Julio was dizzy for weeks. The doctors wanted to perform surgery on his injured sinuses. They had given up on his eye. Julio agreed to the surgery until they warned him about the possibility of getting AIDS if a blood transfusion proved necessary. Not much of a chance, but a chance in a million, and hospitals were required by law to notify patients and obtain a signature. Julio refused the surgery. He would take the chance of surviving without surgery on his damaged sinuses. At least he still had one good eye, he said, but if he developed a serious disease, he might not live at all. When he returned to us, he could see only out of one eye, and his wrist and arm hurt badly. At his next appointment, the doctor checked Julio's blind eye. He could see, though not completely. Without surgery, his sight was slowly coming back. That day the eye doctor also discovered, three weeks after the accident, that his wrist was broken and now had to be rebroken and set. At the next conference of ophthalmologists at the medical center, all the attending doctors took turns looking at Julio's eye and Casa Juan Diego's miracle.

Martín was living in the back of a truck and did not know he had diabetes until his foot had to be amputated. He was referred to us by Adult Protective Services, the arm of the government assigned to help adults who have no one to care for them. They said they could not help him at all because he did not have papers. Martín was very depressed, so we worked with the Mexican Consulate to return him to his family in Mexico.

One month in 1999, we received several calls regarding people who had nowhere to live because their bones had been literally crushed. One man's hands were crushed in a machine at his job; a woman's feet were crushed underneath a train. Another two people walked for days coming north and became very tired, so they decided to sleep along the highway. Unfortunately, a car veered off the road and ran over them.

We brought Samuel back from Ben Taub, the local county hospital. A bus had run over his foot, and it was a mass of red, swollen flesh. The hospital treated him for several days and would not release him unless we came and signed for him. At first, we thought the hospital was attempting to collect money, which we did not have at the time. In fact, it wasn't: the staff did not want to let Samuel go unless there was someone to care for him. The hospital had put Samuel on the third floor, which is almost all obstetrics, but he swore he had not given birth!

When Edwin first came to the United States from Mexico, he lived at Casa Juan Diego for a couple of weeks. During that time, he played guitar with us at our Wednesday evening Masses. He was a wonderful guitarist. A year later, we received a call from him from the hospital. He had been riding his bicycle to work. The pavement was wet from rain, and as a car approached, he slipped and the car slid. Edwin slid right under the car and was run over. The driver told him to move, but he could not. When she dragged him out, he felt a terrible pain in his back. She then fled in her car, never to be found. Edwin asked if he could come back to stay at Casa Juan Diego. He was now a quadriplegic. It was very difficult, but his wife found a way to come across the border to care for him. Later, they found a way to bring their young daughter over. Edwin could never play the guitar again, but he was able to teach his daughter to play when she got older.

At Casa Juan Diego we receive calls every day from hospitals, agencies, wives, or mothers, asking for help for people who have lost an arm or a leg, or who were stabbed or shot in the back while being robbed, or who were unconscious because of an embolism. Sometimes these people are mentally ill. Others have broken backs or spinal injuries that left their legs and sometimes arms dangling uselessly over the side of the bed. For several years, we have been averaging over seventy such sick and injured patients for whom we provide the cost of their care. If they have no family, we assist by paying for their care in a personal care home. If there is family, we help the family with rent, food, and medical supplies. Sometimes, if there is family in another country to care for them, we have helped the injured person return home and have even continued to send a little money each month so that they might survive.

A call came from a policeman who was desperately trying to find help for a quadriplegic man in a wheelchair. He was an honest policeman: he didn't pretend that the injured man was in good health and that all he needed was a place to park his wheelchair. He put it right out there—"This guy is a mess. He can't use his arms or legs and obviously his diaper hasn't been changed. He is half-sitting, half-sliding off his wheelchair. What can you do? No one will help." Since there were no other resources in the City of Houston to help, we said yes.

Sometimes undocumented workers who have made it to Houston in one piece have later fallen from scaffolding while on a construction site and are now paraplegics or quadriplegics. As they hit the pavement, they became casualties of Houston's rapid growth in the 1990s and the first decade of the twenty-first century. Juan fell off a third-story scaffold, broke his back, and now has no use of his arms or legs, no income, and no one to care for him. The contractor had hired Juan for low wages, long hours, and hard work, and had provided him with little safety.

Santiago fell off a scaffold, broke his back in several places, and is now completely paralyzed. He can only talk and see; he cannot move any other part of his body. The only hope for his future is a wheelchair that he can control with a stick for his mouth. Santiago may have difficulty obtaining such a wheelchair. Families and even the county hospital workers call us begging for wheelchairs because there is no funding available to help immigrants who cannot walk. We advertise in our CW newspaper that we need wheelchairs, and people bring them to us a few at a time. We give them out as soon as someone asks for them. In some situations, we purchase wheelchairs for the paralyzed. Motorized wheelchairs are much harder to come by and are very expensive.

Workers who have given many years of their lives to Houston's workforce are abandoned after they are injured. This denial of responsibility leaves many sick and injured people—who had been very productive workers at minimal wages and long hours—without care or support. Their family and friends are faced with the prospect of giving up their jobs to care for their sick relatives, thus having no means of support for themselves or the sick.

Sofia felt bad about calling Casa Juan Diego to ask for help. She said she had never asked anyone for help before, because her husband had always worked and taken care of her and their six daughters. Then he had an accident at work, and now she was caring for him. He was paralyzed, had brain damage, and was in a coma. She couldn't work because the children ranged in age from two to seventeen. The neighbors were helping, but she needed financial assistance. In the several years since then, Casa Juan Diego has been paying her rent every month. On an encouraging note: The oldest daughter now works and goes to college part-time, even though she is undocumented.

Tomás came to the door with a desperate question. "My father fell off a scaffold and is on a breathing machine. They sent him home that way. We finally got an appointment at the county hospital, but we have no idea how we could transport him there. The hospital where he was received in the trauma center did not give us any information on where to find transportation. What can we do?" We did not know either. The City of Houston provides a wonderful service called Metro Lift for the disabled, but this family had never heard of it, much less applied for it. We told them how to apply for it when they went to see the doctor. However, that did not solve the immediate problem. They had to get to a doctor. We tried to think of what to do and began calling private ambulances. When we called, we were told that 911 or a specialized ambulance service would have to handle the transport because the others could not handle a breathing machine. The patient's son was able to explain that the hospital had instructed them on how to disconnect the breathing machine and attach the oxygen tanks during transportation. They could now use the private ambulance service at $150.00 plus $2.85 per mile. Once they had the information, the family was able to come together to pay the ambulance.

Other immigrant workers have had their fingers cut off in work accidents. A nurse called one day from a Houston hospital to tell us to be nice to Pedro. He had lost all his fingers on one hand in an accident and wasn't coping very well. Like many immigrants, he had been recruited to work in the aftermath of Hurricane Katrina in Louisiana, where he was injured. At that time, no hospital there had the staff to work with him. When Mark arrived at the men's house to announce Pedro's arrival, we met a new guest, Juan, who extended his hand when introduced. He, too, had lost his fingers in an accident. He offered a stub instead of a hand.

We found Miguel wandering around a vacant lot near one of our houses. One side of his head had long hair; the other side was clean-shaven, perfect for punk rock, except for the awful gash on the clean-shaven side. He also had a large cut on his arm and, where his fingers used to be, stitches like little bowties that closed off what was left of his fingers. Miguel had fallen out of a tree he was trimming and became entangled with a chain saw. He was lucky his employer took him to the hospital. Many times employers drop injured men off at Casa Juan Diego and run.

Vidal awoke, after a period of unconsciousness, with no hands and only one foot after a worksite accident in which his metal ladder fell on live wires and burned up his hands and leg. He will receive nothing. The contractor who hired him refused to offer any assistance.

A hospital emergency room called us about a patient who was found on the street, disoriented and wearing a diaper. Could we help? He didn't like wearing diapers and kept taking them off. He was a victim of brain damage from a car accident. Ever since, we've been paying each month for his stay in a long-term care home.

Hardly a week goes by that Casa Juan Diego doesn't receive a worker, black and blue from being robbed. Worse yet are the deep stab wounds or broken bones that occur during the robberies. Men often come to us with fractured skulls—baseball bats were big some years.

We also receive or help patients who are HIV-positive or who have full-blown AIDS. Several years ago, we received a call from New Orleans asking if we would receive a man with meningitis. He was recovering, but it was going to take time. Of course, we said yes. When he arrived, however, we were surprised to discover that he actually had AIDS. They were afraid to tell us on the telephone because they thought we would not receive him. The truth would not have affected our decision, but it certainly affected how we would get services for him. Carlos was very ill. The disease was attacking his eyes, and he could hardly see. We were able to help him get medical care, and he is with us to this day.

Sometimes we are called upon to console those who have just discovered that they are HIV-positive. One woman was overcome with sadness because she had just learned that her husband had infected her with AIDS. A man was broken up because his wife had contracted AIDS from working in a *cantina*.

Global poverty contributes to the difficulties that immigrants with AIDS face even in the United States. An HIV-positive woman who came for help with her rent told us that much was unavailable to her because she was unable to obtain a passport from the Honduran Consulate here. We asked what documents she had to present, wondering if she could write to her family in Honduras to obtain what she needed. She had her birth certificate, but needed another document. We asked about her elementary school records, because the consulates here usually accept those as the second document. She said she had never been to school even for one day because her parents did not have the resources to send her.

There are no federal disability funds available for immigrants without valid Social Security numbers and residency cards, no matter now many years they have worked here and contributed to the economy. The injured immigrant worker is basically homeless. This, of course, means that the government saves millions of dollars by not helping immigrant workers find housing once they are disabled. The state of Texas does have a victims' assistance fund for crime victims, and a few lucky people have received help from this fund. Many do not, because the paperwork is so complicated. When injured people do receive help, the hospital, of course, receives most of the money. TV news reports from time to time that the Texas legislature transfers the majority of the money from the victims' assistance fund to other projects and categories in the state budget.

There is no one else to assist the poorest of the sick and injured with supplies, such as catheters, colostomy bags, diapers, gloves, gauze for wounds, special bandages to heal the bedsores caused by sitting in wheelchairs, or tracheotomy tubes. This is another facet of Casa Juan

Diego's assistance to the injured. Some have come to Casa Juan Diego to ask for help after they have reused catheters too many times out of desperation or have reused bandages and have developed infections.

We have learned that it's one thing to be against euthanasia in theory, another to give practical help to the actual folks caring for the wounded and ill. The Sisters of Charity in Houston have helped to provide a visiting nurse for patients. When they have visited, the nurses have been overwhelmed by the high quality of care that the families of injured immigrants give their relatives. Whether the immigrant is a quadriplegic or in a coma, he or she receives loving care. These caregivers are unsung heroes, giving their lives for their family members.

Alejandro had suffered a stroke that completely affected one side. He was unable to talk or walk—he sort of shuffled. So it was an awful sight when he was escorted to jail by two burly policemen, twice his size. The police had come to Casa Juan Diego to ask for him. We were glad we could say he was not there, but they found him a block or so away. We questioned the policemen about taking a man injured so badly. It was unclear why Alejandro, who had been with us a number of months, was suddenly carted off to jail as a hardened criminal. Where were the police all this time?

Alejandro had been sent to us because he was homeless upon discharge from the hospital. He had been shot in the head, which caused his stroke and his inability to speak.

Jail was Alejandro's home for a number of months as he awaited the court's decision. Christmas came and went. We talked to people at the court. The court-appointed attorney told us that if we tried to do anything, it would only prolong Alejandro's time in jail. We became desperate, as Easter approached with no word of release. Alejandro needed a home, not a jail. Finally, the court dismissed all the charges against him. They weren't sure if they even had the right man. In fact, the date on Alejandro's birth certificate was different from the one of the man they had been looking for. When he came back to Casa Juan Diego, still barely able to speak, the first thing he did was to show us his birth certificate.

Alejandro was released on Good Friday, still unable to speak, in time to prepare for Easter Sunday and resurrection. He still can hardly talk and walks very slowly. Nevertheless, he is one of the most reliable and helpful people at Casa Juan Diego. He especially helps other wounded men. The gunshot to his head did not interfere with that part of his brain that says we should help others.

Another group that comes to us is the mentally ill. Research has shown that mental illness has its roots in a chemical imbalance in the brain. Medication can help the mentally ill to manage their symptoms and to have a fruitful life, but it cannot heal them entirely. We trust that they will be healed in the resurrection of the body.

The mentally ill who are undocumented and do not speak English often find it difficult to access mental health services—and so they are brought to Casa Juan Diego. We are fortunate that Mark has years of experience working as a psychiatric social worker before Casa Juan Diego began, so that we can make at least a preliminary assessment of need.

One day in 1984, the police brought us José. He was found lying in the middle of Washington Avenue late at night. Though he had his own room about a mile from us, he gave the police our address, which happens often. José was from a part of El Salvador where there has been much violence. He was mentally ill and thought people were against him. Hospital social workers had sent José to us for temporary placement until they could locate his family. José harassed the other guests of Casa Juan Diego when he was ill. They were afraid of him. We knew that he was harmless, but convincing others of that was difficult. We knew in our heart of hearts that no one else was going to assist us in getting medical help for José and arranging for his hospitalization. It was our responsibility. That is the problem with having a conscience.

The police had already abdicated responsibility. José was ours. At that time, the poor who were mentally ill in Houston could go only to the county hospital. There was no other place. However, that meant hours of waiting and hassle. Things have improved since.

When Mark brought José to the hospital, he began early in the morning, psyching himself up and preparing mentally for a day of waiting. It took a lot of prayer. He told the other Catholic Workers he was going to get help for José and thus would not be back for the rest of the day. They felt sorry for him. It was like going off to jail. José liked and respected Mark, but it took all the strength of the relationship to get him into the car when he knew they were going to the hospital. Mark told him the truth, but promised an awful lot. He felt guilty.

The first stop in "triage" at the hospital went well, although José was uncomfortable and began to act out. He prayed on his knees one minute and was very hostile the next. He harassed the ever-present police who brook no nonsense, but after an explanation, they allowed them to proceed. An ominous sign occurred that Mark didn't take seriously at first—the hospital couldn't find José's chart. José and Mark were sent to the second waiting area where José proceeded to soil his clothes, dress and undress, make hostile accusations, pray spread-eagle on the floor or pray on his knees with arms outstretched, and run around singing and gesturing. He had brought with him a grasshopper, which he put under his shirt, in his underwear, and in his hair. Mark said afterward that he knew he was losing his influence on José, but he stayed with him in the waiting area. People eyed Mark as much as José, wondering about both of them as Mark talked with him.

A social worker who Mark knew tried to hurry things along. They finally saw a physician, which was necessary before they could move on. Mark accompanied José, since the doctor did not speak Spanish.

Mark and José finally made it to the locked unit. It was a great relief, even though they were going to be there for a long time. The locked unit was small, with beds crowded in every nook and cranny, and patients in various stages of medical deterioration milling around, acting like staff— and being staff when someone had to be held down to be restrained. Mark stayed with José, not only because no one there spoke Spanish, but also because they told him they might not accept José. That surprised Mark.

After several hours with one or two Baylor Medical School residents going in and out and giving the appearance of being very indecisive, a young doctor who did not speak Spanish came. Mark was asked to translate for him. The doctor had many questions for José. The hardest were the presentations of riddles and sayings. Translating them into Spanish and then explaining them to José was difficult, but the doctor insisted. For example, he would say, "A rolling stone gathers no moss," Mark would translate it, and then José was to explain its meaning. (Riddles were used to assist in preparing a mental status for patients.) By the time they were finished with them, José was swinging at Mark. Mark was also becoming agitated after the long wait. He had forgotten that neither he nor José had eaten. Mark had forgotten about bringing lunch.

A number of times the young doctor asked Mark what was wrong with José. Mark described José's extreme agitation and psychotic condition. With his experience as a psychiatric social worker, Mark wanted to say, "Just label him with something like 'schizophrenic reaction, paranoid type,' and give him a good dose of phenothiazines, which usually clear up psychotic behavior." But he didn't. The resident left periodically to go to the office of his supervisor and then return with new questions.

The resident and the supervising doctor finally made their decision. They could not accept José. Mark had the same vision as you might upon hearing this news. José was ours, day and night, running through the streets of Houston, escaping his evil fantasies, and trying to escape us—but in the process getting seriously injured by fearful folks.

"Come on, you guys," Mark said.

The supervisor responded, "Just take him downtown to the judge for commitment procedures and then we can accept him."

Mark knew that at this point José would go nowhere with him and said there had to be another way. The solution was for the hospital to accept José as a voluntary patient. Mark turned to José—the same José who wouldn't get into the car to go to the hospital—and said he wanted him to commit himself voluntarily. By then, José was tired of fighting and signed the papers. After receiving medication, José stabilized and Mark went back to work.

Another person with serious problems came into the neighborhood in the early years of Casa Juan Diego. Obviously not in her right mind, Esmeralda (not her real name) was running down Washington Avenue completely nude, singing, "I am a beautiful dove." She was going to be killed by traffic. A motorcycle policeman and patrol car came. The police suggested that we take her to her family, but of course, there was no family.

Esmeralda or people like her are periodically dropped off at our place, with the escort escaping before we get a chance to talk. We were disappointed that the police did not take her to the hospital. Legally, they are the ones who can have a person hospitalized if they are a danger to themselves or to others, or if they cannot care for themselves. We have learned through experience that people who run through traffic or lie down in the middle of Washington Avenue will return to their favorite haunts and run the risk of being injured or killed.

Someone suggested that we could handle Esmeralda at Casa Juan Diego by being nice to her and giving her small chores to do, that this naked "Washington run" was just an isolated incident that "could happen to anyone." Several hours later Esmeralda returned to the streets—the middle of them—just in time for the afternoon rush hour. It seemed that, in addition to Esmeralda being run over (Houston drivers wait for no one), we now were going to lose some of our Catholic Workers who were trying to rescue her.

The police returned but they were not eager to work with us to get her to a hospital. We restated a number of times the seriousness of her condition, but the policeman kept refusing. His response was to criticize the other officer who found Esmeralda naked and didn't do anything. He also said that he couldn't take her to the hospital. *He* didn't see her do anything; therefore, *he* couldn't do anything. Finally, Mark said, "But I am telling you what she did and we have all the witnesses to testify to her need."

"You don't tell me anything!" he shouted, with a gesture that made us think of his nightstick.

Another policeman came along, the nicest guy in the world—very much in the image of the new Houston police. We talked more. I kept insisting that something would happen to Esmeralda if she didn't get treatment. The policeman checked her purse and found addresses of Casa Juan Diego and other places. The sergeant came. He let the officer complete his resource exploration of Esmeralda's purse. Finally, the sergeant said to him, "If you need to send her to the county hospital, just get the papers out of my car, and this man Zwick [Mark] can sign them if she [Esmeralda] refuses to go voluntarily." We hope that the policeman forgave us for our insistence—but we didn't want to put Esmeralda back at the mercy of Houston drivers. (Houston drivers are scary. People ask us if our work is dangerous. It is. The most dangerous part is crossing Durham at rush hour.)

On another occasion, a woman called Marta refused to go to bed at the women's and children's house, although it was late. Not only did she refuse to go to bed, she refused to even go to the second floor, the area where only women and children are permitted to enter. Marta's two-year-old son sensed her agitation and kept screaming and trying to escape her grasp. He was trying to go anywhere and to anyone. He screamed until she let him go.

Marta said there were three men upstairs—one white, one black, and one yellow—who were going to kill her. We knew that there were no men up there because the rule against men on the second floor is strictly enforced. Marta began saying that the food was full of cocaine and the lettuce was laced with marijuana. She said the young Catholic Workers had put it there. She also talked about being dead in the morning and asked us not to revive her or her son—which made us fear that she was both suicidal and homicidal.

Marta was very uncooperative. She absolutely refused to go to the hospital for help and refused to cooperate with us within the house. How could we keep her off the street? A seriously delusional person, who had a two-year-old and who didn't speak English, was not going to be treated kindly by the streets of Houston at night. One solution was to have people block the doors and windows to keep her off the streets for the night. Another was to accompany her on the streets all night to protect her and her son from thugs, thieves, and cars. We knew we had a challenge.

We called 911. They responded quickly with a fire truck with four men and an ambulance with four more paramedics—but they said they couldn't help because Marta wasn't sick; she didn't have any medical problems. We were in the middle of them, putting in our two cents worth about what Marta needed, but it didn't help.

As the firemen and paramedics were leaving, a Houston policeman entered. He had just finished his meal—or we hope he had just finished it—because he had a toothpick hanging out of the corner of his mouth, which he kept working back and forth. He took over as the firemen departed. He seemed cocky at first, but actually, it was probably self-assurance. The policeman spoke fluent Spanish. He also had experience in working with the mentally ill and had a no-nonsense approach. As Marta talked about the three men upstairs out to kill her and about the food and salad, he simply told her that it wasn't true and it was simply "crazy talk." The officer asked us many questions about her antics, about suicide ideation, and about how she got to us: actually, she had jumped out of the car of the people who were trying to bring her to Casa Juan Diego and had run to a police car, which brought her to us. He wanted to write up what happened properly. He took Marta and her son with him to get treatment, something a layman can't do if the patient is unwilling. We have never been so impressed with the Houston Police Department.

In recent years, mental health services in Harris County have greatly improved. A neuropsychiatric center provides emergency evaluation and help, and even sends out staff to the community when a person seeks or needs treatment. One day a deacon from a local parish called to ask if we could accept Julieta, a woman with three daughters—one was a baby and the other two were aged seven and nine. When Julieta arrived with the girls, she was very agitated. They had only the clothes on their backs. She wanted to go home right away to her mother in Mexico. First, she said she lived in Guerrero, and then changed it to Cuernavaca. She had no phone number, however, and we were afraid to send her without a destination.

When Louise talked with her at 8:30 p.m., she noted that Julieta looked familiar and asked if she had been to Casa Juan Diego before. The answer was yes, she knew Louise. Julieta then began to share her great anxieties: She had gone to a women's shelter two days before with her children, but couldn't bear to stay and had taken off. She thought her husband had been poisoning her food. She thought she was going crazy. She could find no peace except in prayer, but a voice in her head kept saying, "Don't pray! Don't pray!" As we conversed with her, we recognized that she needed treatment for mental illness and suggested taking her someplace to get some medication. "Okay, but I have to get my kids to one of my sisters. Can you take me right now?" The place she spoke of was twenty miles away and she had no working phone number for the sister. She kept insisting on going immediately and threatened to walk. Finally, she mentioned another sister at a closer address, and we decided to try to find the family.

We were very grateful when the family answered the door. After we explained to them that help was available at the county neuropsychiatric center, the sister's family, who had had no knowledge of her problems, expressed concern and their willingness to keep the children and take Julieta for treatment. We slept more peacefully that night with that family's help.

The volunteer doctors at Casa Juan Diego's medical clinics give invaluable assistance to immigrants. While many of the sick and injured are referred to us by hospitals, our clinics are involved in the follow-up care. In addition to seeing patients with chronic diabetes or high blood pressure or other standard clinic ailments, the doctors are called upon to take staples out of legs or heads that were placed there by emergency rooms. People bring us their prescriptions after leaving various hospitals. Private hospitals prescribe, but do not provide the medication.

Sometimes serious illnesses are discovered in our clinics. The doctor said that when Edgar came in, he looked not just yellow, but green. The doctor sent him to the lab, which later called us to say that Edgar had to go immediately to the emergency room. We checked our medical records for a telephone number. No telephone. The address was not too far away by Houston standards, so we got into the car and drove over to tell him. When we got there, however, the yard was fenced, the gate was locked, and a dog was barking at us from behind the fence. We tried going to the neighbors to see if someone could help us, but they closed their doors. Finally, a small child's face appeared at the window, and soon the patient himself came out. He had been sleeping. Apparently he slept a lot, even when he was babysitting while his wife worked. We gave him the news along with money to take a taxi to the hospital.

The next day Edgar's wife came to tell us he had been hospitalized to receive blood transfusions and to ask for help for the family while he was in the hospital. Within a couple of weeks, he was diagnosed with liver cancer. He had surgery and will wear a colostomy bag for the rest of his life. We hope he can recover from the depression this has caused him.

As attitudes toward immigrants in the United States seemed to harden and as harangues against immigrants on talk shows and television shows became more common, we wondered whether we would be able to continue to serve so many sick and injured. We tried again to follow the methods of the saints, the methods of Peter Maurin, praying and telling people what we were doing. Our Christmas letter of appeal each year is filled with the stories of the sick and injured, and those left behind from immigration raids. Readers of our newspaper and our Christmas letters have not only continued to respond, but also increased their contributions.

We never realized that we would be dealing with death and burial until one of our guests became seriously ill and died. We turned again to the Sisters of Charity for a recommendation for a funeral home. They referred us to a funeral director who provided an inexpensive burial. The funeral entourage included two limousines and our van, filled with a number of our guests, one person sicker than the other with diseases and broken bones. The funeral director decided to add dignity to the trip by getting a police escort with sirens as we followed our brother in the hearse to the cemetery. Getting everyone to the grave provided by the archdiocese's Office of Catholic Cemeteries was difficult, as some had limited ability to walk, but they made it, albeit slowly. The men had no right to be here while alive, but apparently had the right to be buried in the ground, free at last.

Each November at Casa Juan Diego, we celebrate a Mass for the Day of the Dead, a celebration important in Mexico and Central

America, which encompasses All Saints' Day and All Souls' Day. The skeletons and sugar *calaveras* ("skulls") on the special altar decorated for this day remind us of the dry bones in the Book of Ezekiel. The Day of the Dead is not a day of sadness and mourning, but a joyful affirmation of the very heart of our religion—a celebration of life everlasting. While our guests cannot go to the cemetery where their loved ones are buried, they can pray the liturgy of the Church for them and be conscious of the Communion of Saints, knowing that one day they will be united not only in faith and love, but with transformed bodies.

The Bible passage of the vision of the dry bones from the Book of Ezekiel, which inspired the song "Them Bones," foreshadows how the Lord will bring all the dry bones together again one day and put life in the raised bodies:

> The hand of the LORD came upon me and he led me out in the spirit of the LORD, set me down in the center of the plain, which was now filled with bones. He made me walk among them in every direction; so that I saw how many they were on the surface of the plain. How dry they were! And he asked me: Son of man, can these bones come to life? "Lord GOD," I answered, "You alone know that." Then he said to me: Prophesy over these bones, and say to them: Dry bones, hear the word of the LORD! Thus says the Lord GOD to these bones: See! I will bring spirit into you, that you may come to life. I will put sinews upon you, make flesh grow over you, cover you with skin, and put spirit in you so that you may come to life, and know that I am the LORD."
>
> I prophesied as I had been told, and even as I was prophesying, I heard a noise; it was a rattling as the bones came together, bone joining bone. I saw the sinews and the flesh come upon them, and the skin cover them, but there was no spirit in them. Then he said to me, Prophesy to the spirit, prophesy, son of man, and say to the spirit: Thus says the Lord GOD: From the four winds come, O spirit, and breathe into these slain that they may have life. I prophesied as he told

me, and the spirit came into them; they came alive, and stood upright, a vast army....

Then you shall know that I am the LORD, when I open your graves and have you rise from them, O my people. I will put my spirit in you that you may live. (Ezek 37:1–10, 13–14)

11

DEPORTATION IS A SIN

One of the first questions asked at Casa Juan Diego by groups that visit us is this: Do we help illegal immigrants become legal?

The fees for beginning the process of legalization went up astronomically in 2007 and 2008, making it difficult for anyone to complete his or her application. However, worse than the increase in the cost is the fact that it is impossible for most people to even begin the process. Under present laws, very few qualify to become residents or citizens. The path to legal immigration is closed, for all practical purposes. This leaves people in a state of limbo, unable to establish a normal life without documents, unable to visit family in their home countries because the return journey is filled with dangers of all kinds, not the least of which is the threat of imprisonment and deportation. Even for those who have been able to sponsor family members, the waiting period for their loved ones is often up to sixteen years.

No one in their right mind can say that the terrible, dangerous journey undocumented immigrants have to make from their home countries to the United States is a good thing. No one can say that the separation and destruction of marriages and families of undocumented immigrants is a good thing. It would be better for them to stay home. But they can't and they won't as long as there is no future—or worse, no present—for them there. The days of people quietly starving to death are waning. The desperate poor of the world are on the move.

Both liberal and conservative theologians say that desperate parents have the right to take some food from those who have plenty in order to prevent their own children from starving. This is one of the first lessons of the seventh commandment: the *right to life* comes before the *right to possess*. The *Catechism of the Catholic Church* restates this ancient teaching (no. 2408):

The seventh commandment forbids theft, that is, usurping another's property against the reasonable will of the owner. There is no theft if consent can be presumed or if refusal is contrary to reason and the universal destination of goods. This is the case in obvious and urgent necessity when the only way to provide for immediate, essential needs (food, shelter, clothing...) is to put at one's disposal and use the property of others.

In his message for World Migration Day in 2000, Pope John Paul II called for a change of mentality toward immigrants and criticized "states with a relative abundance [that] tend to tighten their borders under pressure from a public opinion disturbed by the inconveniences that accompany the phenomenon of immigration." The Holy Father indicated that this attitude amounts to tunnel vision on the part of the developed world, which fails to see the "migration of the desperate" that obliges many men and women without a future to abandon their countries amid a thousand dangers.

We know from our experience the damage that deportation can do to individuals and families. Even so, we were surprised when we discovered that the Second Vatican Council had listed deportation as one of the most serious sins, along with murder, abortion, slavery, and the selling of women and children:

> Whatever is opposed to life itself, such as any type of murder, genocide, abortion, euthanasia or willful self-destruction; whatever violates the integrity of the human person, such as mutilation, torments inflicted on body or mind, attempts to coerce the will itself; whatever insults human dignity, such as subhuman living conditions, arbitrary imprisonment, **deportation** [emphasis ours], slavery, prostitution, the selling of women and children; as well as disgraceful working conditions, where men are treated as mere tools for profit, rather than as free and responsible persons; all these things and others of their like are infamies indeed. They poison human society, but they do more harm to those who practice them than those who suffer from the injury. Moreover, they are a supreme dishonor to the Creator. (Pastoral Constitution on the Church in the Modern World, *Gaudium et spes*, no. 27)

John Paul II reiterated this list of serious sins in two of his encyclicals, *Veritatis Splendor* (no. 80) and *Evangelium Vitae* (no. 3).

In recent years, raids on businesses and homes resulting in massive deportations have become the norm. In 2007, newswires reported that six million families had been affected by deportations. With the threat of deportation always before them, undocumented immigrants constantly face possible disruption of their lives, with no security for the future. They are treated as a disposable people—like disposable diapers. Raids have traditionally taken place at the request of employers who no longer need their immigrant workers, or when the workers attempted to organize for better conditions or wages.

Here are just a few people with deportation-related problems who have come to Casa Juan Diego:

> Maria, an eighteen-year-old mother, came to ask for help with rent or a place to stay for herself and her baby because her husband had been deported. We took her in.
>
> Jorge, desperately worried, asked our help in locating his wife, who was mentally ill. He had been deported and had just returned, only to find that she had disappeared while he was gone. We were unable to find her.
>
> Alma came to the door with her husband's brother to ask for help from our clinic. She was seven months pregnant and had been unable to receive prenatal care in any government clinic because she had no ID, no paperwork of any kind. Her husband, the family breadwinner, had been deported. Alma was very worried about her baby and began to weep as she spoke of trying to get some medical care. We were able to get help for Alma.
>
> Three children—two teenagers and a fifth grader—came to us by themselves in 2008. Their parents had been deported. The kids insisted that their parents had been apprehended, not at work, but simply walking down the street. With the help of a neighbor woman, we helped support the children. The parents tried for months to return but were unsuccessful.
>
> A man with a disabled son was desperate for work and watched as someone offered day laborers $8.00 an hour for a job in another part of the city. He didn't go with them. He felt lucky: it turned out to have been a ploy by Immigration.

A mother came to Casa Juan Diego because the building manager had locked her out of her apartment for nonpayment of rent. Her husband had been deported the month before. The doctor had told her that she was on the verge of having a stroke and should be hospitalized. But she couldn't leave her three children alone; instead she was taking pain medication and a blood thinner. We tried to get to the bottom of the situation, in order to understand her options. We learned that the family had left Guatemala to come to the United States when the oldest boy (age fourteen) was threatened if he did not join a gang. He was beaten up twice. We asked, "Do you want to go back to Guatemala to join your husband?" She replied, "I'm afraid my son will be killed like the other boy in the neighborhood who refused to join the gang." Over a year later, the husband told her that he was starting out to try to come back to the United States. He was never heard from again.

The huge increase in deportations and imprisonments in the first decade of the twenty-first century was not publicized until after it had begun in earnest. Citizens gradually became aware of the massive stealth immigration raids all around the country as word spread of the children left behind when their parents were deported.

Sara was deported a number of years ago to El Salvador without her baby. She, like all women in the Houston area who were awaiting deportation at that time, was imprisoned in the Liberty County jail many miles away without legal representation. She did not know that, to prevent being separated from her child, all she had to do was have someone take the baby to the Salvadoran Consulate to obtain travel papers and then take the baby to the airport in time for the scheduled immigration flight. Although the INS would allow someone to help at the last minute, there was no one available. By the time we learned of it, it was too late. The baby was taken to Child Protective Services.

In raids on workplaces or homes since 2006, children have often been torn from their mothers and fathers and placed in the custody of Child Protective Services, perhaps never to be seen by their parents again. Hundreds of children have been separated from their parents because of these deportations. When parents are picked up in a raid during the day, there is no one to receive the children after school or from baby sitters. Elderly people have been left alone. One of the most dramatic stories was that of a seven-month-old infant who ended up in the hospital for dehydration—he had been breastfed and refused to drink the formula given to him while his mother was in custody. Social workers from Massachusetts have traveled to Texas to visit deportation centers to plead that mothers be reunited with their children.

Employees of Child Protective Services declare that they must do a study of the home in the parents' country of origin to see if the children could be returned to the deported parent. It is hard to imagine that CPS in the United States would return children if the parents have no permanent home in their country, perhaps no home at all any longer, having lived and worked here for years. It is also hard to imagine that our government would return children to their parents if they live in poverty, without running water. The parents came here in the first place because of their poverty, to make a better life for their children.

Not only have the raids created an atmosphere of terror , but there has been a campaign by anti-immigrant groups and ICE (Immigration Customs and Enforcement) to redefine undocumented immigrants as criminals and imprison them. The campaign has included creating more jail space to house more immigrants for longer periods. ICE responded to the objection that there was no room for so many detainees by renting jail space all around the country, where sheriffs have been pleased to receive federal money and have sometimes built new jails for their counties, as well as more detention centers, just for that.

A man came to our door to ask for help with bus fare to his family in another state. He did not have a penny. As we talked, we discovered that he had been imprisoned for three months in the Livingston County jail ninety miles away because, when he was stopped by police for a traffic question, he did not have his permanent residence card on his person. He had walked all ninety miles to get to Casa Juan Diego. A lawyer told us that the detention was against the law. The law states that a person not carrying their residency card can be held for forty-eight hours, no more. But who will defend immigrants held in secrecy in county jails? We helped the exhausted man with his bus fare.

Francisca came to Casa Juan Diego to beg for a place to stay with her three children; her husband had been deported for not paying traffic tickets. Any undocumented person who lands in the Harris County

Jail—as well as in many others—may be deported, no matter how small the traffic ticket, even in the case of mistaken arrest.

The expense of imprisoning people is staggering. We couldn't understand the approach of imprisoning more people who were not criminals, building more prisons, and hiring more guards—until we discovered that this is a new business, which, ironically, is thought to be beneficial to the economy. Detention centers have been privatized and are run by corporations, like the Corrections Corporation of America and the GEO Group, who compete for contracts. The government lists not only detention centers but privatized prisons in general as a part of the gross domestic product, showing the outpouring of federal funds for individual gain as "economic growth," instead of the drain on the economy and on human persons that it actually is.

A grand jury in Willacy County in South Texas indicted former Vice President Dick Cheney and former attorney general Alberto Gonzales in 2008 on charges of complicity in the abuse of prisoners in privatized detention centers. The charges were dismissed, but the reality behind the indictment is frightening. Various news services (PR Newswire–U.S. Newswire and AFP) reported that the grand jury indicted Cheney for profiting from the abuse of prisoners by investing $85 million in a mutual fund that holds shares of for-profit prisons—including detention centers. The indictment said this was a direct conflict of interest because Cheney had influence over the federal contracts awarded to the prison companies. The indictment alleged that Gonzalez participated by using his position to stop investigations into wrongdoings, including assaults committed in for-profit prisons in Texas.

Bureaucracy does not necessarily run things well. However, when prisons are moved to the private sector and are on the stock market, the primary motivation becomes profit. Control and oversight may not exist, and concern for the welfare of persons is minimized, even if the detainees are babies or young children.

The public does not have access to the same information on privatized prisons that hold government prisoners—which is what undocumented immigrants are considered to be—the way it has access to information on public prisons. Not only is it difficult to do research on these prisons, it is often difficult if not impossible for families to find relatives who are jailed.

The Associated Press reported in 2008 that the Corrections Corporation of America spent $2.5 million lobbying the federal government in 2007. The CCA has prisons for citizens as well as detention centers. According to the AP article, reprinted in the blog of *Forbes Magazine*, the lobbying of the federal government came in three major areas: (1) lobbying to privatize the Bureau of Indian Affairs prison system; (2) lobbying against the Public Safety Act, which would outlaw private prisons; and (3) lobbying against the Private Prison Information Act, which would give the public the same access to private prison information as public prisons. These corporations are spending millions to lobby Congress and state governments with the very millions given to them by the government.

A large number of children try to come to the United States alone. Most do not make it here, and among those who do, the majority are apprehended and jailed. Fortunately, for some, charitable agencies like Catholic Charities in Houston have contracts with ICE to house the children. Others are not so fortunate. Juan José, a Latin American teenage immigrant who was being held in the INS Detention Center in Houston some years ago, wept as he told his story. For all his life, he had fulfilled the promise he made to his mother of saying three Hail Marys each night for purity, only to lose his virginity to a forty-nine-year-old criminal in a detention center.

In the past, immigrants or refugees often received a piece of paper on arrival that allowed them to travel until their deportation hearing. They didn't understand, thinking that it was permission to be in the United States. If they did not appear in court (the documents were in English), they were judged in absentia and "sentenced" without their knowledge to deportation. Now those that are apprehended at the border are immediately imprisoned. Those who build our homes, clean our offices and hotel rooms, work on our landscapes, and manufacture the inexpensive goods we demand are lumped with some of the worst criminals in this country. Documents on the Web site of U.S. Homeland Security promise that those who are imprisoned will be "safely held." This is not true. Immigrants are cruelly treated as criminals.

Deportation hearings in Texas are held by technology—people do not have a real court hearing. The immigrant, the refugee, is in detention, and the judge is in a city many miles away. The immigrant has no representation, no voice. Everything is done by TV cameras. This might be called one of great misuses of technology of our time.

Families with children tell us how they have been held in darkness, in isolation, in terrible cold for at least three days upon arrival at a detention center after crossing the border. Even after the ACLU won a suit against the government for the inappropriate treatment of children at the infamous Hutto prison in Texas for immigrant families, the Sanchez family told us how their children lost weight, were ill, and were emotionally traumatized there. The mother said, "All of the guards yelled at us that we were criminals and treated us as if we were less than human. They said they were going to take our children, that they were not our children, that we had brought them here to sell them. They woke me up every hour saying they were going to take my children. I said, 'Over my dead body!' I slept in front of the doorway so they could not take them."

When the Sanchezes arrived at Casa Juan Diego, after finally being released on their own recognizance before their asylum hearing, our staff had to reassure these terrified children many times that they were not going to be hauled off by police when they went to school. The eight-year-old had been quite plump, but when the family arrived, both children were skinny. They ate several servings at each meal. When the mother cautioned them to get used to having just one serving since they were going to school, the girls said, "No, it's okay. We are eating in case Immigration picks us up. We will have eaten and won't have to starve."

There was a time when people could fly from their country to another, with a stopover in a U.S. airport, without a problem. No longer. Several years ago, a mother and daughter fleeing Sri Lanka were on their way to Canada to join relatives there. They did not know that the travel agent had routed them through Houston. When they arrived at the airport with a short wait for the other flight, Immigration stopped them. They could not continue their flight to Canada. Fortunately, in this one case, the Immigration officials allowed them to come to Casa Juan Diego, and we were able to work with a refugee group at the Canadian border to get them across. Now even that is no longer possible. A law was passed here that demands that refugees apply for asylum in the first country where they land.

The possibility of humanitarian exceptions was almost entirely eliminated with a cruel federal immigration law in 1996. When that law was implemented, Joe Vail, a friend of Casa Juan Diego, resigned as an immigration judge in Houston. He no longer had leeway in deciding cases and could not make a humanitarian contribution; he felt he could do more working in the community and became a professor of immigration law at the University of Houston. The immigrant community lost an important advocate when Joe died prematurely in 2008.

There was a time when immigration officers did not imprison women who were with child. They would ask us to take them in. This is becoming a dim memory. Now the women have to give birth in prison. There was also a time when people in wheelchairs were not imprisoned, and when hardship cases were recognized and treated accordingly.

In December of 2005, we had just returned from visiting our men's houses for the sick, where many of our guests are disabled and rejected by our society, only to read in the *Houston Chronicle* (December 12, 2005) that the House of Representatives had passed bill H.R. 4437, which would declare all of those men common criminals, subject to a year in prison because they were undocumented. They, like twelve million other undocumented people in the United States, would become felons if that bill became law.

According to that bill, not only would the immigrants receive prison terms, but also anyone who helped them. It mandated the expansion of what constitutes smuggling, harboring, or assisting immigrants—giving a cigarette or a sandwich or a glass of water could make one a felon too. Mandatory prison sentences of up to five years would be imposed on employers, on members of church groups, and on workers in social service agencies who assisted immigrants with their most basic needs. Helping the poor would be considered treason.

It was clear that to implement such a law, new offices would have to be set up throughout the country to receive reports of aliens. Emergency room doctors could report the very sickest to be taken to prison. In addition, teachers could report undocumented immigrants, following the tradition in Communist countries of using children: there, teachers reported parents who disagreed with the government.

We publicized the information as much as we could on our Web site, in our newspaper, and with small groups. Supporters of Casa Juan Diego asked, Where did this sudden increase in hostility and hatred for immigrants come from? How could this poisonous, nativist atmosphere have developed? These friends of Casa Juan Diego were people who believed, with Dorothy Day, that "Catholics may not allow their souls to be clouded with greed, selfishness, and hate. If a man hates his neighbor he is hating Christ."[1]

With the passage of H.R. 4437, we again faced the question: Would we keep doing this work if it became law? Would all of the Catholic Workers be arrested and jailed for long periods? Would those who drop by to bring food and clothing, diapers, and so many other helpful things be jailed? Would the volunteer doctors and dentists at our clinics be jailed? The doctors all said they would continue seeing the sick in our clinics, come what may. Fortunately, in the months that followed, the Senate decided not to pass the bill.

Attempts in 2006 and 2007 to pass legislation for comprehensive and realistic immigration reform were sabotaged by the Minutemen and FAIR, the so-called Federation for American Immigration Reform. Their furious lobbying turned the House of Representatives legislation into the draconian H.R. 4437. It appeared that these groups were trying to repeat the efforts of the Ku Klux Klan in the 1920s, when their hatred and suspicion of people of color, of southern European Catholics, and of Asians were incorporated into intolerant, restrictive immigration law in the United States. The law remained in effect until the 1960s and the start of the civil rights movement. In the 1920s, the Klan had used the scare tactic that Communists were coming across the border with the Mexicans. The cry today is, "Look at all those terrorists who might sneak across the border." Already in 1925, as reported in *Time Magazine*, some factions of the Ku Klux Klan had called themselves the Minutemen.

In April 2006 the anti-immigrant Center for Immigration Studies (an outgrowth of FAIR) published a paper titled "Attrition through Enforcement: A Cost-Effective Strategy to Shrink the Illegal Population." The paper noted that advocates of comprehensive immigration reform contended that deportation of twelve million people was unworkable. The paper's authors urged a war of attrition instead, which would make life so miserable people would want to leave, making deportation unnecessary. The program included stepped-up immigration raids; elimination of jobs for the undocumented by match-checks with Social Security numbers and verification of immigration status, ending all possibility of obtaining driver's licenses; a campaign to pass inhuman state and local laws that would discourage immigrants from living in those areas; and greater cooperation among federal, state, and local law enforcement agencies to identify and deport people.

The same month that "Attrition through Enforcement" was published, the Department of Homeland Security began to implement the policies anti-immigrant groups had recommended, putting out a press release on April 20 announcing what they ironically called "Comprehensive Immigration Enforcement Strategy." By administrative decree, they replaced the hoped-for "comprehensive immigration reform" legislation with harsh measures against immigrants.

Anti-immigrant sentiment has been fueled for many years by FAIR. In the 1980s, FAIR built a watchtower to spy on Casa Oscar Romero in Brownsville, a center for homeless Central American refugees. It was FAIR that mobilized opposition to comprehensive immigration reform and killed the Dream Act for young people in 2007. (The Dream Act, in essence, was a legalization program for children of undocumented immigrants, who had been brought here when very young.) A good example of the importance of the Dream Act is a young woman who came to volunteer in our clinic in 2008. She had just graduated from college and obtained a state license in nursing, but could not obtain a job, even though there is a shortage of nurses in Texas. She had come here as a young child with her parents and had gone through the school system from kindergarten through college. In those years, her parents did not have the opportunity to become legal. She consulted three lawyers, all of whom told her the same thing: In order to become a resident of the United States, she would have to leave the country for ten years, move to a country unknown to her, and pay a large fine. We loved having her as a nurse in our clinic, but it was a shame that she could not get a job. We hated to see her driving around Houston without a license because we knew what might happen if she was picked up for a traffic violation, but there is really no effective way to get around Houston and the surrounding communities without a car.

FAIR presents itself as a nonprofit research organization and is invited to congressional hearings. It appears to be more like a political action group, lobbying at all levels, mobilizing fear and hatred in order to win. A closer look at the passage of restrictive state laws shows the role of FAIR in writing these laws in conjunction with local legislators.

On March 21, 2004, Jason L. Riley published an article in the *Wall Street Journal* that revealed FAIR's background. Riley wrote about the irony of social conservatives, who loved President Reagan, following a racist, nativist group that supported whatever means necessary to ensure there would not be too many people of different colors in the world:

> The Federation for American Immigration Reform and the Center for Immigration Studies…push a cultural agenda abhorrent to any self-respecting social conservative. [And, we might add, to Catholics and other people of good will.]
>
> FAIR's founder, John Tanton, opened the first Planned Parenthood chapter in northern Michigan, accepted more than $1.5 million from the Pioneer Fund, a white supremacist organization devoted to racial purity. Board members of FAIR actively promote the sterilization of Third World women. CIS, an equally repugnant FAIR offshoot, is a big fan of China's one-child policy and publishes books advocating looser limits on abortion and wider use of RU-486.

In February of 2009, the Southern Poverty Law Center published a report titled "The Top Three Anti-Immigration Groups Share Extremist Roots," not only confirming the *Wall Street Journal* article, but also giving information on a third white-nationalist organization, Numbers USA, also closely aligned with John Tanton, who, the report said, still sits on the board of FAIR.

After the failed attempt to pass a national law in 2005–2006, FAIR turned its attention to the states, hoping to accomplish in state law all they had managed to put into the H.R. 4437 bill. They succeeded in lobbying lawmakers in many states and in convincing the Department of Homeland Security to begin raids on workplaces. The hate and misinformation generated by them and their followers made legislators afraid of doing the right thing. Subsequent legislation in some states authorized state highway patrols, and sheriffs and their deputies, to deport people; allowed or mandated hospital emergency rooms to call Immigration to report sick immigrants who came for treatment; and recommended the arrest of those who help immigrants.

The Border Patrol has spent massive amounts of money both on an increased number of agents and on technology to try to intercept all migrants trying to cross the U.S.–Mexican border. In late 2008, the Fides News Service of the Congregation for the Evangelization of Peoples published a twelve-page dossier on immigration in the United States. The report emphasized how enforcement measures were both ineffective and violent:

> More than ten years later we can say, figures in hand, that this strategy only increased beyond all measure the quantity of public money invested in border protection, increased the number of persons killed while attempting to cross the border line, enriched human traffickers (*smugglers*), encouraged in total ambiguity employers who apply norms similar to those of dependence in a regime of slavery, strangled illegal workers with a starvation wage and massacring working-hours, under the blackmail of non-existence.

Nations have always built fences to keep other people out (or in). But in a globalized world, the construction of a fence, a massive barrier between the United States and Mexico, is a symbol of failure. How ironic that the nation that so criticized the Berlin Wall—leading Ronald Reagan to utter the famous words, "Mr. Gorbachev, tear down this wall!"—is creating one of its own.

Local opposition from residents, mayors, and other politicians to the construction of the wall was strong, if not unanimous, all along the U.S. side of the border. It was hard for people in the Rio Grande Valley, one of the poorest areas in the United States, to understand that billions would be spent on a fence—$6 million each mile—which would harm local businesses that depend on customers from Mexico. In one breath-takingly bad decision, Congress gave the government permission to violate every environmental law on the books for the construction of the fence and the Supreme Court upheld its right to do so.

In one of his sermons, theologian Hans Urs von Balthasar described Jesus' attitude toward barriers and fences:

> He accepts us all, whatever nation we belong to. "You are all brethren," Jesus said explicitly to his disciples. The early Church passed what may have been its hardest test, theoretically and practically, when it proclaimed, fought for and implemented the equality of Jews and gentiles, rich and poor, masters and servants or, in modern terms, employers and employees. In all ages men have continually erected these

kinds of barriers, but Christ's Church does not recognize them, because Christ himself has torn them down once and for all.[2]

The war of attrition has divided communities and split families, shattering them with detentions and deportations. The goal to make life miserable for immigrants has been accomplished for those who are still alive.

The media have been complicit, wittingly or unwittingly, in the campaign to redefine immigrants as criminals. When a handful of people who called themselves Minutemen, as if they were like Paul Revere, set themselves up at the border as vigilantes to do the work of the Border Patrol, they received a disproportionate amount of coverage for such a tiny group. As the Minutemen—a small, loud, and vulgar minority—continue their harangues against immigrants, the media continues to feature them.

Even with the best of intentions, the media finds it difficult to make a positive report on what is happening in the immigrant community. How can they report on immigrants without stating the obvious—that these people merely seek survival for themselves and their families. The press could provide many interesting, positive stories if they so chose, but unfortunately, they present the opposite. Immigrants are not described as those who cut our lawns, cook our food, wash the dishes in our restaurants, care for our children, build our buildings cheaply, and thus enrich the economy, but as a group of criminals. We need more publicity about the contributions of immigrants instead of picturing them as lawbreakers.

Young people in the media assess ratings and the popularity of their television or radio station or newspaper compared to others, but they may not consider that their presentation could destroy people. The personal ideology of the owners of newspapers and TV stations is often publicized at the expense of immigrants and the poor. Programs on cable television attack immigrants week after week, influencing many to hate them.

In 1999, we wrote a response in our paper to a picture that appeared in the *Houston Chronicle* that seemed to implicate all immigrants after the arrest of one murderer:

> We knew that the *Houston Chronicle* would want us to clarify the picture that appeared on the City page. Pictured were "twenty-one suspected illegal immigrants" rounded up by police and sheriff's deputies "while searching for suspected

killer Rafael Resendez-Ramirez." These immigrants did not commit a crime. They do look dirty and ugly in the picture because they have been riding a train for days. They probably just participated in family Baptism or First Communion, then headed North (an awful trip) to earn money for their families. They are not here to hurt anyone. They have one great gift that means so much to the United States economy: They are dying to work. After a shower and clean clothes, these "suspected illegal aliens" will look very much like your neighbor or fellow parishioner.

It makes us think of Elie Wiesel's statement about immigrants: "You who are so-called illegal aliens must know that no human being is 'illegal.' That is a contradiction in terms. Human beings can be beautiful or more beautiful, they can be fat or skinny, and they can be right or wrong, but illegal? How can a human being be illegal?"

The animosity and hostility toward immigrants in today's world is hard to fathom. It is partly due to misplaced anger and scapegoating over the state of the economy; it is the result of hate campaigns against immigrants. The events of September 11, 2001, have also been used to demonize everyone trying to cross the Mexican border, even though no terrorists involved in the tragedy crossed that border. In fact, the terrorists had visas.

The campaigns to drum up hatred of immigrants are tinged with racism, as were the campaigns by the Ku Klux Klan in the 1920s and the labor laws in the nineteenth century that led to Chinese workers in California being treated more like slaves than persons. It is as if the Ku Klux Klan is in charge of public relations, spitting out untruths and half-truths about Mexican immigrants as they did in 1920s, when they attacked Slovaks, Italians, Catholics, Jews, and Chinese.

Mark remembers as if it were yesterday the stories his mother told him of the Klan warning his father about being Catholic. The same negative campaign of fear is being built up today against immigrants, as we hear a barrage of comments scapegoating them for the economic situation or difficulties people may find themselves in. The reality is the other way around. Money made off the backs of undocumented immigrants' cheap labor means more profits, which goes to CEOs and stockholders, not to the employees.

A fact often forgotten is that immigrants *do* pay taxes. They pay sales tax, they contribute to property taxes when they rent, and they often pay Social Security taxes.

One of the cruelest tactics is accusing immigrants of identity theft. Identify theft, as practiced by thieves to gain access to people's credit cards and thus ruin their financial lives, is a terrible thing. But when undocumented immigrants use a false Social Security number, it is usually for the purpose of getting a job, which allows them to work and pay into Social Security. Immigrants may contribute Social Security taxes for many years, but will never receive anything in return. Immigrants may single-handedly save the Social Security system because they contribute large sums and get no return.

The climate of fear and dislike carries over to those designated to enforce the laws. While many U.S. Border Patrol agents are courteous, the attitudes and even violent actions of some are a problem. Articles from the Associated Press in 2008 outlined the difficulty of retaining new Border Patrol recruits, with 30 percent of agents leaving their jobs within eighteen months. The articles mentioned factors such as loneliness and boredom. They may have missed the possibility that at least some young recruits realize, as they begin to arrest and deport people who have committed no crime, that it is against their sense of humanity and their beliefs.

The Catholic Bishops of the United States have spoken out courageously and prophetically in favor of comprehensive immigration reform. The Justice for Immigrants Campaign of the USCCB provides information to counteract the lobbying of anti-immigrant hate groups. Individual bishops have responded strongly to inappropriate actions in their dioceses. Cardinal Mahoney of Los Angeles, as well as many other Catholic leaders, has long been an advocate for immigrants.

When Oklahoma passed a restrictive law against immigrants, Bishop Edward J. Slattery of Tulsa published a pastoral letter in November 2007 called "The Suffering Faces of the Poor Are the Suffering Face of Christ." As Bishop Slattery reminded readers in his letter:

> The question of immigration is not simply a social, political or an economic issue, it is also a moral issue because it impacts on the well-being of millions of our neighbors. And because it is a moral issue, it must be examined in the light of our faith in Jesus Christ, Who clearly commands us to "welcome the

stranger," for "what you do the least of my brothers, that you do unto Me" (Matthew 25:40)....It is to Christ's suffering Face, seen in the faces of Oklahoma's immigrant population, that I would draw the gaze of all those who—in whatever manner—find themselves responsible for the passing, the enforcement, or in support of Oklahoma's House Bill 1804.

Bishop Slattery went on to cite the arrival of law enforcement at a diocesan parish before a Mass on Saturday evening:

The sanctity of Saint Francis Xavier Church in Sallisaw was violated by three policemen who knew that Hispanic Catholics trust the Church and come to Mass, even when they would not otherwise venture out of their homes for fear of deportation.... Arriving before the 5:30 Spanish Mass, [the policemen] began to ask the members of the faithful for their papers as they came to offer Christ's sacrifice....

Such intolerable excesses may force the church to go underground, but we somehow will find a way to continue offering the Mass and the Sacraments to our people—for their salvation as well as our own!

Bishop Slattery made a commitment to resist the evil of the law, no matter the cost, announcing that he was even willing to go to jail: "When it becomes a crime to love the poor and serve their needs, then I will be the first to go to jail for this crime and I pray that every priest and every deacon in this diocese will have the courage to walk with me into that prison."

In 2008, Bishop Thomas J. Tobin of Providence, Rhode Island, together with his pastors, took a creative stand and sent ICE a joint letter, not only asking Immigration to stop the raids in their state, but also urging ICE agents to question the morality of their participation in immigration raids. The bishop prophetically introduced the idea of allowing immigration agents to exercise conscientious objection, to make the choice to refuse to participate in raids on workers if they conclude that such actions are contrary to their personal or religious beliefs. Their statement affirmed so much of what the Catholic Worker movement has stood for, applying it to the situation of immigrants:

We the undersigned...urge you to declare a moratorium on immigration raids in the State of Rhode Island, until our nation can implement a comprehensive and just reform of our immigration laws....It is our hope that such reform will make immigration raids obsolete. Until then, we believe that raids on the immigrant community are unjust, unnecessary, and counter-productive....

What we have witnessed is that the police action of ICE against immigrants has divided the community, instilled fear in our streets, disrupted the everyday life of good people and separated family members, innocent of any crime, from one another, the bishop and clergy added. The confusing and secretive detention of those arrested has further complicated the situation. As religious leaders concerned for our people we would be negligent of our pastoral duties if we didn't speak out against these unjust government policies and practices....

We encourage the agents and staff of ICE to evaluate the morality of their participation in immigration raids in the context of their faith and sanctity of their conscience....If their discernment leads them to the conclusion that they cannot participate in such raids in good conscience, we urge them not to do so. If ICE agents refuse to participate in immigration raids in conformity with their faith and conscience, we urge the Federal Government to respect the well-founded principles of conscientious objection.

In late 2008, when his state of Arkansas was considering oppressive legislation against immigrants, Bishop Anthony Taylor of Little Rock published a pastoral letter called "I Was a Stranger and You Welcomed Me: A Pastoral Letter on the Human Rights of Immigrants." His letter emphasized that the second half of the story in Matthew 25 tells us that if we do not receive Jesus in the poor and in the stranger, he will not accept us on Judgment Day.

On the second anniversary of ICE's raid on the Swift meatpacking plant in Worthington, Minnesota, the bishops of that state asked Catholics to renew their commitment to welcoming newcomers, calling for comprehensive immigration reform and strategies to reduce global poverty. Catholic leaders discussed how anti-immigrant sentiment continued to divide communities throughout Minnesota and how recent immigration raids had had a devastating impact on immigrant families and rural communities.

In 2008, the U.S. Catholic Bishops met with Julie Myers, the assistant director of Homeland Security, who had been directing the deportation of thousands of immigrants from all over the country. The bishops objected to the deportations and to the inhumane way they were being conducted. Her response was that Congress was responsible, not she, since they were the ones who had passed draconian laws allowing such deportations. And that was true. This reminded us of the laws passed against Catholics in England centuries ago. Sympathetic observers tried to console the minority of Catholics who had not followed their kings in separating from their church by saying that no one in their right mind would enforce such laws. But the laws were enforced. We do not know if the people were in their right minds or not, but Catholics were systematically persecuted, hung, pressed to death, or drawn and quartered for public display.

A mother with young children came for help because her husband had been deported, even though he did not have a deportation order. Immigration agents had come to the apartment complex to find someone who did and began to fan out into the adjoining apartments, randomly knocking on doors, to take anyone they could find. One of our Catholic Workers remarked, "Don't they know that this is totalitarian? It's like in the worst dictatorships when people are picked up at their homes in the middle of the night." Lawyers from the University of Houston's Immigration Law Clinic confirmed from their interviews with immigrants at the detention center in Houston that this was happening. Several people there told them, "I had done nothing wrong. I did not have a deportation order. They had come for a neighbor. I was in my apartment when they just knocked on the door." A woman who was very ill told us how she fearfully watched from her window while immigration agents searched one apartment after another in her complex in Pasadena, Texas.

On February 4, 2009, the *New York Times* featured an article on a new report from the Center for Migration Studies. It revealed that Homeland Security had done not just what they had told Congress they were going to do, as Julie Myers had protested, but more. The report documented how the project, described to Congress as a search for criminals, had been changed to a general blitz of deportations of anyone they could easily find, at an expense of several hundred million dollars.

Terry McBroom, a new convert to Catholicism, came to visit Casa Juan Diego and stayed with us for a few days. He was considering retiring from his job and becoming a full-time Catholic Worker. While he was here, he helped us mail out our paper. He was taken with the *Houston Catholic Worker*, with the idea of publishing good information about immigrants and immigration along with articles about the Catholic Worker movement and living one's faith in the world. When he returned to Tennessee, he began to request copies of the paper to distribute in Catholic parishes and to immigrants wherever he found them. He found many, got to know them, and discovered people whose lives were based on faith, hard work, and family, in very challenging situations. He eventually began to distribute eight hundred copies of each issue. Terry branched out from giving out the paper to accompanying immigrants to their court hearings and helping them fill out job applications. As he came to know the immigrant families and the difficulties they faced, he became more and more committed to helping them and more disturbed by the raids and local law-enforcement policies. This became his apostolate instead of coming to Casa Juan Diego to work and live.

There are encouraging signs that a majority is not convinced by the campaigns to demonize immigrants—not just among bishops or in the Catholic Worker movement, but in state governments. On August 14, 2008, the *Wall Street Journal* published an article on the efforts of some governors and state legislators (who have rejected FAIR's agenda) to work toward a positive response to immigrants: "Some States Seek Integration Path for Immigrants." Gradually, as more and more bishops speak out, as more parish discussion groups address immigration issues, opinions of Catholics in the pews may more completely reflect Church teaching on immigration, as has happened with the death penalty.

12

CHRIST DID NOT DIE FOR PROFIT

During the Central American wars, people would ask us, Why do refugees come to the United States, to Casa Juan Diego? Why do they come when the journey is so terribly violent?

People ask us the same question today, after the peace accords. They come because they can't feed their children or send them to school because of economics. They come because they haven't worked at a regular job in years. They come because their children are always ill. Decades of the policies of the World Bank and the International Monetary Fund have destroyed their local economies. They cannot make a living on the salaries paid in factories owned by multinational corporations in their countries. However you read it, people are dying by the sword or from lack of bread. An economic death is no better than a political death, just slower.

Stricter, crueler laws; stiffer enforcement; or a new law that imitates the old exploitative *Bracero* Program (which made seasonal migrant workers temporarily legal)—none of these provide simple solutions to the immigration problem. The solution to the influx of immigrants is not more policing to keep people out and deport them, but in the realization that the reason for migration is the global economy. As we were told by politicians in the 1990s, "It's the economy, stupid!"

Our work with the poor, with immigrants, and with refugees repeatedly reminds us of the comments Bartolomé de Las Casas, OP, made centuries ago during the Spanish conquest of Latin America, in response to the cruel behavior and focus of the conquistadors. Las Casas declared to them: "Christ did not die for gold!" Las Casas's answer to the injustices done to the indigenous peoples in Latin America was clear: to appropriate the wealth of others without authorization is to commit a mortal sin of theft or robbery.[1]

As we hear the stories of why our guests come to the United States and see how they fare once they get here, we are as horrified as Las Casas. The conquistadors of today are the multinational corporations and international bankers who make life so miserable for poor workers around the world. We think that Fray Bartolomé would say essentially the same thing to them: "Christ did not die for profit!" Appropriating the lives of workers for the wealth of multinational companies, their CEOs, and their stockholders is a sin of theft and robbery.

You may protest, "But don't immigrants just want what we have, which is the fruit of these profits? Aren't they drawn by the success of our system?" Of course! They, too, want to be able to stay at home with their families. They are unable to scratch out a decent existence in their home countries, and they see the constant barrage of advertisements of what appears to them to be the opulent lifestyle of the United States. Advertising to the poor of the world, accompanying what global economists call "opening markets," makes young people in many countries, who can hardly afford food, want designer jeans and whatever products they see advertised each day. This makes parents even more desperate because they cannot provide these things for their children. Pope John Paul II stated on several occasions that people have a right to migrate, to cross borders, if it is necessary to feed their families—but they also have the right *not* to migrate.

When we force people to leave their countries by our economic policies and then accuse them of being criminals for immigrating to our country, it is unfair. The Holy Father indicated that such attitudes amount to tunnel vision on the part of the developed world, which fails to see the "migration of the desperate" that obliges men and women without a future to abandon their countries amid a thousand dangers.

When a man or woman can earn only a few dollars a day doing backbreaking work, can never get out of debt, and can never afford to feed their children decently, it is understandable that they would take the risk of migration, selling their few precious belongings to make the painful journey. When a mother watches her children die of malnutrition, lack of medicine, or worms that attack the brain—children who never had a chance to learn to read—you can understand why she would leave the children with a grandmother and come to the United States to earn money to send back home. The pain of robbery, of beatings, even of rapes, is devastating, but not as devastating as helplessly watching your child die in your arms.

Within a very few years after we began to receive refugees from the Central American wars, immigrants who were refugees from the global economic system began pouring into Houston. They arrive at our door each day. The system creates migrants. They are very much in need of hospitality and our work expanded to include them. Hondurans started arriving at Casa Juan Diego in large numbers in 1983.

When they arrive, fathers or mothers beg for help until they can earn enough to send money home for the uniforms required by public schools, for shoes, and for supplies so a child can go to school. Guests beg for a few days' work so that they can send some money to their children left at home.

Leticia said her husband encouraged her to come. They sold their small home to finance her journey so she could come here to earn money as a live-in maid to help support their six children. Within three weeks of her arrival in the United States, her husband died, leaving the children back home in the care of her seventeen-year-old daughter. Leticia desperately wanted to return to take care of her children, but they and sympathetic women guests at Casa Juan Diego convinced her that if she went back, they would have nothing. So she continued to work as a maid and came back to stay every other weekend at Casa Juan Diego, where she could speak Spanish with other guests. She called in between weekend visits to ask if there were letters; when she'd arrive she eagerly looked for letters from her family. Casa Juan Diego's post office had many receipts from money she sent to her family.

One woman, who had borne two children here, came to visit us in the 1990s and told us of how she had worked for a number of years in Houston and sent money back to her other children in Honduras so that they could have enough to eat and go to school. However, those children did not understand why their mother could not be with them. When she finally went back to visit them years after she had left them, they would not speak to her.

We try to help our guests find work as much as we can. Those who know of Casa Juan Diego call to offer a day's work—cleaning, yard work, or carpentry. A number of times we have asked parishes to put notices in their church bulletins about the availability of workers. Some have responded and continue to respond. A high percentage of those who have hired immigrants are delighted with their work. Employers are impressed with their work ethic. Mrs. Jones was delighted with the work José did with her plants, her landscaping. Mr. Smith said the workers were great. They did a lot of work and they did it well.

After the 1986 immigration law passed, our hiring hall/work center, which has space for day laborers and cooperatives, has provided a way for undocumented men and women to work legally. If only this were true in Central America, where cooperatives were a part of the ideas of the social movements of the 1970s that brought repression and death squads down on the people's heads. Even many years after peace accords were signed, people in Central America have told us they dare not touch the idea of cooperatives for people who are on the margins economically, because they will be accused of being Communists.

Sandra was seven months pregnant from a rape by a coyote, who had promised to bring her safely to the United States. She was so happy that a woman came to Casa Juan Diego to work with our cooperative in order to find someone to clean her house. Sandra was able to earn $50.00 this way to send to her mother to help her sick grandmother get medical care in Honduras.

Some employers who are not a part of our cooperative take advantage of the vulnerability of undocumented workers. Those who are skilled and aggressive are absorbed into the work force. But it is difficult for those who are not highly skilled, especially if they don't have family or friends in the States. The men must often face not being paid at all, and without a doubt being underpaid. They must face the fact that if they are injured, the contractor will disappear. Some of our guests first came to us after they had found unsatisfactory employment.

Women immigrants are often limited to live-in housework, sometimes six or seven days a week. They are able to earn enough this way, without living expenses, to send money back for their children. Unfortunately, there are always people here ready to exploit women. At Casa Juan Diego, we try to screen those who want women for work. When people come to the door to ask for women to work in clubs, bars, or *cantinas*, we always say no. We do not provide prostitutes. Although the word *cantina* does not always refer to a disreputable place, in Houston it frequently does. It didn't occur to us that those same people who wanted desperate immigrant women for their *cantinas* would try us again after they'd been refused, this time sending other women with babes in arms asking for a live-in maid. One of our guests responded to such a request and found, when she arrived at the job, that she was not to be a live-in maid as she thought, but a worker in the type of *cantina* related to prostitution. We were glad that she called us right away and returned to the safety of Casa Juan Diego until she could find work that was more appropriate. She was lucky that they let her go.

"Rita is a thief," one woman said. Rita, like all the immigrants, wanted to work, to get any kind of work. An American couple asked her to work with their children and offered to pay her $100 per week. She was happy to have work and have money to send to her mother, who was caring for her children, as her husband was deceased and her family was poor. The downside of this job was that the husband stayed home some days and insisted on having sex with Rita. She was uncomfortable and refused. "We may be poor *mojados* [wetbacks]," she said, "but we are decent." She threatened to tell the spouse, but the husband was relentless. Rita told the spouse and was fired for being a thief. No proof was given. Rita found refuge at Casa Juan Diego.

Rosa fared no better than Rita did. She was hired by a woman who was a front for a divorced man with two little girls. She was told the job was with a married couple. She was to be a live-in babysitter, since the couple worked different shifts in their jobs. The problem was that it was not a couple, but a single man who actually employed her. When it was time to go to bed, the man said that she would have to sleep with him, since there was only one bed. When she refused, the man accused her of being a prostitute and fired her.

Rosa's friend, a live-in maid, didn't have a bed, either. She slept on the floor in the baby's bedroom. There was a crib for the baby, but no bed for her. The employer said there was a new carpet, however, where she could sleep. There was another woman who paid her new maid with old clothes.

Mercedes worked for a year as a live-in, available almost fourteen hours a day to cook, clean, and care for the children. One day, the lady of the house was missing some jewelry. She accused Mercedes of stealing it, reported the theft to the police, and fired her. Mercedes came in tears to Casa Juan Diego, proclaiming her innocence. A few days later, the woman found the missing jewelry and called to tell us so. However, she did not go to the police to withdraw the charges against Mercedes.

Brenda planned to send her baby to Guatemala to live with her mother as soon as he was born. She knew her opportunities for working here and possibilities for saving money would be much less if she kept the baby with her. Her mother had mortgaged the house to pay for her trip to the United States, and the coyote was threatening to take the house. In the meantime, she was a new mother, worried about little things that might endanger the baby. He cried all the time at night. What should she do? We asked if she was burping him well, and she assured us she was. When she saw the doctor in our clinic, though, it turned out that she had to burp the baby a little more enthusiastically. She would not hurt him by patting him harder on the back. Problem solved. Time dragged on as the woman who had promised to take the baby to Guatemala repeatedly postponed the trip. As he grew, Jorge developed an interesting personality and became a favorite in the house. His mother's attachment to him also grew. Soon he was six months old, but she still spoke of sending him back so that she could work. We discouraged her, because he was so young and had become very attached to her. Fortunately, she found some friends who would take her in and help by taking turns caring for the baby so he could stay until he was older.

The *maquiladora* system, known in the United States as outsourcing, was developed to help multinational companies. In the mid-1980s, we began to understand the problem that outsourcing is for the people of Central America and Mexico, when we saw a segment on the television program *Sixty Minutes*. Officials of the U.S. Agency for International Development (U.S. AID) were shown calling out to businesses: Come on down! You cannot imagine the advantages of moving your factories out of the country. There will be no local taxes (none to help the community), labor leaders will be blackballed so that wages will be kept very low, and there will be fences around special compounds built for your companies. U.S. AID promised the multinationals that it would name all "troublemakers" trying to organize unions, people trying to make wages high enough to at least survive with their families. Julian, who came to Casa Juan Diego, had been blackballed by a U.S. government agency in his country because he was active in his labor union. In the *maquiladoras*, teenage girls are enticed to leave school to work; they are given employment only for a few years, and then are left without a future.

After he made it to Casa Juan Diego, one man who had worked in a *maquiladora* in Honduras, a factory of a multinational company, told us he could not live on the $14 a week he was paid. He could not pay the rent, provide food for his family, and buy shoes so the children could go to school. He explained that his father was able to survive because he had worked for many years in a different job there and made $28 a week. He said, "I came here to work to feed my children." This was at a time when many factory workers in the United States were making $14 an hour.

Betty had worked in a *maquiladora* in Honduras, but the company closed that location and left for another country. She was almost nine months pregnant when she arrived here:

> I'm Honduran. I love my country, but it was time for me to leave. Why? There is no work. They closed the factory where I was working, leaving a great number of us without jobs.
>
> Even though we worked from 7 a.m. to 5 p.m., they gave us only 40 minutes to eat lunch. We had to ask permission to get a drink of water. We were not allowed to stand up if our work was done sitting. If your work was done standing, you couldn't sit down. They'd warn us, they'd put out a goal of 1,000 pieces of clothing; it would depend on your particular job. If you did it quickly, the next day they would raise or multiply the amount of work you had to do and lower the wage for that job or the price, so that someone would kill herself working, but earn less than what she had before. I thought, and I continue to think, that this is unjust, that it is robbery, because the worker deserves a good salary, a decent wage. It doesn't matter if you work all day, as long as they pay what they should pay. When our government put some pressure on the companies so that they would pay overtime, some of them removed their factories from Honduras in order to go to even cheaper countries. They left thousands and thousands without work.
>
> When I found myself without a job, I decided to become an emigrant, because I have two children to provide for. Without work, I couldn't give them what they needed.
>
> In addition, the father of my baby insisted that I get an abortion. He almost convinced me because we couldn't afford the children we had, let alone another. He almost convinced me in my head, yes, but in my heart, he couldn't. He

gave me a little bit of money for it, but with the money, I embarked upon my journey, five months pregnant.

People have always come from Mexico, but it was after NAFTA (the North American Free Trade Agreement) went into effect in the early 1990s that Mexican immigrants began pouring in to Casa Juan Diego. They were unable to compete with U.S.–subsidized agribusiness (large-scale farming), or with Walmart, which had moved in under the new rules and undermined small local businesses. These immigrants all found us through churches, individual people, schools, the police department, and almost any agency you could imagine. Much had been promised by those trade agreements, but the people had to emigrate because their livelihood was gone.

One of the key conditions of NAFTA was that Mexico not subsidize agriculture. The United States, of course, continued and continues to provide enormous subsidies to farmers, mostly agribusiness that does not need subsidies. Local agriculture around the world has not been able to compete with the heavily subsidized agribusiness of the United States.

After NAFTA was implemented, we began to receive those who had to leave their homes because they were part of the 1.2 million farmers who lost their land or whose small businesses had been destroyed by NAFTA policies. Dawn McCarty of the University of Houston Downtown wrote in the May–June 2008 issue of the *Houston Catholic Worker* about what had happened to agriculture in Mexico with NAFTA and the causes of increased migration:

> The causes of the changes in immigration patterns are varied and complicated, but the key factor is the policies associated with the North American Free Trade Agreement (NAFTA). Nowhere is this clearer than in the rural, agricultural areas of Mexico, where working-age men and, increasingly, single women are scarce, unable now to make the living that their ancestors had made for centuries on land they used to own. Protected by the 1917 Constitution of Mexico, *ejido* lands, as they are called, belonged to the people in common and could not be sold. Communally owned lands that giant agribusiness interests could not legally buy was the polar opposite of the free-market ideology of NAFTA. Against years of precedent,

then President Salinas managed to change the Mexican Constitution in 1992 so that *ejido* lands could be made the "private" property of individual members of the collective, who then could sell their plot of land to private individuals. This privatization of *ejido* land was a critical component of NAFTA, since these communal lands comprised 29,000 communities and three million producers, encompassing 75% of all agricultural production at the time....

As *ejidos* were broken up and title given to the individual *campesinos*, these poorly educated farm laborers tried to make a living on their small plots of land, just as their ancestors had done for centuries. But now that they owned the land individually, they found that the rules of the game had been changed. The government subsidies that had allowed *ejidos* to survive were now disallowed by NAFTA. The tariffs that protected them from the much more "efficient" agribusiness of the United States were gone. But somehow U.S. agribusiness still got *their* government subsidies, and that fact, together with the economies of scale available to giant corporations, meant that it was cheaper for a *campesino* to buy American corn shipped across the border than to grow it himself on his own plot of land. There was no way the individual farmer in Mexico, left by himself to the mercies of the "free market," could compete with the Colossus of the North. Unable to make a living on the land, no matter how hard they worked, the *campesinos* had to sell their patrimony, and, with no bargaining power, they sold it for a pittance. The predictable result was that much of the land that supported the rural Mexican economy now belongs to the same major corporations, and their affiliates, that own the land in the United States.

Some of the former *campesinos* still get to work on the land, but it is no longer their land, and they get paid what the corporations are willing to pay. The minimum wage in Mexico is a little more than four dollars a *day*. Some corporations pay twice that, or more, but to get that kind of money you have to work very hard for very long hours, and be very lucky. There are many people desperate for a job, and few jobs offered. And the work is sporadic.

Those who lost their livelihoods in their own countries often found people ready to take unfair advantage of them when, in desperation, they came to work in the United States. It is common for undocumented workers to be cheated by employers. Millions of dollars are saved by contractors each year because of wages that are never paid—a real contribution to the economy! An immigrant can go to jail for many months for traffic tickets and be deported, but the person who cheats him of his wages—thousands of dollars—usually goes scot-free. It is not considered a crime to neglect payment of wages, simply poor business practice.

Some employers have developed a special way to cheat immigrants. They pay them well for a few days or two weeks to secure trust, and then for the following weeks pay them nothing and put them off. Soon they disappear from the face of the earth. Another way to cheat immigrants is to pay them with checks that bounce. We cash checks for workers who have no ID. For the most part the checks are good, but we cannot rely on this. On one day, we had three bounced checks worth $1,000. Another employer paid two men $800 each. Both checks bounced. We began to be able to recognize the types of checks used for this purpose. Often the checks had no address or an out-of-town address.

"Pedro is a fake," the man said. Pedro's hand was swollen out of all proportion and looked more like a melon. Pedro was in great pain and burning up with fever. He had been injured on the job, he said. His boss dropped him off at Casa Juan Diego. When we asked the boss why he didn't get help for Pedro, he said there wasn't anything wrong with him. "Pedro is a fake and doesn't want to work. He is not getting my money!" The boss refused to pay him for two weeks of work that was due. Pedro sought assistance at Casa Juan Diego. The doctors told us later that he almost lost his hand.

Pablo, a refugee from El Salvador, made the mistake of working for a carpet layer who habitually cheated refugees, but he was desperate since he had a wife and two children at Casa Juan Diego and wanted to get out on his own. The employer was in a powerful position. His usual response when people awaited their pay was to tell them repeatedly to come back and then finally refuse to pay them. Pablo became impatient. He went one evening to the carpet layer and refused to leave until he was paid. He said if he wasn't paid, he was going to take some carpet from the back of the truck and began to do so. The employer became very angry and beat Pablo until his face was black and blue and bloody. As Pablo dragged himself off the ground, he turned back to the cheating carpet layer, waved his fist at him, and said, "God is going to get you for this!" We nursed Pablo with his cuts and bruises and retired for the night. But just as we were going to sleep, the phone rang. It was the wife of the carpet layer—calling from the hospital and demanding to speak to the people in charge. She wanted to give them the money owed to Pablo immediately. Her husband had just had a terrible automobile accident and had been hospitalized.

Juan's boss had not paid him in over a month, not a penny for six weeks, which meant no funds for rent, food, utilities. His boss did promise—as he talked to Juan from his beautiful, expensive home in Sugar Land, Texas (a suburb of Houston)—that he would pay him someday. Two of Juan's friends had not been paid, either. Someone was ahead $10,000 or so, and it wasn't them.

Fortunately, most employers who hire our workers at Casa Juan Diego do pay. There are many workers who come to us for help, however, who do not live with us. There is generally no recourse when workers are not paid. We have tried the most high-powered lawyers in Houston at the recommendation of the AFL-CIO; we have tried the most powerful government agencies. Not a penny has ever been recovered by the lawyers or agencies.

Robbing immigrant workers of their pay is such a common occurrence that one wonders how many houses have been built, how many new roofs put on, how many ditches dug, and how many houses painted by these "volunteers." The refugee or immigrant is a very valuable commodity in the job market because he is dying to work. What he faces in the United States, however, is often very unpleasant. He is treated more like chattel—like a farm animal by some contractors, who sometimes even ask for "bulls." No matter what country they are from, immigrant workers are called Mexicans, illegals, or wetbacks.

If you want to experience rage, speak to the men who have been robbed of their wages. They haven't been robbed at gunpoint: they have been robbed at shovel point. When it comes time for paying wages, the employer tells them that they need to wait until tomorrow. He might say, "I haven't received *my* money yet." And he may disappear for days or weeks until he thinks the workers have forgotten about him. It is hard to imagine how those who cheat workers can sleep at night—especially if they could know the story of each worker, who is trying to send money to a family on the edge of survival.

We hate going through the ritual when we accompany immigrants and refugees to their bosses who have refused to pay them. The violence is mostly verbal in this ritual, but we feel like physical violence could erupt at any moment. It's always the same old song and dance. It is as if these small-time bosses have gone to the same school to learn the ritual of robbing people of their wages. First, they attack the worker: "He steals, he is lazy, he ruins things, he is no good." Then comes the chorus: "He's illegal anyway." Next, they start on us: "Who are you?" (A few haven't asked that; they already know us.) "Why are you doing this? Are you trying to make a name for yourself? You think you're somebody. I'll show you a thing or two, and how I am somebody, too." These bosses try to crush us with insults and threats. Usually in these direct encounters, the wage robbers pay something. Unfortunately, it's often a compromise.

One of the cruelest responses to the attempt to collect wages occurs when the worker actually meets a gun when he or she visit the employer's home to demand owed wages, after days and weeks of not being paid. Some warn them: You come to my house even with Don Marcos (as Mark is often called), and you will be met with a gun.

Economists tell us that the undocumented labor force is good for business, since undocumented status forces the immigrant to work for less with fewer complaints. Keeping people illegal to limit their ability to pursue justice in the marketplace is hardly a good practice. It is rather like the old idea of keeping your wife barefoot and pregnant in order to control her. "But it keeps down prices!" the economists say. Mistreatment of immigrants feeds the economy.

A special list of sins that used to appear in old catechisms was entitled "Sins That Cry to Heaven for Vengeance." One of the sins on the list was to deprive the laborer of his hire—in other words, his wages. Among immigrants, there is a lot of crying out to heaven. Whoever compiled the list of sins knew what they were doing when they included depriving a person of their wages. This comes from the Bible. In James 5:4–5, the writer exhorts the corrupt employer: "Behold, the wages you withheld from the workers who harvested your fields are crying aloud, and the cries of the harvesters have reached the ears of the Lord of hosts. You have lived on earth in luxury and pleasure; you have fattened your hearts for the day of slaughter."

The ink had not dried on the first newspaper stories about the devastation in New Orleans caused by Hurricane Katrina when vans began appearing at Casa Juan Diego with drivers seeking to recruit workers to begin the cleanup and restore power. Guests discouraged each other from going with some clearly disreputable recruiters, but they enthusiastically joined the representatives of major corporations working on the power grids. One group said they would pay $8 per hour and one meal a day. We talked with a worker later who said they were on the level, it was all true—many hours of work, but they were paid. There was, however, only that one meal a day, because there were no stores or restaurants anywhere near where the people stayed. We later heard stories of workers with other groups who were involved in the worst of the cleanup with no protective clothing, where dead bodies and contaminated earth were everywhere. Once immigrants had done much of the dirtiest work, deportations began. The mayor actually announced that immigrants were welcome to do the cleanup, but now it was time to *leave*!

In 2008, Eleazar, who had gone to work on the post-hurricane cleanup and had stayed on, became very ill. He had very high blood pressure, diabetes, and renal failure. He told us that when he went to the emergency room in New Orleans, Immigration was called to deport him. When he told them that he had been a policeman in Mexico and of the pressure on him there to join the drug cartels, he somehow was not deported, but was told to report in to Immigration each week. He came to seek help at Casa Juan Diego and lived in one of our houses for sick and wounded people.

People from different walks of life make money off poor immigrants, from stockholders of companies where they work and stockholders of the detention centers that imprison them, to people who call themselves *notarios* (notaries) to actual immigration lawyers. In Latin America, a *notario público* can do much more than a notary here, so it is easy to trick an immigrant into believing they are doing a lawyer's work. One man told us he spent eight years on the waiting list for people from Mexico seeking family reunification, so he could help his wife and children become legal. He asked for help with the expensive sponsorship because he was disabled. When we talked with his "lawyer," we found that it was a *notario*, who had done absolutely nothing. His hopes were ruined. In many other cases, real lawyers accept immigrants' money and do nothing to advance their cases. Nothing happens to lawyers who commit this malpractice.

Sharing the sufferings and tragedies of the workers, we felt obligated to look into the kind of economics that caused this situation, in which people have to leave their countries and families to work in an underground where they are so easily abused. Why are they migrating all over the world (not just to the United States) at a rate greater than that of the fourth century, when the Roman Empire fell? It became clear that immigration questions have everything to do with economics. They also have everything to do with our Catholic faith, our Scriptures, our magisterial teaching, and our tradition of welcoming the stranger. As we listened to the stories of those who come to Casa Juan Diego, we knew there was something wrong with the global economic system.

We were never very interested in economics as a theoretical field, although Mark was conscious of the ideas of Milton Friedman, the famous professor from the University of Chicago, who was publishing his ideas when Mark studied there for his master's degree. At first glance, some of the ideas seemed interesting, such as a negative income tax. As we saw the impact of his influence in economics, however, it became clear that his other ideas were destructive for the poor around the world. In fact, the ideas he taught turned out to be so harmful that if he were still alive, we might recommend that he be jailed. We are not the only ones. In 2008, when the University of Chicago planned to establish a research institute named after Friedman, it caused an uproar among the faculty. More than a hundred tenured faculty members signed letters and a petition opposing the plan.

As we have listened to those who have just crossed several countries on foot, on freight trains, or in trailer trucks tell about the global impact of such economic policies, we have realized that it is in direct opposition to the teaching of our Church (for example, Pius XI's encyclical *Quadragesimo Anno*, Paul VI's *Populorum Progressio*, John XXIII's *Mater et Magistra*, and John Paul II's *Laborem Exercens*). In *Laborem Exercens*, John Paul II declared that the key to the evaluation of any economic system is the way workers are treated: "In every case a just wage is the concrete means of *verifying the justice* of the whole socioeconomic system and, in any case, of checking that it is functioning justly."[2] Current economics, under this grading system, would receive an F.

We discovered that people in poor countries are obligated to work day and night to pay off loans given to dictators who did not use the money for the good of their country. When we first started studying the economics of immigration, we were very surprised to learn that the interest rate on these loans has been raised over and over again, so that even though the countries have paid enough to pay off their loans, perhaps several times, all was applied to interest and they were unable to reduce the principal. This seemed immoral; it seemed to be robbery of poor countries.

We discovered that the World Bank and the International Monetary Fund (IMF), which so closely control the lives of those in poorer countries, have imposed detailed economic regulations on them, calling them "reforms" or "structural adjustments." The promise has been that, given time, these programs would stimulate growth, provide development, and work miracles for the economies of poor countries so that even the poorest would be better off. That hasn't happened yet. In structural-adjustment programs, the focus is on debt reduction. The priority is exporting products that bring in the most cash, even if it means paying slave wages, using environmentally destructive methods of production, and, especially, exporting the best and most nutritious food.

We witnessed this firsthand at a banana processing plant in Guatemala. Mammoth semitrailer trucks headed for the United States were loaded with the best bananas. The rejects were put on a small dump truck for local consumption. A man who arrived at Casa Juan Diego from Honduras saw bananas in the dining room and picked one up. He stood looking at it and exclaimed: "This is a miracle! A miracle banana! I have never seen a banana like this!" We understood that he had not seen bananas at the market in Central America—they were all shipped to the United States.

At the same time that these programs have been creating an economic crisis for the mass of people in their countries, the IMF has insisted absolutely on privatization of services that the government used to provide, such as health care and even the public water supply. The basic resources of the countries have been sold to multinationals, companies like Enron, that famous Houston company that purchased much of Argentina's water supply. It is hard to imagine that Enron executives, who were so busy making money, had the good of the people of Argentina at heart. The multinational corporations that have been taking over business operations all over the world and purchasing the public services that are privatized are often closely aligned with police and military operations in order to keep out labor organization and competition from local groups.

One of the key aspects of structural adjustment has been that governments stop helping the people. The IMF and the World Bank allow no "socialism"—no free medical help, no government help for the poor. They demand that agricultural products be grown for export, rather than for the country's own people. The IMF has also dictated what crops can be grown and what industries can exist. In recent years, even the IMF has admitted that its policies have not worked and that economies collapsed after its policies were imposed. In their own reports, the IMF has admitted there is little evidence that globalization and the enforcement of its policies helps poor countries, and instead may actually increase their risk of financial crisis. Yet, the IMF continues.

When Pope Benedict XVI said loans from international institutions must not be tied to structural adjustment, the majority of people who listened did not know what he meant, had not even heard the term *structural adjustment*, and had no idea of the damage done to local economies by the "experts" dictating how they must be operated.

John Paul II called for rapid action to correct the economic tendencies that allow powerful individuals to manipulate the markets of less developed countries. He expressed his fear that workers in the least developed countries could be reduced to the condition of new serfs of the world. At Casa Juan Diego, we receive these former serfs, who seek work that will pay enough to enable their families to survive in their countries.

The inequality between "North and South" was dramatically illustrated for us when we took in a Guatemalan mother who had just arrived to register her two little girls at school. The birth certificates had been lost on the journey, and the school asked the mother the children's ages so that they could make a placement pending receiving new birth certificates. The mother said the girls were in first and second grade. The school secretary stared in disbelief and laughed at the mother. "There is no way these tiny girls can be in first and second grade!" she said. The mother turned to Louise, weeping and speaking softly in Spanish: "Here you have a lot to eat; we have so little, it is not surprising my girls are so small!"

The recent crisis of the price and availability of food around the world has not just been related to the use of corn for biofuels or the fact that India and China are eating more, as some have indicated. The food crisis is related to the destruction of local agriculture and the imposition of policies of growing plants for export instead of for one's own people. One of the worst outcome of the past thirty-to-forty years of these policies has been that local economies and local businesses have been destroyed and multinational corporations have moved in to replace what local people once did.

Publishing articles on economics has sometimes irritated the readers of our newspaper. Some have disagreed, hoping that we would leave out the subject altogether. They preferred personal stories of charity. Some have forgiven us for our writings on economics because we help the poor. For example, one not-so-pleased recipient of our Christmas letter of appeal wrote: "We love the work you are doing. Here is a check for $1,000, but STOP sending that newspaper." Later, the same person wrote again, "You didn't stop sending it. Here is a check for $500, but please stop sending it."

We are sometimes invited to speak to small groups in parishes about the work we do, about social justice, and about how Catholics and others of good will can participate in making a better world. Sometimes when we make such a presentation at an upscale parish, we quote the popes on economics and then try to give practical examples of how people, without starting a Catholic Worker house themselves, can make a very real contribution to the lives of the poor.

What would happen, we say, if a person with a quarter-million-dollar house who is thinking of buying a half-million-dollar house, something they could well afford, would give up the idea and instead buy houses for the poor? With that "extra" quarter million they could buy a number of houses for the poor. We continued on the same theme with automobiles. Suppose a family was thinking of buying a new car for $45,000, but instead purchased a $20,000 car and saved the rest for housing or cars for poor families.

It took a businessman from one parish to help us explain why people generally do not do this. He responded ironically, "You don't understand! You don't understand! That is *virtue*. People who work hard, behave themselves, and pray hard deserve to be rewarded by material things for their virtuous life. God has blessed them, and it is something to leave to their children." As for those who don't have much, not even a house—it may be because they didn't practice virtue. If people are poor, there must be something wrong with them. "You have to understand," he continued, "that so-called 'accumulation Catholicism' has respectable status. Purchasing bigger homes, bigger cars, and elegant clothing is not seen as a vice. God has given individuals talent and ability, and if they use it to create more possessions, then God surely approves. God is on their side, rather than on the side of those who have been unsuccessful in creating wealth and maybe don't even have enough to support their families."

However, this is not Catholic thinking. It is Calvinism, in which material success is a sign of God's blessing: money—instead of the Sign of the Cross! Catholic teaching insists that we respect the dignity of each person, even the poor. Most Catholics know well that bigger houses, bigger cars, and fancy clothing are not prerequisites for gaining eternal salvation. On Judgment Day, the Lord is not going to ask about bigger and better. In fact, he had some comments to make about people who build bigger barns. As the saying goes, "We take to heaven what we have given away."

One couple (who were not Calvinists) sold their big house to live in a smaller one and used the money to help Casa Juan Diego. But they didn't want others to know—not just because the right hand should not know what the left is doing—but because they were embarrassed, not yet ready to confess in our society, where status and comfort are everything, that they had implemented different values.

Our great consumerist society, which utilizes the majority of the world's resources, flourishes because of the low wages paid to those who make our goods. One could almost say: "To live as we live, kills." The good life of a few is planned and built without pity on the misery and death of the many. It has become almost a cliché—but a useful one—to say that we should live simply so that others may simply live. Our desire for more and more inexpensive goods drives companies to pay less and less. The dignity of the human person requires a wage that will allow a family to live in at least somewhat decent conditions.

Dorothy Day and Peter Maurin spoke of locating the center of value somewhere other than wealth and accumulation. That would go a long way to helping this situation. Making a living and having a place to live is important, but we are called to more—to a destiny. Dorothy and Peter emphasized the primacy of the spiritual in our lives. It is easy to see how economic factors predominate in people's lives. What one *has* is what counts, not what one *is*. What you drive, what you wear, where you live, what house you live in, what parish you belong to, what wealth you possess: this is what counts. The problem is that this hurts other people. It goes like this: *my* house, *my* car, *my* yard, *my* clothes, *my* vacation, *my* money, *my* investments, *my* figure, *my* body.

Consumerism and individualism severely limit human freedom and divine grace and thus limit human destiny and vocation. We have learned the hard way that only grace overcomes self-interest.

Peter Maurin quoted the prophets of Israel and the Fathers of the Church as the best guides, who recognized economic injustice when they saw it and prophetically addressed the issues. Peter and Dorothy defended workers against a brutal capitalism that took advantage of labor to acquire wealth for the few. They called these capitalists robber barons.

Dorothy Day spoke about the need for a revolution—a revolution of the heart—to break away from the grip of materialism that tries to replace our values and take possession of our souls. For her, to tempt people constantly, barraging them with advertisements, is immoral and unethical. She wrote in the April 1953 *Catholic Worker* that to entice people into materialism is contrary to the law of God:

> There have been many sins against the poor which cry out to high heaven for vengeance. The one listed as one of the seven deadly sins, is depriving the laborer of his share. There is another one, that is, instilling in him the paltry desires to satisfy that for which he must sell his liberty and his honor....Newspapers, radio, TV and battalions of advertising people (woe to that generation!) deliberately stimulate his desires, the satisfaction of which mean the degradation of the family.

When the depth of the financial crisis became evident in late 2008, it also became clear that those who maligned immigrants, blaming them for every economic ill, had been—as everyone should have known—quite wrong. Greg Erlandson said it well in his article entitled "An Inside Job: Our Best and Brightest—Not Illegals—Pushed Us to the Brink of Financial Disaster":

> They did it again. They distracted us with all their talk of illegal immigrants stealing our jobs and draining our resources. They told us how we had to put up barriers, distrust anyone

who wasn't American. They made us suspicious of others, just the way they did in the past with blacks and Jews, Italians and Irish.

We talked about walls to keep those people out and keep us safe, and we let commentators on talk radio and cable television whip us into a frenzy over the folks they said threatened America.

Once again, the fingerprints on the knife in our back belonged not to the poor and minorities, but to the best and the brightest.

Instead of statues of a bull and bear on Wall Street, we should erect a Trojan horse, because what's pushed America to the brink of financial disaster was not all those illegals coming in and "stealing" our jobs as busboys and janitors and underage laborers in meat-processing plants.

This was an inside job. It was made in America. It was all the hotshot brainiacs, our best college graduates, the brokers and bankers pulling in bonuses that weren't just in the hundreds of thousands but in the millions.[3]

Immigrants have made a tremendous contribution to economic growth because of their willingness not only to work for less, but to also to work harder and longer. They are driven by the needs of their families in their home countries. Everything in Houston is less expensive because of this cheap labor market. The economy of Houston depends on immigrants. Houston's citizenry should be grateful for the contribution of the immigrant, whether it means cheaper housing, cheaper food, cheaper cleaning services, cheaper landscaping, and a myriad of other cheaper services. Employers have depended on immigrants to do the dirtiest work, such as plumbing, or the most dangerous work, such as toppling large trees. The immigrant carried the burden of Houston's economic success and growth. Now, with the downturn in the economy, they are expendable and unwanted.

As we reflect on economics, consumerism, materialism, and the plight of immigrants, we remember the old proverb quoted by Martin Buber and Cardinal Joseph Ratzinger: "Success is not one of the names of God, but consuming fire is." With this understanding, the poor in despair who come to us can find hope in the fire of God's love, so far beyond worldly success, as can the rest of us.

Perhaps if we all pray to God as fervently as the Franciscan missionaries did in Mexico at the time of the Spanish conquest and ask Our Lady of Guadalupe and Juan Diego to join in our prayers, a just solution will be found in a new, surprising way that will change hearts.

13

ANGEL'S STORY
"I Almost Suffocated in the Trailer"

Reporting on the trial of the truck driver accused of making a smuggling run into the United States in 2003 in which many immigrants died, the *New York Times* wrote that when authorities found the truck in Victoria, Texas, it was piled with dead bodies and fifty-five survivors. The truck had been traveling from Laredo to Victoria. The *Times* reported, "How many were crammed into the 18-wheeler remains unclear. The dead and survivors total 74, but some riders may have escaped when Mr. Williams unlocked the doors" (*New York Times*, December 4, 2006).

Two of those who escaped came to Casa Juan Diego. They were from El Salvador. The local press reported at the time that the Honduran Consulate might bring Honduran survivors from the truck to Casa Juan Diego if the Immigration and Naturalization Service released them. In the days following the tragedy, reporters from television stations and newspapers called or came to ask if the surviving victims had arrived; they wanted to speak with them in order to report a more personal story of what had happened. We had to say that they had not arrived, because they hadn't. Immigration kept those who were detained hidden in a hotel, interviewing them as witnesses against the coyotes. A few days later, when the press had stopped calling, we were surprised to receive two men who had managed to leave the trailer and escape before Immigration had arrived. Angel was one of those two men.

On Wednesday, May 21, 2003, before our Mass, he told his story. It was a week after the abandoned truck full of immigrants was discovered. After listening to him speak for a half hour about the terrible sufferings during his journey, and especially those of his sister, we tried to tactfully mention that, while we were very interested, as well as concerned about his sister, the priest was waiting to begin.

It was only then that Angel said he almost died with the others in Victoria and started to tell the guests gathered for Mass the details of those terrible hours trapped inside the trailer. We all listened, spellbound. This is his story. Angel wanted to be sure it would not be published in the *Houston Catholic Worker* before he left town. He had suffered too much on the journey to be captured by authorities now.

I was working in a *maquiladora* in El Salvador, called Consul Tex. In this *maquila*, we made the shirts for the football and basketball teams of the NFL and NBA. They didn't pay us enough to live on. I have four-year-old twin daughters and another younger daughter, and I couldn't provide for my family on the salary they paid me. For example, a pair of shoes for my daughters costs $20 in El Salvador, and they don't last more than a month or two. We now have to pay for school, not only for registering a child, but also for electricity and water for the school, in addition to supplies, uniforms, and all. Many children are out of school because their parents do not have enough money to send them. The company paid us $35 or $40 a week—and we knew that they sold the shirts for $200 to $500 each. If they had paid us $60 a week, we would have been able to live and and I would have been able to send my daughters to school.

When the three of us—my brother, my sister, and I—left El Salvador, we were happy that we were coming to the United States. We started out in a bus from the border of El Salvador and Guatemala. We changed buses for one to Esquintla and then on to Tecún Umán. We arrived at 2:30 in the morning. When in Tecún Umán, we went toward the Suchiate River, the border of Mexico and Guatemala. On the other side of the river seven *mañosos*—clever, crafty robbers, rapists, and murderers—came out. They tied up my brother and me and raped our sister before our eyes. They laughed when they were doing the act and they beat us. When they got bored, they left. We were very discouraged and didn't want to continue toward our destination, but the three of us talked and decided to go on.

We started to walk and arrived near Hidalgo just as the train was leaving. We jumped on and went toward Tapachula, where we spent the rest of the day. In the afternoon, while we were waiting on the platform for the train, more thugs arrived. My brother ran, and I grabbed my sister's hand and we began to run. Another migrant stayed behind; they caught him and beat him until he couldn't stand up. My brother and our sister and myself got together again and at about 1:00 a.m. the train came and we got on. We hadn't gone five kilometers when gangs stopped the train. We ran and lost my brother. The guy running behind us had not crossed the fence when they shot him, and he cried out for us to help him. I couldn't help him because I was bringing my sister.

We began to walk toward Huistla, and arriving there, we walked along the train track. Arriving at the checkpoint la Arrozera, there were more *mañosos*. When we saw them, we began to walk back the other way. When we arrived in Huistla, I asked a man how we could get through. He told us to circle around, and we started to walk through the canals.

When we arrived at another town, we went to a house where the lady told us no when we asked for water. She said that it was already enough what they had done to her. She told us to leave, and if not, she would call Immigration.

We continued walking to catch the train. It was already going, but we managed to get on and there was Immigration. On the train, there were about three hundred of us and they caught more than half. We were lucky to escape. When we got off, we went around the checkpoint and walked five hours, got on the train again, and arrived in Tonelá, where we spent two days.

We got on another train, and there more *mañosos* awaited us. They robbed us, took our clothes, and left my sister and me both naked. I only had undershorts. I left my sister in some trees and found a house where I sought help. At first, the woman didn't believe me, but then she went to get my sister, brought her to her house, and helped us. From there we took the train to Tierra Blanca where the *mañosos* followed us again. My sister went into a nearby house and they beat me. They told her to come out or they would kill me. I told her not to come out, and finally they left. I couldn't stand up because they had beaten me hard, but the woman from the house where my sister was came out and helped me. She took me to her house and gave us food. We were there four days until I could walk. Then we went out to catch another train that went to Orizaba, and there again the thugs pursued me to get my sister. We ran until we arrived at a shelter and they let us in. We stayed there eight days.

We went out again to catch the train and when we got off, we went to a nearby house where the woman gave us food, but called Immigration. When we saw the Immigration van, we ran. At that moment, the train came and we were able to get on. We continued our journey to Monterrey, and then went to Nuevo Laredo where people helped us and I was able to find work for my sister. She stayed in Nuevo Laredo at her job, while I swam the Rio Grande to this side.

I met another Salvadoran in Laredo, Texas, and we went walking. A man asked us if we had anyone in Houston who could help us and we said we did. He agreed that in two days he would take us in a van.

When we got into the van, he told us to get down on the floor. The van started off and when we reached the trailer truck he told us to run and get on, so we did. Soon more people started to get on, both men and women, and the container, the trailer, was filled and the door was closed. The truck started to move. At first, it was cool, but after a while on the road, the trailer started to heat up. There were about seventy people inside. Soon there was no air and we started to become weak, with an immense sweating. The women started to become agitated, to run, to cry out, and to try to open the trailer. A baby began crying and crying. Nobody could open the door. Then two men became angry and said if the baby would not be quiet, they would kill it.

Then began a total disorder, chaos. People began to fall to the floor, all desperate to get out. They grouped and massed by the door, one on top of the other, and thus it happened that many more people died. Those who were already on the floor kicked them. Some died of heart attacks and others of asphyxiation.

We stayed at the back of the truck. I fainted from the heat, from not drinking water, without eating, without pure air. We didn't even know when the truck stopped. When I came to, someone was already opening the door. When it was opened, several bodies fell to the ground. Then the driver unhitched the cab and left. People began to throw themselves out of the truck and fell, lying down, all dizzy and faint.

The other Salvadoran and I woke up a little in the fresh air. We were not the first to leave the truck, because some had not fainted, as we almost had. As we began walking, we came to ourselves and went into the brush because we saw helicopters belonging to Immigration and patrol cars. After this, a man drove by and gave us a ride. We explained by signs what had happened, since he didn't speak Spanish. He had seen the trailer, with the bodies falling to the ground. He took us to his house and gave us food and a place to bathe. That is how we were saved. His friend at his house spoke Spanish and he told us of all that was coming out on the news about the truck and the migrants who had died. We watched the news. We spent two days at his house and later they sketched a little map for us of how to get to Houston.

We started to walk along the highway at night, going off the road when a vehicle was passing. We walked six hours and then tried to get a ride. First, a truck passed and didn't want to stop for us, then a trailer that didn't want to either. Then another trailer with bunk beds inside gave us a ride to the edge of Houston. We saw the police there and we were afraid. We stayed there and spent the day hidden in some trees.

When it got dark, we started to walk again, into Houston, where we slept in the unfinished construction of a house. At dawn, the workers arrived, including many Mexicans. We asked them if they could get us a job. They said, "We are immigrants also. You'll have to wait for the *patrón* [the boss] to ask. We cannot say." We asked them where we could talk on the telephone (to make a call to the relatives of my Salvadoran friend in Houston). They sent us to a store a few blocks away to buy a phone card. We bought the card, but couldn't make the connection. We didn't know the codes.

We came back and asked a man waiting for a bus to help us dial the phone number. He looked like he didn't trust us, but he dialed the number. He couldn't get through, either, and he lent us his cell phone. Unfortunately, the other Salvadoran's uncle said he couldn't help us, because his family in El Salvador had had its own tragedy and he had sent all his money there for a funeral. We asked the man who had let use the telephone if he could help us. "Let me think, and ask my life's companion," he said. He called his wife and she said yes. His mother-in-law came for us, took us to their house, and gave us food and a place to bathe and clean clothes, because we were very dirty. We asked them if they knew of a church or somewhere that could help us. Yes, they said, and they brought us to Casa Juan Diego, where they received us. We spent two days at Casa Juan Diego before going to be with my family in another city. This was the fifth house of hospitality run by Catholics that we had stayed at on our journey through Guatemala and Mexico to the United States.

I can hardly believe I am alive. I never want what happened to us to happen to another person. I came to the United States to work and help my family get ahead a little. I still don't know anything about my brother who was lost, even though I have spoken with my family in El Salvador.

I knew before coming that the trip to the United States was very hard, but I had never seen things like these. If I had known, at no time would I have allowed my sister to come. But now I will go on to try to begin work right away so I can send money to my family in El Salvador.

Afterword
"HOW DID YOU GET THAT WAY?"

Once, when we were making a presentation to a small group in a parish in Houston, we were startled by the question, "How did you get that way?" At first, we thought it was a hostile question. We soon realized, however, that people were not attacking us, but asking how they might be freed from their imprisonment in the bourgeois, middle-class environment in which they lived and worked. They had their credit card debt, their homes, their two cars—so many things to be responsible for—as well as looking ahead to college for their children. They wondered how we had found the freedom to live in a different way, rather than to be formed by the culture. They asked how we managed to get away with changing our lifestyle in order to be free to create programs for the poor immigrant, who is a nonentity or nonperson in our world.

We tried to present the Catholic Worker movement envisioned by Dorothy Day and Peter Maurin as an alternative way of living. We weren't always successful. We told the questioners about the freedom of giving one's work as a gift, about commitment to nonviolence and peace in our world, about the joys and sorrows of giving hospitality to those who have no home, and of giving hospitality to the lost and wounded. We also talked about the Christian economic theory called distributism, which emphasizes small businesses and vibrant local economies; it has been endorsed by Peter Maurin and Dorothy Day, as well as a number of popes. We could only begin and share a little on each topic.

However, people still asked, "How did the two of *you*, with your children, find that you could take this path? What inspired you to do so?? They asked why we chose refugees and immigrants as those we would receive in hospitality. We believe, we told them, that we are only doing what any committed person would do. We just happened to be in the right place at the right time and had had experiences that led us to begin the Houston Catholic Worker house.

Although we are very much influenced by Dorothy Day and Peter Maurin, the roots of our life and work at Casa Juan Diego are in Mark's family. For his parents and their twelve children, the Catholic faith was a vibrant, living thing. Mark always remembered seeing his father on his knees with the family as they prayed the Rosary together during Lent. For the Zwick family, faith did not depend on the personality of priests. Often those assigned to their country parish and later to their small town were struggling; some were even alcoholics. Realism and practicality went along with their strong faith, not sentimentality. Mass and frequent confession were essential. There was never a doubt about going to Mass. For example, when, as a teenager, one of Mark's brothers came in very late, overslept, and missed part of the early morning Mass, he immediately went to another Mass in order to be there for the complete liturgy.

Mark's father died when he was seventeen. After his father's death, he decided to go to the seminary. It was when Mark was a student working in the seminary library at St. Mary's College in Kentucky that he began to read Catholic periodicals, including the *Catholic Worker*. He became friends there with Jim Clark, who had been a captain in the New York Fire Department and had later joined the seminary. Jim shared with Mark about his friendship with Dorothy Day and his reasons for becoming a pacifist.

Mark visited the Catholic Worker in New York several times and met Dorothy Day, along with Michael Harrington of *The Other America* fame, who gave him his first tour of the Worker. Mark and his mother, who sometimes accompanied him on the visits, helped with requests that Dorothy made of them. Once Ed Willock of *Integrity Magazine* was ill. Dorothy asked them to drive Willock's children up to Massachusetts to Mary Reed Newland (who was a writer of children's liturgical books). Louise also visited the New York Catholic Worker in the 1960s. We still have a letter that Dorothy wrote to us. Many years later when we visited the New York Catholic Worker after we had begun in Houston, whom did we find there celebrating Mass but Fr. Jim Clark, who was also visiting.

Mark knew Fr. John Hugo, Dorothy's spiritual adviser for many years, the person who put flesh on the bones of the famous retreat of Fr. Lacouture that Dorothy Day recommended so highly. Mark had the opportunity to make the retreat with Fr. Francis Meenan, and he knew the other priests who gave the retreat as well. He participated with a small group that met periodically to follow up on the retreat, inviting one another to follow the Gospel. People called them "Hugo-ites." These eight-day silent retreats, with several conferences a day, are based on the first week of the Ignatian retreat. The retreat is still being given. We made it together in the 1990s.

When Dorothy published her classic book, *The Long Loneliness*, Mark was able to promote it in his newly founded apostolate in bookstores he started in Ravenna and Warren, Ohio.

Although she went to a little Protestant country church on Sundays and sang in the choir while growing up, Louise had not had a faith experience. She began seeking God when she was in college. She took several philosophy classes taught by a Catholic priest at Youngstown University where she did her undergraduate work. She met Mark on the steps of St. Columba's Cathedral in Youngstown, Ohio, where he was stationed as a priest. Louise, a student at the university, had become interested in the Church. When she visited the sisters at a nearby Catholic bookstore, they sent her to find Fr. Zwick because he was the one who organized and presented classes for those interested in joining the Church. She had gone to Mass that day for the first time and was very moved by the liturgy, by the sense of the sacred, and by the devotion of the congregation. She had not seen people kneeling in prayer before. As we look back, it strikes us that we met on December 8, 1962, almost thirty years to the day after the historic meeting of Dorothy Day and Peter Maurin.

It was through Mark that Louise came to belief in God and faith in Christ, and became convinced of the truth and beauty of the Catholic Church. Mark had instructed many dozens of people in the Catholic faith. When he taught inquiry classes for possible converts, he always included the famous passage from Matthew 25 in which the Bible tells us how one day we will be judged on caring for Christ in the poor—the passage that became so much a part of our lives in the Catholic Worker. Mark was known in the Diocese of Youngstown as a priest who reached out to the poor.

As a part of her preparation for entering the Church, Mark introduced Louise to Catholic writers, including St. Thomas Aquinas and those of the Catholic renaissance in the twentieth century that had prepared the way for the Second Vatican Council. He shared with her authors such as Henri de Lubac, Hans Urs von Balthasar, and Louis Bouyer, and presented the Catholic Worker as one way to live out the Gospel. She entered the Catholic Church in 1963.

After graduating from college, Louise worked for a time at Catholic Social Services in Youngstown and then for St. Columba's parish. Working with Mark on community organization in that inner-city parish, she visited homes there. In the community adjacent to the cathedral, there was much violence and few resources for families. The residents told of the need for a neighborhood center where there would be programs for the youth.

So together we founded Gilead House, a neighborhood center and council to address the poverty, the violence, and the concerns of the community. We rented an old building, found volunteers to help, and began a variety of programs, including softball teams for kids from the ghetto, which Mark coached. Music lessons were taught by people Louise knew from the university, where she had studied. Growing up in a rural community, Louise had participated in the 4-H. Representatives from the 4-H came to provide programs.

During this time in the 1960s, we participated with other active Catholics around the liturgy, attended national liturgical conferences, and participated in the *Cursillo* movement. We protested racism and the Vietnam War with others both in and outside the Catholic community. Louise considered a vocation to the religious life, but was discouraged by the vocation director at the order where she made inquiries. This was near the end of the Second Vatican Council and many religious sisters themselves were considering leaving their order.

After we had known each other for about five years, we became especially good friends and fell in love. Mark was laicized and the Vatican gave him permission to marry within the Church.

We moved to Chicago where Mark studied at the University of Chicago and received his master's degree in social work in 1969. It was there in Chicago that our first child, Jennifer, was born and took her first steps. When Mark finished his studies, we moved to Modesto, California, where we had our second child, Joachim.

Mark had good work as a psychiatric social worker at the Stanislaus County Community Mental Health Center in Modesto. He was also asked to work overtime on the psychiatric emergency team, as California began to close mental hospitals with the idea of providing more care in the community. In addition to his daytime position, he was called out at all hours of the night to evaluate the psychiatric needs of people who came to the hospital emergency room, to determine if they needed to be hospitalized or if they might remain in the community to receive help. His experience in diagnosing and recommending treatment for psychiatric problems has been invaluable in our work at Casa Juan Diego, as we receive so many people in Houses of Hospitality, some of whom, as in any population, are mentally ill.

Louise stayed home with the children in the first years of our marriage, something we both valued very much. We got to know the Lamaze method for assisting with childbirth, and the La Leche League for helping with breastfeeding. We learned about babies and colic. We learned a lot about washing cloth diapers and plastic pants, and about treating diaper rash. We learned what it meant to be up all night with a child with a fever, and the importance of waiting two hours after a child threw up so his or stomach could rest and recover before giving even a teaspoon of water. We discovered the practical remedy of using dark molasses as a gentle laxative for babies. As Louise took the children to parent-participation nursery schools, we had a good introduction to early childhood education. It did not occur to us that all these practical lessons and skills would be most helpful years later in giving hospitality to mothers with babies and children.

Weekly trips to the library brought stacks of picture books and children's literature to the house. Louise taught the children to read at home, using the ideas of a book called *Montessori in the Home*. It was during this time that we became aware of what a public library committed to community outreach could do, and Louise's interest in library science grew. It was also in California that our children began their music lessons in the Suzuki method, in violin and piano. We soon became committed and seasoned "Suzuki-ites." Louise had studied music and enjoyed sharing it with the children. To this day, they appreciate their music background.

Some might have thought we had it all! We had purchased a house and, over a period of several years, saved a year's salary, or even two. We had what might be considered usual for middle-class people—a four-bedroom, two-and-a-half-bathroom house, two babies, two cars, two bank accounts, and a good salary. People respected us at the city gates, as the Bible would say. What would be next? A cottage on the lake, a boat, a larger home with six bedrooms, a Mercedes, an upper-middle-class parish? We knew that there was more than this to life.

We joined a small discussion group with a membership made up of Christians and Jews, where we read and discussed books by authors such as Martin Buber, Dietrich Bonheoffer (*The Cost of Discipleship*), and Graham Greene. One young man in the group, who was a recent graduate from Yale Law School, kept challenging us by asking where we were going with our lives and where our careers were going to lead us. He challenged the traditional career ladders and the idea of professionalism. "What is next?" he kept asking, or the old, "And then?"—which reminded us of the question of St. Alphonsus Liguori we had heard years ago: "What is all of this in the light of eternity?" The young attorney's message was loud and clear, and we took it to heart. He is probably a Wall Street lawyer today, while we are here at the Catholic Worker.

During those years, the life and vision of Peter Maurin and Dorothy Day continued to be in the background, haunting us, challenging us to live out the Gospel in a radical, practical way. In the meantime, we tried where we were, while working and raising children, to live out some of their ideas and inspirations. We were conscious of social issues and concerns. We were reading Frances Moore Lappé and about her conviction that those who said population growth caused all the hunger were incorrect. The problem, she said, was that a third of the world's grain was being fed to livestock, making grains, the heart of the world's diet, too scarce and expensive. The planet was not really out of food and did not have to throw some people off the lifeboat. Her book *Diet for a Small Planet* was half explanation, half recipes. It didn't turn us into vegetarians, but gave us ideas in preparing combination dishes with less meat and more grains, vegetables, and dairy products.

We supported the efforts of the United Farm Workers in California, where those who picked the fruits and vegetables for our tables labored so long and hard in the fields, picketing with them at the Gallo ranch a half a mile from where we lived, and joining the grape boycott. It was frustrating, though, not being able to speak Spanish with the farm workers.

We brought Dan Berrigan, SJ, closely associated with the Catholic Worker, to speak several times in California during the Vietnam War. Fr. Dan encouraged us to learn Spanish and move to the Southwest. He also shared with us his great interest in the writings of Jacques Ellul. Friends formed another discussion group with us where we read and discussed eight or ten of Ellul's books. Ellul, a French Protestant and a profound thinker, encouraged again our reflection on the way we would live our lives. We have never fully recovered from reading his books—thank

God. Peter Maurin and Dorothy Day would have been at home with him in raising doubts about the technological society, the evils of the "city," and shallow activism.

The two of us began to meditate more and discuss more. We took a risk—one never knows where prayer, meditation, and discussion can lead a person. It is not only a way of avoiding the ennui and boredom of life, but it helps one avoid falling prey to the syndrome that Thoreau talks about when he says that most men lead lives of quiet desperation. We concluded that even with two little children, there was another way to live. We could each work half time and thus have more time for the family and for participation in social justice actions, for example, with the United Farm Workers. However, changing our lifestyle was not that simple.

Mark had a difficult time even thinking about working less, because he was respected and had a good future in one of the most creative and innovative mental health centers in the United States. He published articles in professional journals on the mental health prevention programs he was organizing among the poor. He was paid well and we could save money. It was hard to argue with the need to save for the children's future, especially since we had been penniless when Mark finished graduate school. But working overtime so many hours, Mark didn't see Louise or the children as much as he would have liked. One day he suggested that maybe he should quit the job that took him from the family so much. Maybe Louise could go to graduate school, after which they could both work part-time.

Mark said later that Louise never had an iota of doubt. She broke all records for being accepted into graduate school in the least amount of time. It seemed that by the time he returned from buying milk for the children, Louise was on her way to being accepted in a children's literature and library science master's program at the University of California at Berkeley. She would become a children's librarian, and Mark would help to take care of the children during her graduate studies. And so it was! Mark had saved up a lot of vacation time and was able to commute a couple of times a week from Modesto to Berkeley, some ninety miles, in order to help care for the children while Louise studied. They were five and three years old at the time and attended kindergarten and preschool, which helped with some child-care hours. Louise was pleased with the library classes, especially in children's literature. However, we were surprised to discover that at the university in Berkeley, after all the turmoil of the 1960s, the overwhelming interest of graduate students was how to find a job and how much money they would make when they received their degrees.

After Louise completed graduate studies, we kept to the half-time idea, although it was difficult to find professional half-time positions. Working half time put us on the slippery slope of living differently.

Louise began her first half-time library job as a reference librarian for a research company that wrote environmental impact studies. It wasn't a job as a children's librarian, but the job that was available part-time. She had a positive experience in her library work as she developed a report-and-document collection for the company. She was disturbed, however, by a lack of depth or commitment there to genuine evaluation of environmental dangers. They seemed more concerned over losing contracts.

Mark became director of group therapy for children, his specialty in graduate school, at a community mental health center near Louise's work on the San Francisco Peninsula, which is south of the City. That half-time job as a group psychotherapist for children was challenging and rewarding. He also trained psychologists, psychiatrists, and social workers to conduct group therapy. He enjoyed his work, but wondered about the overwhelming influence of Freudian dogmas in the mental health field in the interpretation of everything a child did. Their faith in Freud was more profound than many Christians' faith in the Nazarene.

Our income was cut by two-thirds by the move to half-time work, even though two people were now working. We moved to a two-bedroom apartment, which was more than adequate since the children were still small. The people at the city gates were unimpressed—in fact, people felt sorry for us. This was unnecessary, as we were surviving very well with our simple lifestyle and were still saving money "for the children." We did not give up our savings, which allowed us liberty to survive if things went wrong. Living with less income did not destroy us, but in fact prepared us for future moves.

Our lifestyle change was not precipitous but something that occurred over a period of years. We continued our part-time work as we related to a small community and talked about Catholic Worker possibilities with them. Our discussion-group community volunteered at the soup kitchen of the San Francisco Catholic Worker, participated with local people committed to reducing the risks of nuclear destruction, and continued to aid farm workers on a part-time basis. During this time, we read more about Dorothy Day and the Catholic Worker movement in William Miller's classic book, *A Harsh and Dreadful Love.*

It was around this time that we became friends with Tom and Mella Trier. Tom was Jewish. Mella was raised Catholic. As we celebrated the Passover with the Triers (including our children and their children), our discussions took on special significance in the light of the experience of "exodus." Together we read the ancient story of the Jewish Passover and the exodus. Tom's own exodus from Nazi Germany at age seven came just in time for him and his parents to escape. Tom told his story of escape to freedom, and we sang the songs of Passover in Hebrew and English. We prayed that the Passover might become a reality to us, and we thanked the Lord especially for Tom's Passover. The Trier experience remains with us still, influencing our feelings about refugees from persecution in any country.

For a number of years, we had been interested in Latin America, in the small base communities there, in the Spanish language, and in Hispanic culture. We had tried learning Spanish without much success. We couldn't shake our knowledge of French, Italian, and Latin, and we couldn't concentrate, even though working half time. We talked about taking a sabbatical in Spain when the children got older. Friends living in Mexico, however, convinced us that the best time to travel with children is when they are young. Adolescents don't travel as well with their families, they told us, and may need a stable environment during the teenage years. Moreover, why not go somewhere closer to home, in this hemisphere? We began to explore possibilities that would include learning more about the *comunidades de base* in Latin America.

By the end of 1976, after many months of thinking about moving to Latin America, we were ready. We had been through a number of groups and read a number of books. We had prayed and saved money and talked to a number of people. We had studied Spanish for a semester. We decided it was time to go. We were ready to learn Spanish, to live with the poor, and to participate in the life of the Church in Latin America. The previous chapters tell the story of our time in Central America.

By the time we were back in the United States, working at St. Theresa's parish in Houston, the onslaught of homeless and desperate refugees began to arrive. We knew we should do something to help. We had few funds, but we had experience and we had come to know the people in El Salvador and Guatemala. We could speak Spanish now, more or less. We had known about the Catholic Worker movement for a long time before we went to Central America. We knew it was possible to start a Catholic Worker house. We had fallen in love while working with the poor. Our love began and flourished in the middle of service to others, so there were no excuses for not responding—we thought—and so we began. After having lived with the poor in Central America, giving hospitality to the immigrants and refugees pouring into Houston was a natural response.

Louise worked at the Houston Public Library during the first eleven years of Casa Juan Diego, while Mark laid the groundwork for and did the work of founding it, receiving the refugees and immigrants who have become so much a part of our lives. As he had done before in various projects, Mark quietly but enthusiastically spoke to various people and groups and gradually developed support for the work. He rented what we called the ugliest building in Houston and began to receive refugees. Both Central American refugees and full-time volunteer Catholic Workers from the United States came to join in the work.

It hasn't always been easy to balance family life with the busy Catholic Worker. When we started, our children were in the sixth and fourth grades. Since Louise worked from 9:00 a.m. to 6:00 p.m., Mark learned to cook various dishes and left the House of Hospitality each afternoon so that dinner would be ready when the children came home from school. The children continued their music studies and both played violin in the Houston Youth Symphony. Louise was able to leave her library work and join Mark full-time without a salary when the children were almost finished with college.

Jennifer went to high school at Incarnate Word Academy, where the Sisters of the Incarnate Word and Blessed Sacrament were an inspiration to her. She wrote several articles for the *Houston Catholic Worker* during high school and college, and lived and worked at Casa Juan Diego for a time during college. Jennifer married at nineteen and had two children, all the while studying at the University of St. Thomas in Houston, where she got her degree in bilingual education.

Joachim attended St. Thomas High School, a few blocks from Casa Juan Diego, and played clarinet in the band there. He studied at Notre Dame for three years and then studied music at the University of Houston and played viola in the Galveston Symphony. His hobby in computers later became his full-time work.

In the mid-1990s, Joachim came to us and said that our newspaper had to be on the World Wide Web, which was in its early stage of development. Joachim and his friends set up our Web site at www.cjd.org, where the stories of the people who come to take refuge with us are recounted, along with articles about immigration, economics, the Catholic Worker movement, and faith and culture. Joachim spent many hours formatting articles from our newspaper for the Web site, preparing articles that existed in electronic files. In the earliest years, we had typed our copy on paper and sent it to a typesetter; those issues are still not in electronic form, except for the stories reprinted in this book. Gradually, Joachim taught us to work with a program for the Web site, using the simple method of taking a template of an already-existing article, erasing the article, placing a new one from a current issue of the paper there, and using the "Save As" function to create a new page.

Jennifer's marriage did not work out. She taught bilingual education for several years as a single mother and then became ill. She and the kids came to live with us, and so we have had another generation of young people raised in the Catholic Worker environment.

Our granddaughter Noemí Flores volunteered at Casa Juan Diego through high school and wrote some articles and book reviews for the paper. Her first book review, of a children's book about Dorothy Day, appeared when she was eight years old. Noemí attended Incarnate Word Academy, her mother's alma mater, and is currently a college student at the University of St. Thomas in Houston, where she has received scholarships. She continues to volunteer part-time as her schedule permits, organizing donations or working with the children of Casa Juan Diego. Our grandson, John Flores (officially Juan, but he goes by John), is two years younger. He sometimes has helped to send out the newspaper, and he has brought his high school classes to volunteer. He and his sister protested the Iraq War with us and with other Catholic Workers. They picketed with us when we went to Alvin, Texas, to protest with Vandana Shiva the biopiracy of the "copyright" of rice from India by U.S. companies. While we did not anticipate helping to raise our grandchildren, we have continued to live as Catholic Workers. We do not own a home, but live in one of the Catholic Worker houses.

People keep asking us the same question today: "How did you get that way?" This work is fine, they say, for a year or two right after college. "Why would you want to spend the rest of your life as Catholic

Workers?" The examples of Dorothy Day and Peter Maurin gave us the inspiration and the courage to take the New Testament seriously and try to live it out, even though that seemed like a radical thing to do. When we are asked what has kept us going and why we are still here, we realize that part of the answer is that we also continue to read and have conversations and discussions with others. In addition to weekly discussions with Catholic Workers in Houston, we continue to participate in other groups, such as a *communio* group that meets at Casa Juan Diego, and to dialogue with those who visit. Peter Maurin called this clarification of thought.

When the Catholic Worker movement was criticized in several Catholic magazines in the early 1990s, we wondered how to respond. We decided to look more deeply into the ideas that had formed Dorothy and Peter and inspired them to start the Catholic Worker. We began to read some of the authors Dorothy and Peter had read and quoted in their writings. Those writers inspired us again, helping us to express what we had already found to be true through our experience. One reader from the East Coast loved the series in our paper beginning in 1995 on the roots of the Catholic Worker movement, about the philosophers and saints who influenced and inspired Peter Maurin and Dorothy Day. He sent sizable contributions and made copies of the relevant pages in our newspaper, printing up the first small version of what later became our book published by Paulist Press, *The Catholic Worker Movement: Intellectual and Spiritual Origins*.

By now, serving the poor in a personalist way is a part of our "habits of being," as Emmanuel Mounier described it. Mounier, who developed the ideas of French personalism that so influenced the Catholic Worker, wrote that personalist action begins with a change of heart and a sense of one's destiny. We are transformed when we act, when we live out our destiny. Mounier said, "Every person is responsible for incarnating and living out the values of his or her vocation. The values of one's vocation form a person, form the habits of being."[1] Mounier emphasized that a Christian has a responsibility to act in the world. This engagement in the world makes life unpredictable. We have certainly found this to be true. We have to say that life at Casa Juan Diego has rarely had a dull moment. As Mounier reminded his readers: "Availability is as essential as loyalty, the test of history as much as intellectual analysis."[2] Anyone who has ever been a Catholic Worker or worked in the service of the poor knows how demanding availability can be.

Those involved in the Catholic Worker movement realize that the Works of Mercy benefit not only those served, but also those who serve; the action of serving leaves traces, marks, in a way that impacts the future of those who serve, as well as of those around them. Anyone who has ever spent a few months or even days at a Catholic Worker is changed forever in some way. Mounier spoke of how a person becomes a person through acting. John Paul II called this the "intransitive." His intransitivity thesis told us that "in acting we change the world around us, but more importantly we change and transcend ourselves."[3]

There have been a number of times when we have been overwhelmed or discouraged, especially when we hear tragic stories from our guests. The world is too hard on them. Our faith is what keeps us going. As Hans Urs von Balthasar put it:

> From a worldly point of view everything may seem very dark; your dedication may seem unproductive and a failure. But do not be afraid: you are on God's path. "Let not your hearts be troubled; believe in God; believe also in me." I am walking on ahead of you and blazing the trail of Christian love for you. It leads to your most inaccessible brother, the person most forsaken by God. But it is the path of divine love itself. You are on the right path.[4]

We would say with Dorothy Day that we have been disillusioned this long, long time in the means used by *anyone* but the saints to live in this world God has made for us. She said that the great mystery of the Incarnation is a joy that makes us want to kiss the earth in worship, because his feet once trod that same earth. The poor can identify with the Lord's life:

> To begin to understand this mystery that we as Catholics accept, there are also the facts of Christ's life, that he was born in a stable, that he did not come to be a temporal king, that he worked with his hands, spent the first years of his life in exile, and the rest of his early manhood in a crude carpenter shop in Nazareth. He trod the roads in his public life and the first men he called were fishermen, small owners of boats and nets. He was familiar with the migrant worker and the proletariat, and some of his parables

dealt with them....He died between two thieves because he would not be made an earthly king. And he directed his sublime words to the poorest of the poor, to the people who thronged the towns and followed after John the Baptist, who hung around, sick and poverty-stricken at the doors of rich men.[5]

In the middle of our consuming and comfort-oriented society, reflection on the Incarnation reminds us that people are more important than the latest gadget, even if they are born in the place where animals live, even if they have to drink out of the troughs where animals drink on their journey to the United States. They are more important even if they spend their lives doing menial, backbreaking work and traveling to different countries to find that work and the smallest, crowded room in which to live.

Dorothy's words about the Incarnation help us at the Houston Catholic Worker to accept the new immigrants who end up in our doorway every day of the year—those who, as she described it, hang around, sick and poverty-stricken at the doors of rich countries, allowing us to practice the hospitality of the Gospels, which tell us that when we accept the least ones we accept Jesus himself.

People have a little trouble with us after all these years of being at the Catholic Worker. They say: "You used to be nice liberals, talking about politics, books, movies, and good wine. Now you have become so darned pious, talking about carrying the cross and the crucifixion and all that old pious stuff. Give us a break!" Others encourage us. Give us a break!

Appendix 1

FAQS

The Truth about Casa Juan Diego

Question. *You have just talked to thirty-to-forty guests at the men's house. There are many women and children housed in the other centers. You have provided food, clothing, medicine, medical care, dental care, and eye care to hundreds of others in Casa Juan Diego's neighborhoods. You help so many sick and injured. Aren't you and the other Catholic Workers tired?*

Answer. Yes.

Q. *How can you and the other Catholic Workers do so much?*
A. We work as if all depended on us and pray as if all depended on God.

Q. *How can you face all the suffering, pain, sickness, disease, oppression, and abuse the immigrants face day after day?*
A. We don't face it! We couldn't survive if we did. We try to do something about it. We are foot washers rather than hand holders.

Q. *But don't former guests call, write, and visit to say, "How great thou art?"*
A. No.

Q. *Don't you get warm fuzzies at the end of a long day walking between houses and looking up at the stars and haze, and thinking about all the people you helped?*
A. No—we frequently get a headache.

Q. *Don't you think it is important to really "feel the love" every time you help someone?*
A. The work at Casa Juan Diego is hard. The days and sometimes the nights are long. You have to be tough to survive. Sometimes the work with the poor is romanticized. The real compensation is not in feeling, but in believing—believing that it makes a difference to try to change

things, instead of cursing the rich or the government or even the poor for that matter. The real compensation in working with those in need is not in feeling but in knowing—knowing that one's humble efforts may make a difference. Casa Juan Diego is a faith operation. You have to believe in people and in the Gospel. The work is not done because it "feels good."

Q. *Do you get angry with the people who are trying to get help from you?*
A. You have to see each person as a special human being. Each person has to be seen through the eyes of faith; otherwise, if you look through tired, faithless eyes, each person coming through the door—and there are dozens each day—is a threat to you and may be seen as the enemy, seeking something that is yours. The eyes of faith know otherwise.

Q. *Some of you miss daily Mass sometimes because of the needs of the poor. What do you say about that?*
A. We need to be better organized.

Q. *You are a large organization. Aren't you ashamed of being so big for a Catholic Worker house when "small is beautiful"? [The phrase comes from E. F. Schumacher.]*
A. Yes, we are trying to do better. We recently gave some of our houses to the Missionaries of Charity.

Q. *Aren't you taking a risk by having sick adults, sick children, high-risk pregnancies, and so on, in your houses?*
A. If you are housing Jesus in the poor, it is easier to take the risk.

Q. *How can you do so much?*
A. We pray a lot.

Q. *Tell the truth. How do you do it?*
A. The truth: we don't pay anyone. The money that comes in goes to the service of the poor.

Q. *You mean that there are no wages?*
A. We have totally abandoned the wage system, and we have embraced giving our work as a gift.

Q. *Isn't it un-American not to pay people?*
A. It may be against the Calvinist and Puritan ethic, but it is not un-

Catholic, or un-Catholic Worker, or un-Gospel not to pay people who *choose* this way. It is quite another question, however, when we are speaking of cheating a poor worker out of his wages.

Q. *Just because all of you are workaholics, does that mean everyone has to be?*
A. No. Young people seem more balanced and more adept at avoiding workaholism. So we don't worry too much. Occasionally a young person may look like a workaholic for the poor, and we give thanks. Our volunteers are not volunteers in the popular sense. They are totally dedicated people who would not do this work for any amount of money. Once they have the vision, it's easy. And they have a day off a week.

Q. *How are Catholic Workers compensated?*
A. By being given the opportunity to live out the Gospels, the social teachings of the Catholic Church, and the ideals of Peter Maurin and Dorothy Day, founders of the Catholic Worker movement.

Q. *Sounds like you hope to get to heaven by serving the poor.*
A. Yes.

Q. *Aren't you ashamed of getting to heaven on the backs of the poor?*
A. Is there another way? We are afraid of the "half a loaf" attitude that accepts Jesus in the Eucharist, but does not accept Jesus in the poor, which is the other half of the loaf.

Q. *Are all the workers in Casa Juan Diego Catholic?*
A. No. At times, half the workers present have not even been raised Catholic.

Q. *What is the religion of the immigrants whom you serve?*
A. We don't know.

Q. *You mean, you serve Protestants?*
A. We also serve Protestants, Jewish people, and people of other religions, including Politically Correct). Many of our guests are not Catholics. In fact, some really despise Catholics and the Church.

Q. *Do you ever serve African Americans?*
A. Yes, especially if they are Spanish speaking. We have had a number of guests with African roots from several countries, such as Colombia and especially Honduras, from the Garífuna community.

Q. *Do all immigrants come to the United States?*
A. No. There is enormous migration between other countries, for example, migration between countries in Latin America, or migration between countries in Africa. The new global economy has made life so hard for people that they desperately travel to other countries looking for work so their families can live. Some estimate that the current world migrations are the largest since the fourth century. But, percentage-wise, very few come to the United States.

Q. *Are you in favor of immigration without legal papers?*
A. Absolutely not! We oppose undocumented immigration because it destroys families, separates parents and children, and ruins marriages. We believe immigrants should be able to stay in their own countries with their families. We believe we, the United States, should make that possible by insisting our companies in Latin America pay a living wage, instead of the slave wages that force people to emigrate (to a place where they'll then be attacked for migrating).

Q. *That doesn't sound like someone who has had over 60,000 immigrants pass through their doors, does it?*
A. We pick up the pieces, as it were. After people are at your doorstep, it's hard not to accept them. Not to accept the homeless at your doorstep is tantamount to rejecting one's belief system. When someone comes to your door all black and blue or with their toes coming through their shoes or with feet swollen like melons, it's a little late to worry about asking for papers. Besides, we know what happens to those who say no. (See Mathew 25:31ff in the Bible.)

Q. *Why do immigrants come?*
A. They can't make it in their own countries. Our government, our multinational corporations, and the international financial institutions we sponsor have a huge role in creating a global economics that uproots people and forces them to migrate in order to feed their families.

Q. *Why do you use the word* undocumented *instead of* wetback *or* illegal?
A. It is actually very difficult to sort out at what stage people are in arranging their legal papers, and so it is more accurate to say *undocumented*. In addition, as Nobel Prize recipient and holocaust survivor Elie Wiesel tells immigrants: "You who are so-called illegal aliens must know that no human being is 'illegal.' That is a contradiction in terms. Human beings can be beautiful or more beautiful, they can be fat or skinny, they can be right or wrong, but illegal? How can a human being be illegal?" Weisel "gave" the last sentence to the Sanctuary Movement for their campaign "No Human Being Is Illegal."

Q. *What would help stop people from immigrating to the United States?*
A. The United States could insist that U.S. factories in other countries pay a living wage. Something is wrong if a teenage girl in El Salvador is paid 16 cents to make a shirt that the GAP or another company sells for $20 or $25 in the United States. Wages in China, where so many companies have moved, are even worse.

Q. *If U.S. companies in other countries paid more to the workers, could they still make a profit?*
A. They could still reap tremendous profits. For example, if they doubled the $.37 an hour wage, which is the average hourly wage in Honduras, they could still be rich with much more dignity.

Q. *Why doesn't the United States implement a Marshall plan in Latin America, as they did in Europe after World War II, to help these countries get on their feet economically?*
A. Great idea, *if* we would also eliminate the policies of institutions like the World Bank and the IMF tied to "assisting" countries, which actually make the people poorer.

Q. *Aren't slave wages better than no wages?*
A. No! Absolutely not, any more than being a prostitute is better than no job.

Q. *Don't immigrants come to the United States to get on welfare?*
A. That's the great radio-talk-show lie! It is impossible for undocumented immigrants to receive welfare. Those seriously injured on their jobs here cannot receive any kind of disability either.

Q. *We notice Spanish-speaking people using food stamps at the checkout counter at the grocery store. Isn't that the same?*
A. Not all Spanish-speaking people are illegal and thus they *can* receive benefits. Hispanics have been citizens for generations longer than many Anglos who also receive food stamps.

Q. *Aren't you worried that some of the people you serve may be illegal?*
A. No. Matthew 25 says, "What you do to the least of the brethren you do to me." The "least" are often undocumented.

Q. *Do you accept money from the poor you serve?*
A. Never. They must keep their money, so they can get on their feet.

Q. *They must pay in some way.*
A. Yes! When a poor person crosses their path in the future, we insist that they help that poor person as a way of paying us. We insist on this! Matthew 25 is for everyone. Our former guests will have more opportunity to meet other poor people in need than the average person who lives in the suburbs.

Q. *Aren't you worried that agencies will not respect your work as "professional" because you're just a bunch of volunteers without salaries?*
A. Agencies call us daily and hourly, seven days a week. They can distinguish between "being professional" and "professionalism," which is the curse of agencies. Instead of focusing on professionalism, we focus on personalism.

Q. *What agencies commonly call you?*
A. Hospitals and clinics, mostly, but also the Houston police, schools, all the women's groups and centers (including in other counties and states), churches, and even the Immigration Service.

Q. *Do other agencies do good work?*
A. Yes, of course. Sometimes better than we do. We can be Catholic shirkers as well as Catholic Workers.

Q. *What are the important things in the Catholic Worker movement?*
A. There are many facets. One of the most important things is hospitality, and that's the hardest thing we do each night for many people. When people live with us, we share their problems. Matthew 25 and the

Sermon on the Mount are key. Also important are voluntary poverty, pacifism, and personalism—that is, the Works of Mercy as opposed to the works of war.

Q. *Why don't you have public relations and fund raising?*
A. Our work is our public relations. That seems to be sufficient, along with our newspaper.

Q. *Would you do this work for money?*
A. Society could not afford it.

Q. *Do you do this work to be famous in the Andy Warhol style?*
A. It hasn't happened!

Q. *Do you want to be like Dorothy Day and Peter Maurin and the saints?*
A. Yes.

Q. *Why haven't you succeeded?*
A. Good question!

Q. *Your work is hard and the hours are long. How many years do you plan to continue this work?*
A. We are just going to try to finish out today.

Q. *Why do you do this work?*
A. Apparently, the Lord wants us to work out our salvation among immigrants and the poor.

Q. *Aren't you ashamed of hiding behind the skirts of Holy Mother Church in your work with immigrants?*
A. Well, we are Church, too—or part of the Church, the Body of Christ. We are grateful that the Church is with us in our humble efforts with immigrants. So many other groups have abandoned the immigrants.

Q. *Who are the immigrant men on the street corners in your neighborhood? Are they from Casa Juan Diego?*
A. They are not from Casa Juan Diego, but come to our neighborhood to get work, which is meant for our male guests.

Q. *Why are you so conservative?*
A. If trying to follow the teachings of Jesus and the Church, if trying to implement Catholic social teaching, and if trying to live out the ideals of Dorothy Day and Peter Maurin the best we can makes us conservative, then we are conservative.

Q. *Why are you so liberal?*
A. If trying to follow the teachings of Jesus and the Church, if trying to implement Catholic social teaching, and if trying to live out the ideals of Dorothy Day and Peter Maurin the best we can makes us liberal, then we are liberal.

Q. *Why are you so radical?*
A. Radical means going down to the roots, in this case, the roots of the Gospel and Catholic tradition. If taken seriously, this means living in a different way.

Q. *When you distribute food and clothing to the poor, you seem to be all business. There is no hand shaking and hugging.*
A. It's bad enough that the poor have to suffer the humiliation of being in need, much less of having to hug the giver.

Q. *Are you strict?*
A. All receive the same.

Q. *Isn't it uncomfortable with all those poor people who have no food or attractive clothes?*
A. We have not accepted acquisitiveness (acquiring many things) as a transcendental value. The worth of the person is primary since *being* comes before having.

Q. *How do you know that the people deserve what you give them?*
A. What we give them is not ours, but theirs in the first place. Our role is serving; God's role is judging.

Q. *What is the worst thing we have done to the poor?*
A. Making them think that they do not possess human dignity because they do not possess as many things as other people.

Q. *People accuse you of Band-Aid work. What is "Band-Aid work"?*
A. It is a phrase invented by those who believe we shouldn't help poor people with things, but instead focus on the structures that cause their poverty. Giving them things or a place to stay is "Band-Aid work." To those who believe this, the only real help is changing structures. Mother Teresa does not appeal to them. Dorothy Day was accused of doing Band-Aid work. She and Peter Maurin responded by pointing out how the monasteries in earlier centuries changed the structures, changed society, by living in a different way, living their faith and at the same time helping the poor. Actually, living in a different way is revolutionary, they said.

Q. *Where do you stand on Band-Aid work, as opposed to changing structures?*
A. We think they cannot be separated.

Q. *Does your Band-Aid work do any good?*
A. Recently, a battered woman and her five children came from Casa Maria, our Catholic Worker house in Southwest Houston, to live with us at Casa Juan Diego, after working up courage to leave her battering husband. Her battering husband purchased beer and milk—that's all!—over a period of several years. The only food the mother and children had was what they received from Casa Maria's weekly food distribution. Ditto, clothing: the only clothing they had was what they received from Casa Maria's clothing distribution. So, yes, Band-Aid does good.

Q. *What is your most difficult Band-Aid work?*
A. Providing hospitality. When you receive people into your home, you also receive their illnesses and problems, and must respond no matter how much you believe in changing structures.

Q. *What do you do with all of the people in the houses?*
A. We provide beds, food, clothing, medical care, transportation, jobs, English classes, and so on—basically, a place to rest a little and begin anew.

Q. *What do your guests say about Casa Juan Diego?*
A. That it's an oasis of peace, where they can rest for a time after experiencing violence, exhaustion, or deprivation.

Q. *Aren't you afraid of working with poor people? You know: they may be violent.*
A. No. What we fear most is trying to cross Shepherd and Durham Avenues during the rush hour.

Q. *Do you work with people with AIDS?*
A. Yes, we work with whomever comes to our door. We are supporting a number of people who are very sick with AIDS.

Q. *How can you do so much?*
A. We practice voluntary poverty. No one is paid.

Q. *How do you know if you are practicing voluntary poverty?*
A. If you offer your shoes to the poor and they refuse them.

Q. *What keeps you going after thirty years?*
A. If we didn't study and pray, we would be dead.

Q. *Aren't you ashamed of bringing in all these foreigners?*
A. We have never brought anyone to the United States. We think the people should stay home with their families. However, we can't expect them to stay home and starve to death. The millions used for border control and for prosecution of immigrants should be spent on providing people decent jobs in their own countries to keep them at home.

Q. *What is xenophobia?*
A. Fear of foreigners, which is condemned in the Bible.

Q. *What upsets some people?*
A. When we use old-fashioned ideas like, We must be in love with God, must love God passionately, and must love him in his poor. People are not sure how to respond.

Appendix 2
HOUSES OF HOSPITALITY
(Albergues) IN MEXICO AND
GUATEMALA

MEXICO

Casa San Juan Diego
Calles Abdul y Castaño
Colonia Matamoros Mariano
87380 Matamoros, Tamaulipas, México
Tel. (868) 817-4511 (Parroquia de Nuestra Señora de Lourdes)

Casa San Francisco de Asís
Calle Golfo de México 149
Col. Ampliación Solidaridad
Matamoros, Tamaulipas, México
Tel.   (868) 822-2213
         (868) 822-4649

Albergue del Migrante Nuestra Señora de Guadalupe
Boulevard Luis Echevarría S/N
Zona Centro
Reynosa, Tamaulipas, México
Tel.   (899) 922-4268

Casa del Migrante Nazaret
Calle Francisco I. Madero
Colonia Victoria
38030 Nuevo Laredo, Tamaulipas, México
Tel.   (876) 714-5611

Casa Madre Assunta (mujeres y niños migrantes)
Calle Galileo 2305
Colonia Postal
22350 Tijuana, Baja California, México
Tel. (664) 683-0575

Albergue del Ejército de Salvación
Av. Aquiles Serdán
Col. Libertad parte Baja
22300 Tijuana, Baja California, México
Tel. (664) 683-2694

Casa YMCA (jóvenes)
Boulevard Cuauhtemoc Sur 3170
Colonia Chulavista
22410 Tijuana, Baja California, México
Tel. (664) 686-1359
     (664) 686-2212

Casa del Migrante (hombres adultos)
Calle Galileo 239
Colonia Postal
22350 Tijuana, Baja California, México
Tel. (664) 682-5180

Casa Beato Juan Diego
Boulevard Lázaro Cárdenas
Fraccionamiento Murua
(Central Camionera)
22540 Tijuana, Baja California, México
Tel. (664) 621-3041

Albergue San Vicente
Calle Novena 691
Colonia Bustamante
22840 Ensenada, Baja California, México
Tel. (646) 176-0306

Casa del Migrante—Nuestra Señora de Guadalupe
Av. Hidalgo Int. 401
Colonia Centro
Tecate, Baja California, México
Tel. (665) 554-2662

Albergue Juvenil del Desierto (jóvenes)
Carpinteros #1515
Colonia Industrial
21010 Mexicali, Baja California, México
Tel. (686) 654-5364

Casa del Forastero Sta. Martha
Bocanegra 801
Colonia Industrial
Monterrey, Nuevo León, México
Tel. (818) 372-3355
       (818) 374-3637

Albergue Ejército de Salvación
Carvajal y De la Cueva 1717 N.
Col. Primero de Mayo
64550 Monterrey, Nuevo León, México
Tel. (818) 375-0379

Casa del Emigrante
Cerrada de Paz 120
Barrio de Tlaxcala
San Luis Potosí, San Luis Potosí, México
Tel. (444) 812-9019
       (444) 812-5672
E-mail: magdalenaasistencia@hotmail.com

Casa del Emigrante
Father P. Martín Martínez
Jonuta, Tabasco, México
Tel. (913) 367-0366

Santuario de Nuestra Señora de Guadalupe
Latinos #193
Colonia Moderna
Nogales, Sonora, México
Tel. (631) 313-5824

Casa del Migrante
Calle Neptuno #1855
Colonia Satélite
32540 Ciudad Juarez, Chihuahua, México
Tel. (656) 687-0676

Casa YMCA (menores)
Calle 3, Av. 10, No. 999
Agua Prieta, Sonora, México
Tel. (633) 338-4000
     (656) 615-5803

C.A.M.E.
Calle Sexta y Anahuac
Agua Prieta, Sonora, México
Tel. (633) 338-7694

Centro Comunitario de Atención al Migrante y Necesitado
Av. Gonzalo Senday #79
Col. Buenos Aires
Altar, Sonora, México
Tel. (637) 374-0360
Fax (637) 374-0032

Casa Emmaus: Casa del Emigrante
Prol. Victoria y Dr. Coss 47
Antigua Escuela Miguel Hidalgo
Ciudad Acuña, Coahuila, México
Tel. (877) 772-5717

Casa de la Peregrina
C. Quintana Roo #253
Colonia Monumento
32020 Cd. Juarez, Chihuahua, México

Iglesia de la Santa Cruz
Villahermosa, Tabasco, México
Tel. (993) 312-0647

Casa YMCA (menores)
Calle Tlaxcala #267
32000 Cd. Juarez, Chihuahua, México
Tel. (656) 612-6138

Belén, Posada del Migrante
Calle Juan de Erbaez 2406, esquina con Prolongación Salazar
Colonia Landin
25070 Saltillo, Coahuila, México
Tel. (844) 414-8317

Casa del Peregrino
Anahuac #605 Nte.
Zona Centro
26000 Piedras Negras, Coahuila, México
Tel. (878) 782-3620
    (878) 782-4788

Casa YMCA (jóvenes)
Xicotencatl No. 1802 Nte.
Colonia Mundo Nuevo
26010 Piedras Negras, Coahuila, México
Tel. (878) 703-5037

Albergue Ejército de Salvación
C. Gutierrez Nájera #514
Colonia Centro
82000 Mazatlán, Sinaloa, México
Tel. (669) 982-3453

Albergue Ejército de Salvación
C. Labradores #85
Colonia Morelos
15270 México Distrito Federal, México
Tel. (5) 5789-1511

Albergue Belén—Casa del Migrante
Apartado 87
Sn. Antonio Cahuacan
Av. Hidalgo S/N
27900 Tapachula, Chiapas, México
Tel. (962) 625-4812

GUATEMALA

Casa del Migrante
O Av. "C" del Migrante 8–22
Colonia Olguita de León
Tecún Umán, Guatemala
Tel. (502) 776-8416
Fax (502) 776-8417

Casa del Migrante
30 Av. "A"–26, zona 7
Colonia Tikal
Ciudad de Guatemala, Guatemala
Tel. (502) 474-3359
    (502) 474-3367

Catholic Relief Services
10. Av. 10-57 zona 10
Ciudad de Guatemala, Guatemala
Tel. (502) 331-0682
Fax (502) 332-0107

NOTES

CHAPTER 1

1. Oscar Romero, *The Violence of Love*, compiled and translated by James R. Brockman, SJ (Maryknoll, NY: Orbis, 2004), 1.

2. Carmen Elena Hernández, quoted in *Oscar Romero: Memories in Mosaic*, ed. María López Vigil (UCA Editores, El Salvador, 1993); trans. Kathy Ogle (EPICA, 2000). Contact EPICA (Ecumenical Program on Central America and the Caribbean), reprinted in *Sojourners*, March–April 2000. www.sojo.net.

3. Romero, 202–3.

4. Quoted in James Brockman, *Romero: A Life* (New York: Orbis Books, 1989), 241–42.

5. *Catechism of the Catholic Church*, no. 2562.

CHAPTER 3

1. See *Juan Diego, una vida de santidad que marcó la historia* (Mexico City: Editorial Porrúa, 2002), 46–51, 121–28.

CHAPTER 4

1. Dorothy Day, *Selected Writings: By Little and by Little*, edited and with an introduction by Robert Ellsberg (Maryknoll, NY: Orbis, 1992), 330.

2. Martin Luther King, Jr., "Letter from Birmingham Jail," *Why We Can't Wait* (New York: Harper & Row, 1963).

3. Houston Independent Media Center, http://houston.indymedia.org/news/2007.

4. Day, *Selected Writings*, 95–97.

CHAPTER 6

1. Dorothy Day, *The Duty of Delight: The Diaries of Dorothy Day*, ed. Robert Ellsberg (Milwaukee: Marquette University Press, 2008), 192.

2. See Mark and Louise Zwick, "Nicholas Berdyaev, Particular Prophet of the Movement," in *The Catholic Worker Movement: Intellectual and Spiritual Origins* (Mahwah, NJ: Paulist Press, 2005), 75–96.

3. Hans Urs von Balthasar, "Setting Out into the Dark with God," in *You Crown the Year with Your Goodness: Sermons Throughout the Liturgical Year* (San Francisco: Ignatius Press, 1989), 279.

4. Dorothy Day, *The Long Loneliness* (1952; repr. San Francisco: Harper & Row, 1997), 171.

5. Ibid., 170–71.

6. Emmanuel Mounier, *Personalism*, trans. Philip Mairet (Notre Dame, IN: University of Notre Dame Press, 1952), 63.

7. Ellen Cantin, CSJ, *Mounier: A Personalist View of History* (New York: Paulist Press, 1973), 64.

8. Antonio Socci, "Divo Barsotti," in *30 Days*, April 1990, 53.

CHAPTER 7

1. One retelling of this folktale is Becky Reyher's *My Mother Is the Most Beautiful Woman in the World* (New York: Lothrop, Lee & Shepard, 1966).

2. Hans Urs von Balthasar, "Setting Out into the Dark with God," in *You Crown the Year with Your Goodness: Sermons through the Liturgical Year* (San Francisco: Ignatius Press, 1989), 277.

CHAPTER 8

1. From William D. Miller, *A Harsh and Dreadful Love: Dorothy Day and the Catholic Worker Movement* (New York: Liveright, 1973; repr. Milwaukee: Marquette University Press, 2004), 24–25.

2. Marc Ellis, *A Year at the Catholic Worker* (New York: Paulist Press, 1978; Waco, TX: Baylor University Press, 2000), 72.

CHAPTER 9

1. Tom Roberts, "Guatemala: Truth Commission Report Details Years of Military Abuses," *National Catholic Reporter*, NCROnline, March 12, 1999; http://www.natcath.org/NCR_Online/archives2/1999a/031299/031299a.htm.

2. Margaret O'Brien Steinfels, "Death and Lies in El Salvador: The Ambassador's Tale," *Commonweal*, October 26, 2001, Volume CXXVIII, No. 18.

3. Manuel Roig-Franzia, "Former Salvadoran Foes Share Doubts on War: Fifteen Years Later, Problems of Poverty Remain at Forefront, *Washington Post*, January 29, 2007; www.washingtonpost.com/wp=dyn/content/article/2007/01/28/AR2007012801353.html.

4. *Testigos de la fe en El Salvador: Nuestros sacerdotes y seminarista diocesanos mártires 1977–1992*, collected by Father Walter Guerra and others, 2007.

CHAPTER 11

1. Dorothy Day, quoted in Stanley Vishnewski, *Wings of the Dawn* (New York: Catholic Worker, n.d.), 63.

2. Hans Urs von Balthasar, "You Too Were a Stranger in Egypt," in *You Crown the Year with Your Goodness: Sermons through the Liturgical Year* (San Francisco: Ignatius Press, 1989), 261–62.

CHAPTER 12

1. See Gustavo Gutiérrez, *Las Casas: In Search of the Poor of Jesus Christ* (Maryknoll, NY: Orbis, 1993).

2. John Paul II, *Laborem Exercens* 19, emphasis in the original.

3. Greg Erlandson, "An Inside Job: Our Best and Brightest—Not Illegals—Pushed Us to the Brink of Financial Disaster," reprinted from *Our Sunday Visitor* in the *Houston Catholic Worker*, November–December 2008 issue.

AFTERWORD

1. William Griffin, "A Study of Emmanuel Mounier's Philosophy of Personalism, Its Philosophical Roots and Its Contemporary Relevance" (master's thesis, Fordham University, 1992), 11–12.

2. Emmanuel Mounier, *Be Not Afraid: A Denunciation of Despair*, trans. Cynthia Rowland (New York: Sheed and Ward, 1962), 132.

3. Karol Wojtyla, *The Acting Person*, trans. Andrzej Potocki (Dordrecht, South Holland: Reidel Publishing Company, 1979), 149. *See also* Karol Wojtyla, *Person and Community: Selected Essays*, trans. Theresa Sandol, OSM (New York: Peter Lang, 1993), 265–69.

4. Hans Urs von Balthasar, "Setting Out into the Dark with God," in *You Crown the Year with Your Goodness: Sermons through the Liturgical Year* (San Francisco: Ignatius Press, 1989), 279–80.

5. Dorothy Day, *The Long Loneliness* (1952; repr. San Francisco: Harper & Row, 1997) 204–5.

THE CATHOLIC WORKER MOVEMENT:
INTELLECTUAL AND SPIRITUAL ORIGINS
Mark and Louise Zwick

Brings to life the philosophers, theologians, economists, and saints
who influenced Dorothy Day and Peter Maurin in the development of
the ideas and spirituality that supported their radical following of the
Gospel in the movement they founded.

0-8091-4315-1 Paperback

DOING FAITHJUSTICE (REVISED EDITION): AN INTRODUCTION TO CATHOLIC SOCIAL THOUGHT
Fred Kammer, SJ

Shares the Roman Catholic experience of faith intertwined with justice, reviving a common language of public and civic virtue that grounds a political vision for the 21st century.

0-8091-4227-9 Paperback

THE RISING OF BREAD FOR THE WORLD:
AN OUTCRY OF CITIZENS AGAINST HUNGER
Arthur Simon

The book is an autobiographical account of the launching and
development of the nation's foremost citizens lobby on hunger.

978-0-8091-4600-0 Paperback

GREAT MYSTICS AND SOCIAL JUSTICE:
WALKING ON THE TWO FEET OF LOVE
Susan Rakoczy, IHM

Demonstrates that the fullness of the Christian life must include commitment to social justice by examining the lives of a number of Christian mystics and the implications their insights hold for contemporary Christians.

0-8091-4307-0 Paperback

MY LORD & MY GOD:
ENGAGING CATHOLICS IN SOCIAL MINISTRY
Jeffry Odell Korgen; Foreword by Jack Jezreel

Provides Catholics with all the tools they need to build successful
parish social ministries through invitation, conversion,
and empowerment.

0-8091-4370-4 Paperback

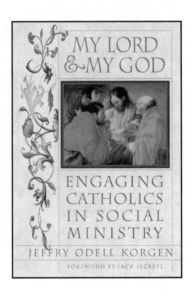

RESPONSES TO 101 QUESTIONS
ON CATHOLIC SOCIAL TEACHING
Kenneth R. Himes, OFM

An explanation of Catholic social teaching using the most frequently asked questions posed to this experienced teacher and lecturer on the topic.

0-8091-4042-X Paperback

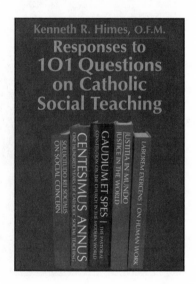

JUST PEACEMAKERS:
AN INTRODUCTION TO PEACE AND JUSTICE
Mary Evelyn Jegen, SND de N

This timely and urgent book does more than describe societal problems—it gives concrete methods and means toward resolution. Each chapter is designed for personal study and also for use by groups.

0-8091-4350-X Paperback

THE CATHOLIC PRAYER BIBLE (NRSV):
LECTIO DIVINA EDITION
Paulist Press

An ideal Bible for anyone who desires to reflect on the individual stories and chapters of just one, or even all, of the biblical books, while being led to prayer though meditation on that biblical passage.

978-0-8091-0587-8 Hardcover

978-0-8091-4663-5 Paperback